ANGLO-IRISH TRADE
1660-1800

TO
MY PARENTS

ANGLO-IRISH TRADE
1660-1800

by

L. M. CULLEN

Augustus M. Kelley · Publishers

New York · 1968

© 1968 L. M. CULLEN

MANCHESTER UNIVERSITY PRESS
MANCHESTER 13, ENGLAND

First published
in the United States
1968
by AUGUSTUS M. KELLEY · PUBLISHERS
24 East 22nd Street, New York, N.Y. 10010

PRINTED IN THE REPUBLIC OF IRELAND
BY HELY THOM LIMITED, DUBLIN

PREFACE

THIS work is based on researches commenced at the London School of Economics in 1956 under a travelling studentship from the National University of Ireland and awarded for a Ph.D. degree of the University of London in 1959. My research was also facilitated by a grant from the Research Fund of the University of London. Some further research on Anglo-Irish trade was carried out between 1959 and 1961.

Revision for publication was drawn out over the years 1959 to 1963: I had only limited time to devote to the task in those years, much of which were spent outside the British Isles and hence away from its library facilities.

As revised for publication, the work also takes account, especially in the introductory and concluding chapters, of subsequent research undertaken into wider aspects of Irish economic development in the eighteenth century. Although some of this research involved a study in some detail of the smuggling trade in the eighteenth century, I have resisted the temptation of rewriting the chapter on the smuggling trade, both because to do so would have taken me far beyond the confines of Anglo-Irish trade, and because it is hoped to publish the results of this enquiry fairly shortly.

In the study of relations within these islands, 'English', 'England', and 'Anglo-Irish' are often employed where relations between Ireland and Britain rather than between Ireland and England are concerned. Where however a strict geographical location or identity is implied by the context in these pages, the term 'England' or 'English' should be taken as referring invariably to Britain south of the Cheviots, and 'Britain' or 'British' to the island as a whole. I also hope that no Scotsman will be offended by the inclusion in a study of Anglo-Irish trade of trade relations between Ireland and Scotland, but it is inevitable that such a work should take some account of trade with Scotland. Irish statistics of overseas trade in the eighteenth century do not always distinguish between England and Scotland; Scotland, whose trade with Ireland was of some consequence for much of the eighteenth century, was also an alternative source of supply for some important imports from England, and its ports were successful rivals of English ports in re-exports to Ireland.

Over a period of twelve years a student accumulates obligations to many people. My greatest debt is to Professor A. H. John, London

School of Economics, who suggested Anglo-Irish Trade to me, acted as supervisor, and has commented patiently and at length on successive drafts. I am greatly indebted also to Dr D. C. Coleman of the London School of Economics who supervised the section of the thesis dealing with the seventeenth century and whose advice and comments have also been forthcoming on repeated occasions. I am grateful also for comments on the work in one stage or other of its progress to Professor Síle Ní Chinnéide, University College, Galway, and Professor K. H. Connell, Queen's University, Belfast.

It would be invidious to single out individuals among the many archivists, librarians and officials who have gone out of their way to help me, but I owe a special debt to the staffs of the National Library of Ireland, Dublin, in particular Dr R. J. Hayes, its former director, and Mr. John Ainsworth; the Public Record Office of Northern Ireland, Belfast, Mr. Brian Trainor especially; and the Custom House Library, London; and to the officers of H.M. Customs and Excise in a number of English and Scottish ports. I am also indebted to Professor Liam O Buachalla, University College, Galway; Dr E. R. R. Green, University of Manchester; former colleagues in the Irish Diplomatic Service, and my friend, Mr. John H. Talbot, who has read the proofs. My wife also has given advice or assistance on a number of points.

I am grateful also to the Editor and Editorial Board of *Economica* for permission to reproduce chapter X, 'The exchange business of the Irish banks in the eighteenth century', which first appeared in *Economica,* November 1958.

L.M.C.

Trinity College, Dublin
February, 1968

CONTENTS

ABBREVIATIONS

Add. MSS.	Additional Manuscripts
B.M.	British Museum
H.M.C.	Historical Manuscripts Commission
Ir. MSS. Comm.	Irish Manuscripts Commission
P.R.O.	Public Record Office (London)
V.C.H.	Victoria County Histories

NOTE

Attention should be drawn to the method of quoting Anglo-Irish exchange rates. The exchanges are quoted, following eighteenth-century practice, in terms of the number of Irish pounds purchased by £100 sterling; or simply in terms of the surplus of Irish pounds acquired by £100 sterling, this surplus being generally described as a percentage, though not strictly one. The par rate, for instance, was £100 sterling=£108⅓ Irish or simply '8⅓ per cent'. High exchange rates in Dublin (i.e. when rates exceeded '8⅓ per cent') therefore signified a movement of payments unfavourable to Ireland; low exchange rates (i.e. when rates fell below '8⅓ per cent') a favourable movement.

CHAPTER I

THE IRISH ECONOMY AND OVERSEAS TRADE

I

IRELAND at the Restoration was recovering from the turmoils of two decades in which almost twelve years of war between rival Royalist, Parliament and Irish Confederate interests had been followed by the most ruthless and widespread confiscation in its history. With a population depleted by famine, plague and the sword, and with all the more powerful elements of opposition banished or exiled, the country's dependence on England was extreme. For the greater part of the next thirty years the island was ruled without a Parliament.[1] Moreover, the executive in Ireland was appointed in England. The policy of the Irish government was, as a result, dictated from London; and in the early Restoration the viceroy, despite Ireland's sufferings in the Stuart cause, had clear instructions to further Ireland's interests only in so far as they did not conflict with England's. The new Irish tariffs[2] passed in the first and only Parliament of the Restoration period reflect this policy.

The ease with which England pursued her economic and political policy towards Ireland resulted, however, primarily from the infrequency of Irish parliaments at this time. Once parliaments came to be held regularly in Ireland, political tensions were bound to arise between the two countries. The constitutional pretensions of the English parliament to legislate for Ireland[3] were inevitably challenged, and on the Irish side the claim was put forward that Ireland was the equal under a common crown of the sister kingdom in constitutional stature and in the independence of its parliament. Many of the measures binding Ireland were in the economic field, the most famous being the act of 1699 prohibiting the export of woollen goods from

---

[1]A Parliament meeting for the first time on 8 May 1661, and dissolved on 7 August 1666, had ten brief meetings, some of them lasting as little as a single day. It was the last Parliament until 1692, excepting the Jacobite 'Patriot Parliament' of 1689.

[2]14 & 15 Car. II c. 8 (Ir.); 14 & 15 Car. II c. 9 (Ir.). Books of rates appended.

[3]See T. J. Kiernan, *History of the financial administration of Ireland to 1817* (London, 1930) pp. 94–105.

Ireland to foreign parts.[1] This act was doubly celebrated, firstly, because it was regarded as a particularly high-handed measure, and secondly, because the circumstances leading to it were the occasion for the publication of Molyneux's tract, *The case of Ireland stated,* which determined Irish constitutional thinking during the eighteenth century. English policy was largely political in its general motivation. Moreover there were many in England who gained by existing Anglo-Irish trade. In consequence economic measures directed against Ireland were in no small measure the achievement of pressure groups rather than the product of a clearly defined economic policy which English governments sought to pursue. The over-representation in the English parliament of some of the cattle-breeding counties and of the wool manufacturing districts of the south-west was therefore an important factor in over-riding the considerable opposition in England to some of the legislation directed against Ireland.

English policy was in some respects colonial. The later Navigation Acts excluded Ireland from much of the direct trade with the colonies themselves, for example. Ireland's inferior position was also reflected in the often unilateral advantages conceded in the Irish tariff regime to English products. But, as has already been mentioned, English policy was primarily political, and where vested economic interests did not prevail, Ireland's position was in some respects a favourable one. This was strikingly evident in two ways. Firstly, while many of the products of Irish agriculture and industry suffered directly or indirectly from the effects of British protectionism or policy, this was not true of all Irish products. A favoured position in the British market was a powerful factor in the expansion of exports of linen, worsted yarn and after the 1750s, provisions. Grudging and incomplete though it was, the encouragement of the Irish linen industry in the form of the removal of import duties was one of the decisive factors in its evolution. Secondly, Irish shipping as such was treated as British and hence experienced no discrimination. Even where Irish ships were debarred under the Navigation Acts from carrying commodities from the colonies to Ireland, they were still free to engage in the direct trade from the colonies to Britain.

Apart from the attempted reversal of English policy by the short-

[1] 10 & 11 Wm. III, c. 10 (Eng.). The act did not prohibit exports to England, but the duties there were already effectively prohibitive. For the general background to the passing of the act, see H. F. Kearney, 'The political background to English mercantilism, 1695–1700', *Economic History Review,* second series, vol XI, no. 3 pp. 484–96.

lived 'Patriot Parliament' in Dublin in 1689, English supremacy was not in any important respect successfully challenged until the final quarter of the eighteenth century. The failure, despite French intervention, of the Jacobite and Irish forces in the Williamite campaigns of 1689–91, the subsequent confiscation of most of the remaining landed property in native ownership, and the imposition then and in the early eighteenth century of legal disabilities on Catholics reduced the native Irish to political impotence. Parliament, itself imperfectly representative of the Anglo-Irish minority, was manipulated in the English interest by the executive in Dublin Castle, which dispensed patronage and 'places' to ensure a majority for its measures. Discontent with economic policy there was, even in Parliament itself, but it was minority discontent, tempered by the realization that English support was the ultimate line of defence against the Catholic and disenfranchised majority of the island's population. Strong opposition both inside and outside Parliament was first inspired by the defection of the American colonies in the 1770s. But economic factors were also important. The constitutional crisis of the late 1770s and the less acute one of the 1720s coincided with serious economic difficulties. The passage in 1778 of the first substantial measure of relief for Catholics[1] suggests also that the Anglo-Irish community was at last outgrowing its sense of dependence.

Under the threat of armed rebellion by the Volunteer forces of the Protestant gentry and the inhabitants of the towns, formed to protect the country against the possibility of French invasion (after the bulk of the troops had been withdrawn to assist in the attempted suppression of the American colonies), England was forced at the end of 1779 to concede 'free trade'. This meant the opening of the colonial trade in the Western hemisphere to Ireland, and the removal of the prohibitions laid by the English Parliament on the export of Irish glass and woollens. It was the first break in English economic policy towards Ireland, and was followed five years later by Pitt's unsuccessful attempt to reach an Anglo-Irish commercial arrangement.[2] Earlier favours—the removal of the duties on Irish plain linens in 1696, on

---

[1] 17 and 18 Geo. III, c. 49.
[2] See W. E. H. Lecky, *History of Ireland in the 18th century* (London, 1892), vol. ii, pp. 430–53; A. E. Murray, *The history of the commercial and financial relations between England and Ireland from the Restoration* (London, 1903) pp. 236–63; G. O'Brien, *The economic history of Ireland in the 18th century* (Dublin, 1918) pp. 249–68.

woollen and worsted yarn in 1739,[1] and even the relaxation of the
Cattle Acts at the end of the 1750s were isolated concessions, justified
by England's economic circumstances. The suspension of the Cattle
Acts, despite its significance to Anglo-Irish trade relations, was at
first regarded as a temporary measure, not as the overthrow of the
controversial legislation introduced a century earlier. Suspension became repeal only in 1776[2] when there was no longer any doubt that
the state of supply and demand had changed fundamentally in the
English livestock economy.

The success of Irish opposition in 1779-80 appeared to be crowned
in 1782 with the repeal of the Act of 6 George I which asserted the
right of the British Parliament to bind Ireland by legislation. Victory,
however, was more apparent than real. No change was effected in the
position and power of the Irish executive, nor were any measures of
reform introduced in the Irish Parliament, many of whose members
indeed had a vested interest in parliamentary corruption. As a result
the opposition victories of 1780 and 1782 bore little fruit, Parliament
remained under control of the executive, and Irish government policy
was still in the last analysis directed from London. The failure of the
United Irishmen, a movement inspired by the principles of the French
Revolution, and of the 1798 rebellion, paved the way for union with
England, a measure which by its political achievement offset the
drawbacks of a narrower agreement such as the commercial one proposed in 1785. The union was effected in 1800, when in the aftermath
of rebellion it had become politically feasible and had been made by
persuasion and bribery to appear desirable. Nor, in the continuing
transformation of the English economy, did the prospect of the removal of trade barriers between the two countries encounter opposition among English commercial and manufacturing interests, similar
to that on which only fifteen years previously Pitt's other measure,
the ill-fated Commercial Propositions, had foundered.

II

In 1660 Ireland by comparison with England was a less developed

---

[1] Excluding 'worsted yarn of two or more threads twisted or thrown, or cruel'.
The removal of the duties was to take effect only from 1 May 1740.

[2] For details of the legislation repealing the Cattle Acts, see J. O'Donovan, *The
economic history of livestock in Ireland* (Cork, 1940) p. 110.

community. Exports of manufactured goods were negligible,[1] and essential imports were financed by exporting cattle and wool to England. Even the English Cattle Acts[2] of the 1660s served to effect little change in the Irish economy, producing only a swing towards dairying and sheep-raising and a reorientation of the cattle trade to meet the growing demand for salt beef in the English and foreign islands of the West Indies. The main Irish industries were the making of woollen cloth and the tanning of hides. Moreover, both industries were greatly limited by the extent of the export of the raw materials. In addition, the principal cloth export was frieze, which was spun and woven in the homes of the largely self-sufficient peasants and was not subject to the more capitalistic methods employed in the making of the finer cloths. The export of woollens was therefore of minor importance in Irish foreign trade, and was brought to an end in 1699 when it was prohibited by the English Parliament at a time when the industry was showing signs of benefiting from immigrant capitals and skills. The rapid rise of the Irish linen industry in the eighteenth century did little to change the predominantly rural and agricultural nature of the Irish economy. Most of its workers were peasant tenants of the north-east who in their free time from farming wove the linen in their homes and in the spring and early summer sold the un- bleached webs to the drapers. A degree of capitalist organization was, of course, introduced into the industry during the century. Some weavers became small 'manufacturers', while drapers and bleachers distributed yarn to others who worked on commission. But even these weavers, who by comparison with the independent weavers were probably still in a minority at the end of the century, wove their linens at home on their own holdings or on agricultural plots held from their employer. An urban proletariat was unknown, and the factory system was only slowly introduced in the nineteenth century.

Ireland had no large mineral resources. In consequence there was no marked concentration of industry, and little urban development apart from the growth of inland market towns and of the seaports. The maritime towns were as a result the main centres of industry. Dublin and to a lesser extent Cork, Waterford and Belfast were all

[1]According to Petty, 'the manufacture bestowed upon a year's exportation out of Ireland is not worth above 8,000£'. *Political anatomy of Ireland*, 1672, in Hull, *Economic writings of Sir William Petty* (Cambridge, 1899) vol. 1, p. 197.

[2]For details of this legislation see J. O'Donovan, op. cit., pp. 50–60; A. E. Murray, op. cit., pp. 24–32; G. O'Brien, *Economic history of Ireland in the 17th century* (Dublin, 1919) pp. 153–7.

such centres based on imported raw materials, supplying the breweries, salt works, glass and sugar houses. Dublin, the capital and by far the most populous town, was easily the principal site of this activity, and its importance was enhanced by its being the site also of the silk industry and of much of the woollen industry. Belfast's industrial importance, originally smaller than that of Dublin or Cork, grew steadily over the century, and in the last decades, Belfast, now the third port of the kingdom, also developed a prosperous cotton industry organized on capitalistic lines.

Ireland, therefore, remained primarily a rural community throughout the century, the vast majority of her growing population living on the land or deriving their income directly or indirectly from it. The land system, however, has been frequently misunderstood by historians who have represented it as one in which land was occupied mainly by cottiers with no security of tenure or at best short leases. In reality the cottier class was but one element among the occupiers of the soil, and it was only in the second half of the century that their numbers multiplied. The prevalence of cottiers far from being something which always existed was itself a consequence of accelerated population growth in the second half of the century. In other words accelerated population growth was not superimposed on an existing social structure, but instead was responsible for altering in the long run the original system almost beyond recognition.[1]

The spread of the potato diet itself was a reflection of growing demographic pressure. Peasants, conservative in their food habits, do not change their diet readily and without reason, and in fact the potato had been widely known in Ireland for over a hundred and fifty years without it becoming a staple of the diet. The Irish diet was far from dependent on the potato in mid-century. Grain was important, and a large home output, augmented by a sharp rise in grain imports in years of harvest failure, normally ensured an adequate food supply. The change from a largely grain diet to a largely potato one is something which took place only in the course of the second half of the century. The spread of a potato diet was most evident among the cottier class, and widespread dependence on the potato accompanied rather than preceded the accelerated growth of population.

[1] L. M. Cullen, 'Problems in the interpretation and revision of eighteenth-century Irish economic history'. *Transactions of the Royal Historical Society*, 5th series, vol. xvii, 1967.

Until Irish society was engulfed by the demographic expansion, the most representative member of Irish society was the small tenant. A balance existed between the tenants working by far the larger part of the land area, and the cottiers supplying the labour needs of agriculture additional to the supply of tenant family labour. It was only with accelerated population growth that this balance was altered. Society was distorted in the late eighteenth and early nineteenth centuries by the multiplication of the cottier class both on the margin of leasehold land and within leasehold farming itself by the process of sub-division of land among peasants themselves often in defiance of the wishes of the landlord. Leaseholding tenants were not only in a favoured legal situation, but were also in a favoured economic situation, when prices were rising. The leases which tenants enjoyed were long ones (typically three lives or 31 years). Indeed, far from the tenants suffering from insecurity, the length of the leases and the consequent rigidity of contractual obligations were at times a serious difficulty in the first forty years of the century, when prices were low. With rising prices during the rest of the century, except in the difficult 1770s, the tenant farmer, even if paying a much higher rent at the renewal of a lease, stood to gain subsequently from the upward trend in commodity prices while his rent remained unchanged. The cottier, of course, and the insecure occupier of subdivided leasehold land had no such protection and suffered directly from the impact of growing competition for land. With the shift in the balance between cottier and tenant the proportion of the population in a vulnerable legal and economic position rose sharply. Even when prices fell after the Napoleonic wars, the cottier stood to derive no advantage from his flexible tenurial arrangement, because with growing population pressure, rents were ceasing to be determined by economic forces and the competition for cottier holdings and for sub-divided plots was fed by mounting population numbers.

Tillage never receded to the extent suggested by contemporary pamphleteers and later historians. The worst imbalances between the supply of and the demand for food were the consequence of harvest failure, not of a wholesale movement out of tillage. Tillage itself remained substantial, and within it there was evidence of intelligent substitution of one crop for another in accordance with movements in relative prices. Tillage was still widespread in mid-century in Leinster. In other parts of Ireland not only was much grain produced for subsistence and local needs but where transport facilities were at hand grain was also produced for more distant markets. However, extensive though tillage remained, relative prices encouraged farmers with access to capital to switch from tillage to grazing. This switch itself, by enabling Irish farmers to avoid ruinously low grain prices, was a factor in keeping rural poverty and depression at bay.[1]

Animal husbandry was of course the more important branch of Irish farming, although even in the middle decades of the eighteenth century grazing was never pursued to the extent suggested by some historians. Grain growing was not only considerable but, at times when relative prices warranted expansion, spread rapidly. In the first decade of the century arable cultivation was extended substantially. Some decline took place subsequently under pressure of low prices, but, because of substitution of crops within tillage, the decline in arable cultivation as a whole was far from dramatic. Moreover, the rise in cattle numbers was not exclusively at the expense of tillage. Apart from short-lived reversals, the long-term trend was out of sheep pasturage in the eighteenth century in Ireland, and much of the rise in cattle numbers therefore took place on existing pasture lands.

The livestock trade was important not simply because of its extent but also because through its intricate market organization it helped to develop from an early stage an interdependent economy throughout the country. After the Cattle Acts of the 1660s had ended the trade in lean cattle to England, the division of the country into breeding and fattening lands became much sharper. Calves and yearlings from holdings throughout the country, more especially from the dairying counties of the south and south-west (Carlow, Kilkenny, Waterford, Kerry and parts of Cork and Limerick), were fattened on richer lands. There was, therefore, a movement of stock from the poorer to the richer lands, and in particular an outward movement from the dairying areas as a whole. The fattening lands were spread widely across the Irish midlands and in the more fertile eastern part of Connaught. At the age of 3 or 4 years the cattle were purchased by the graziers in the finishing lands of Meath, Limerick, Tipperary and North Cork. This was the general pattern of the livestock industry, varying locally where soil conditions permitted. Sheep were numerous, to some extent in the maritime counties of the south-west and west, but mainly in the inland counties of Roscommon and Tipperary,

---

[1]L. M. Cullen, 'The value of contemporary printed sources for Irish economic history in the eighteenth century', *Irish Historical Studies*, vol. XIV, no. 54 (September, 1964) p. 153.

where they were grazed along with cattle. Dairying and sheep or cattle grazing were thus spread across three of the four Irish provinces. Tillage was practised everywhere though as one would expect it was more important relatively on small farms and in areas where such farms predominated. The counties of the north-east stood to some extent apart from the general pattern of Irish agriculture. There was relatively little grazing of sheep or cattle but tillage and dairying were carried on mainly for local requirements, though leaving a surplus of butter for export.

The holdings of tenant farmers were generally small. Typical farms of this kind were in the region of 20 to 50 acres. In Ulster, where the growth of the linen industry offered the possibility of secondary employment, holdings were smaller than elsewhere, acreages of 10 or 12 being quite common. Farms of 100 or 150 acres and larger were found mainly in grazing areas. On the great sheepwalks of Roscommon, flocks of sheep as large as 20,000 were not unknown, though by Young's time the largest flocks had fallen to 6,000 or 7,000. In the grazing counties there were a number of farms of 4,000 acres, and a few of 10,000 acres or exceptionally 13,000 acres (21,000 English acres). It would be deceptive, however, to judge Irish agriculture simply by the size of holdings, which is a rather meaningless yardstick in some respects. A more significant measure of the efficiency of farming is the availability of capital. Even in the more prosperous eastern counties, the tenant's capital was generally very inadequate, amounting, in Young's opinion, to less than one-third of that employed by an English farmer on the same acreage[1]. On poor lands, more especially the barren lands of the north-west and west, the large size of holdings, often running into hundreds of acres, is deceptive, because farmers often overcame their want of capital by taking a large tenant farm in partnership. Despite the fact that their large flocks of cattle and sheep showed that they had some access to capital, the large tenant graziers themselves had limited resources, which were very far from being commensurate with their vast acreages. Their profits were in an economic sense very low: 'so low', in Young's opinion, 'that nothing but the ease with which grazing bullocks is carried on could induce a man to be satisfied with it'[2].

But the lack of investment in Irish agriculture has been greatly exaggerated. There is too much concrete evidence of investment by

[1]Young, *Tour in Ireland* (London, 1780) part II, p. 16.
[2]op. cit., part I, p. 370.

landlord and tenant to justify the view that Irish agriculture was starved in a chronic way of capital. Many landlords both invested themselves and sought to encourage investment by tenants, often by rent abatements or by the inducement of the renewal of the lease at a favourable rent. It was in fact their interest in improvement that was in part responsible for the conscious attempt on the part of land-owners from the 1760s to eliminate middlemen. In any event, middle-men, to whom many of the inadequacies of management and invest-ment have been attributed, were not as universal as many have imagined them to have been. They were entrenched in particular areas, more especially in the south-west, where barren soil and poor communications made personal management or management through the hands of an agent far from attractive. While the utility of the function of the middleman is debatable in many respects, it must be admitted that they served a useful function in providing capital in the development of the dairying industry in the more backward areas. The switch from tillage to dairying entailed what was for the small peasant producer a substantial investment in a herd of cattle. Without the investment of capital by middlemen in dairying herds the ex-pansion of dairying would have proceeded much more haltingly in these areas. The small peasant farmer had not the resources which would enable him to build up his own herd.

If capital had not been made available by the middlemen, the move from unremunerative tillage and the decay of subsistence conditions would have been much slower in these areas. The middlemen leased land and invested in herds from as few as 40 or 50 animals up to 200 or 300 or even as many as 2,000. Grazing land along with herds of cattle of up to 40 or 50 were then let to dairy farmers in return for an annual payment, in cash or part in kind, per cow. This system was not necessary in the expansion of dairying in Carlow and Queen's County, because farmers' capital, modest though it was, proved adequate to the task of building up small herds of dairy cattle. But it was essential to the growth of dairying in Waterford, Cork and Kerry. In more advanced parts of the regions embraced by the 'dairyman' system, such as Waterford and parts of Cork, the condition of the dairy farmer improved with the rise in butter prices in Ireland in the second half of the century. But in the more backward parts of Cork and Kerry, which were on the verge of a demographic crisis, the dairyman's living was mean, his profit negligible and, often paying a substantial part of his rent in kind, he gained much less than others from the rise in prices. Moreover, he was often part of a growingly oppressive social system. Significantly, the middleman system was much more complex here than in the rest of Ireland. The middlemen themselves often had remarkably small herds, and an element of personal exploitation of one peasant by another was involved.[1]

III

The Irish economy, therefore, was predominantly rural and peasant. There were few inland towns, and in one only of them, Clonmel, did a banking business of any consequence develop during the eighteenth century. In the seventeenth century even the ports were small. In Dublin £32,562 was collected in customs and import excise duties in 1664 and £33,137 in 1668. No other port paid more than £12,000, and apart from the 5 more prominent ports of Dublin, Cork, Waterford, Galway and Limerick, 16 ports contributed only £23,661 to the revenue in 1664 and £23,943 in 1668.[2] These figures suggest that Dublin already dominated overseas trade. This is especially true of imports for as early as the 1660s the Dublin importers supplied most of Leinster and were already dealing with the other provinces. The smaller ports of the east and south-east had been hurt by the Cattle Acts, which ended the livestock trade with England: most of the Irish ports, however, engaged to some extent in the growing provision trade with the continent and the colonies. This trade, with its emphasis on the fattening of cattle in Ireland, gradually centralized on the ports serving the richer fattening areas, and thus led to the decline of the provision trade in the smaller harbours, some of which, like Galway, Kinsale and Youghal, had a substantial provision trade as late as the 1680s. By the 1740s the trade was centralized almost completely on four ports, Cork, Limerick, Waterford and Dublin. These four ports controlled 63 per cent of total Irish beef exports

[1]Around 1765, a south of Ireland landlord attributed the deterioration of the tenants to the dairying system. 'This is in great measure owing to the pride, drunkenness and sloth of the middling sort among the Irish. Every one of them thinks himself too great for any industry except taking farms. When they happen to get them, they screw enormous rents from some beggarly dairyman and spend their whole time in the alehouses of the next village. If they have sons, they are all to be priests, physicians or French officers. . .' Ir. MSS. Comm., *The Kenmare MSS*, ed. E. MacLysaght, p. 230.
[2]*Calendar of State Papers Ireland, 1663–5*, pp. 460–61; ibid., *1666–9*, pp. 672–3; B.M., Harl. MSS. 4706, ff. 7–8.

in 1683; 80 per cent of the trade in 1701, 86 per cent in 1717 and 92 per cent in 1734. Concentration was particularly marked in the French trade in which by the middle of the century, the four ports controlled 99 per cent of beef exports. The division of the country into breeding and fattening lands, evident in 1697 and fully developed by 1730,[1] necessitated a large internal trade in livestock and led to the intricate pattern of fairs and markets for the buying and selling of stock,[2] which by the middle of the eighteenth century was an important factor in unifying the Irish economy. Yearlings from the dairying areas, after fattening on the richer lands throughout the country, were eventually disposed of at the fairs, especially the great midland fairs of Ballinasloe, Banagher and Mullingar, to the graziers of Tipperary, Limerick and Meath. The finished beasts were purchased in the slaughtering season commencing in August or September by the butchers and merchants of the exporting ports.

In the seventeenth century there was a pronounced swing to dairying in no small measure at the expense of beef production. Butter came to be exported from most of the Irish ports. But as the price of beef recovered in the 1710s and 1720s with the growing colonial demand for salt beef, the emphasis, as prices for grain and wool remained unattractive, moved again towards beef production. Butter exports were already declining sharply in the smaller ports and from the end of the 1730s had virtually ceased, suggesting that the cottiers and tenants in the hinterland of these ports were now selling their butter to merchants from the larger ports or, as was probably the case in the west of Ireland, selling their calves to graziers rather than keeping them for dairies. Butter exports as a whole declined somewhat during the 1720s and 1730s, reflecting a decline from the high level of prices of the years 1713-1718, and the trade was now largely a specialized business of part of the expanding hinterland of the growing ports of Cork and Waterford and to a lesser extent of Dublin and Limerick. The four ports had shipped only 36 per cent of butter exports in 1683, but this percentage was 66 per cent in 1701, and increased to 81 per cent in 1717, 85 per cent in 1734 and 94 per cent in 1753.

The developments in the livestock trade, making the different sectors of the economy more dependent on one another, were paralleled in other fields. Much of the wool sold at the Ballinasloe fairs—

---

[1]e.g. see H.M.C., *Egmont Diary*, vol. 1, p. 48.
[2]See National Library of Ireland, Dublin, MS 498, Herdbook and Farm Accounts of a midland grazier, 1734-86.

where even as late as the 1770s, when the wool trade was in decline, over £200,000 worth was purchased every July[1]—was taken to Cork and there spun into worsted for the English market by peasants employed throughout the county by the master-combers. Legislation from 1689 onwards, restricting the number of Irish ports entitled to export wool,[2] had a limited—if any—significance in centralizing the trade in Irish wool and worsted yarn, for even before 1689 the small amount of wool exported from the western ports suggests that most of the supply was already being conveyed overland to Cork and Dublin. In 1739, the limitation of the wool export trade to a few ports in the east and south-east was removed,[3] but the removal of this restriction had no effect whatever in reviving a wool export trade in the other ports. The supplies continued to be disposed of by Dublin merchants or purchased by the agents of the Cork and Leinster combers, worked up in the country, and exported principally to Manchester and Norwich.

More striking still as a sign of the growth in volume of inland trade, is the dependence of Belfast's foreign trade on Dublin. Even by the second half of the seventeenth century when Belfast was still a small port, much of the butter produced in the north was sent to Dublin from Belfast, or shipped directly overseas from Belfast on the account of Dublin merchants. As the linen trade developed in the eighteenth century, its export branch was also dominated by Dublin drapers and shippers, who purchased the linens, either on their own account or to fulfil buying commissions received from London or the north of England, from North of Ireland drapers who came to the Irish capital to dispose of them.

Dublin and, on a more modest scale, Cork, as the major centres of Irish foreign trade, built up larger exchange and discounting facilities than any other Irish town. This in turn contributed to the further growth of the two cities, and enabled them to oust the merchants of the smaller ports from much of the provincial trade. As Irish internal trade needed cash, and as in the butter trade, often entailed advance payments to many of the producers, the merchants of Cork and Dublin, in having banking facilities at hand, had a great advantage over merchants elsewhere. In the early decades of the eighteenth century this advantage was still somewhat limited by the fact that in

---

[1]Young, op. cit., part I, p. 277.
[2]1 William & Mary, c. 32 (Eng.); 10 & 11 William III, c. 10 (Eng.).
[3]12 Geo. II, c. 21 (Eng.).

the more primitive parts much of the trade was barter. But when by the middle of the century a money economy became general, the position of the Cork and Dublin merchants was greatly enhanced. Though Cork by the early eighteenth century had already displaced Youghal in the butter trade, much butter continued to be exported directly from the more inaccessible parts of the mountainous counties of the south-west. Rents were paid in kind in many of the remote dairying areas, and the butter was exported directly by small legitimate traders or by smuggling concerns like that of the O'Connells of the Iveragh peninsula in County Kerry, who were partners in a small business shipping to the French port of Nantes.[1] By the middle of the century, however, business of this nature had decayed greatly and it ceased in the course of the 1750s. Rents increasingly were paid in cash, and the 'dairymen' of remote districts like the Iveragh Peninsula were sending their butter to Cork. The impetus for this development was supplied by the emergence before 1750 of inland butter merchants acting as intermediaries between the producers and the Cork exporting merchants, and paying cash or making advances to small producers over a wide hinterland.

Dublin was by far the largest port. It had sizeable exports of provisions and especially of wool and worsted yarn, and for most of the century dominated the exports of linen, the largest single item in Irish export trade. The import of finer goods like drapery, silks, tea and wine, and of raw materials like sugar and hops, was largely centred on the capital, and to an increasing degree its merchants ousted the provincial interests from this business and extended their operations into all four provinces. Galway, for instance, had once been an important centre for the distribution of wines in the west of Ireland, and its wine trade continued to flourish in the early eighteenth century despite the fact that the town's commerce generally was already decaying rapidly. But from the middle of the century the local merchants succumbed to the competition of the Dublin importers, and the wine trade fell away.[2] This dependence on Dublin affected ports much larger than Galway. In 1791, for instance, Coquebert de Montbret, the French consul, wrote of Limerick, then the seventh port of Ireland, that 'almost all the small traders live on Dublin spirits, wine and especially sugar as there is no refinery in Limerick

---

[1]Library, University College, Dublin. O'Connell Papers.
[2]See L. M. Cullen, 'Tráchtáil is Baincéaracht i nGaillimh san 18ú Céad' (Trade and banking in Galway in the 18th century), *Galvia*, vol. 5 (1958) p. 52.

and about a dozen in Dublin'.[1] Even in the cotton industry, established in the north of Ireland in the closing decades of the eighteenth century, much of the cotton was supplied through the Dublin wholesale importers, and the finished goods were likewise disposed of in Dublin. The capital controlled so much of the inland and foreign trade because it was easily the largest—indeed apart from Cork virtually the sole—centre of exchange and discounting. Its merchants were therefore better able to cope with the demand for cash in purchases of Irish commodities and for long credit in the sale of imported goods than were the merchants in the outports. Dublin's control of imports was most striking in the case of drapery, manufactured or wrought goods, certain raw materials for processing, tea, or wine, the commodities in which in fact credit terms were likely to be longest. The existence of these facilities meant also that when in the second half of the eighteenth century export dealings in linen were shifting from Dublin to the north, Dublin continued to handle the bulk of exchange transactions concerning linen.

During the greater part of the century, more than half of the total shipping coming to Ireland was entered in Dublin and over virtually the whole century more than half the customs duties were collected there.[2] Though Dublin's share of total tonnage 'invoiced' declined in the last few decades, its percentage share of the total customs collection did not decline below 50 per cent until the last decade—and then only slightly—suggesting that Dublin merchants were still able to dominate much of the import trade, despite the new trends towards direct dealings in imports and in exports, especially in the linen trade. As might be expected, Dublin controlled the exchange business with London, and as the great growth of internal trade over the first half of the century simplified internal remittance, the provincial centres of exchange became more than ever subsidiary to the Dublin market. Significantly, a major Dublin bank was founded by the merchant family of Dillon, dealing in the provision trade and carrying on a country-wide business in wine. They had correspondents all over the country, and, when their banking house failed in 1754, had assets

---

[1]S. Ní Chinnéide, 'A Frenchman's impression of Limerick town and people in 1791', *Journal of the North Munster Antiquarian Society,* 1948, p. 100.

[2]Figures for the number and tonnage of shipping invoiced in the various Irish ports, and for the revenue collection are available in P.R.O., Customs 15. The shipping statistics are somewhat ambiguously described as those of 'shipping employed in carrying the trade of Ireland', but are in fact those of shipping 'invoiced'.

scattered in three of the four provinces. Dublin's importance was of course enhanced by the fact that, with a population of around 200,000 at the end of the century, it was the main home market for much of Irish production. In particular, with the aid of parliamentary bounties on the transport of corn and flour it became the centre of a large flour trade, drawing on mills all over the country.[1]

Yet, though the capital at the end of the century continued to dominate the inland and foreign exchange business, signs of a changing organization of commodity trade and exchange business were already abroad. Dublin's share of direct exports of linens to Great Britain had fallen to 35 per cent in 1800, and in the same year its share of the total tonnage of shipping 'invoiced' in the Irish ports had fallen to 41 per cent. Although much of the overseas trade of the island was still dominated by the merchants of the seaport towns, specializing in the international transfer of commodities, the growing volume of trade and improving communications were already altering the channels of distribution. By the end of the century many northern linen bleachers, by-passing the shippers and drapers in Dublin and the importing merchants in London, dealt directly with the English inland wholesalers. On the other hand many English manufacturers, dispensing with the services of wholesale importers in Ireland, dealt directly with their Irish customers. Similarly, in the early nineteenth century, English importers of agricultural produce frequently by-passed the merchants in the Irish ports and dealt directly with inland merchants and with the producers. These changes were bound to lessen the degree of concentration in Irish trade and exchange business, and in the early nineteenth century Dublin and Cork both lost the dominant position.

Next to Dublin, Cork was the most important Irish port. It was the main centre of the trade in butter, beef and worsted yarn and dominated the agricultural economy of the south, west and part of the midlands. By the 1760s and 1770s its exports were valued at £1,000,000 per annum,[2] and the balance of its commodity trade was highly favourable. As the centre of the provision trade, it was the seat of a victualling agent of the Admiralty, and in the final decades of the century of a Portuguese consul and a Spanish vice-consul.

---

[1]Mills were established in the provinces rather than the capital, since the bounties were much more generous in the case of flour than of grain.

[2]Young, op. cit., pt. I, p. 275. On the trade of Cork, see also W. O'Sullivan, *The economic history of Cork* (Cork, 1937).

Contemporaries were highly impressed by its great trade. Arthur Young, for instance, found there 'the most animated busy scene of shipping in all Ireland.'[1] Excluding the coal trade which was particularly prominent in Dublin, the tonnage of shipping invoiced in Dublin was apart from the opening decade of the century only 20 to 60 or 65 per cent greater than in Cork, and exceptionally in some years the tonnage entered in Dublin was below that in Cork.[2] But Cork's position in the import trade remained markedly inferior to Dublin's. Other rapidly developing ports were Waterford, over most of the century the third port of Ireland;[3] and the ports of the northeast. In the 1660s no port in the north was among the first seven Irish ports, but already by 1700 Belfast was the fourth port in Ireland. With the development of the linen trade the relative importance of the north in the Irish economy expanded. By the middle of the century three northern towns, Belfast, Londonderry and Newry, were among the first seven Irish ports, and at the very end of the century Belfast itself was the third port of the kingdom. The concentration of trade on the larger ports entailed decline for most of the smaller ports. In many, the decline was absolute. In others, the percentage growth was generally less than that of the country as a whole, suggesting a relative decline. So small was the trade of most Irish ports that of the 26 in the island the revenue collected at 19 failed to cover the costs of administering them.[4] In Kinsale the costs of collection exceeded receipts by 39 per cent, in Dingle 1877 per cent and in Baltimore 2200 per cent.[5]

Ireland's foreign trade reflected, of course, the nature of her economy: largely an exchange of a few agricultural and textile products for a wide range of raw materials, luxuries and manufactured goods. England naturally was the main centre of this exchange, because of her proximity, her political dominance and the interde-

---

[1]Young, op cit., pt. I, p. 282.

[2]As calculated on the basis of tonnage of shipping invoiced *less* tons of coal imported. Figures from P.R.O., Customs 15.

[3]See L. M. Cullen, 'The overseas trade of Waterford as seen from a ledger of Courtenay and Ridgway', *Journal of the Royal Society of Antiquaries of Ireland*, vol. LXXXVIII, pt. 2 (1958) pp. 167–8.

[4]*Irish Parliamentary Register*, vol. 2, p. 111. It should be added that an eighth port, Drogheda, had a very large volume of shipping invoiced in each year, but had a very small trade in dutiable commodities, with which it was supplied largely from Dublin. The tonnage of shipping invoiced in Drogheda was however inflated by the relatively very large coal trade centred on that port.

[5]Ibid., vol. 3, p. 113.

pendence of the two economies. In the 1660s England's and Ireland's economic activities were still competitive enough to warrant the exclusion of Irish cattle, beef and butter. But the rapid changes in the following years obliged England, with no general relaxation of her illiberal trade policy towards Ireland, to admit Irish plain linens free of duty from the end of the seventeenth century; and from 1758-9 to re-admit Irish beef, butter and cattle and to remove the duty on tallow. The two economies thereafter became increasingly complementary, and Anglo-Irish trade became by far the most important, and an ever-growing, portion of Irish foreign trade. But immediately after the Cattle Acts, Ireland had to seek new continental markets: in 1683 only 30 per cent of Irish exports were consigned to England. Once the Irish linen industry began to expand, however, Ireland's dependence on England again became very obvious. By 1730 43.4 per cent of Irish exports were sent to Britain and by 1770, a decade after the re-admittance of Irish provisions to English ports, 76.2 per cent.

Ireland's trade with the continent or with the West Indies and America was therefore relatively small, and played a major role in Irish overseas trade only in the two decades immediately following the passing of the Cattle Acts. Apart from the effect of the exclusion of Irish cattle from English markets, the growth of continental trade owed much to the growing French and Spanish demand for salted beef and butter. A wholly inadequate production of these products on the continent and the growth of traffic with the West Indies and the Americas had as their consequence an increasing need for beef and butter for ship crews and for the growing slave populations of the crowded plantation islands. The cheapness of the Irish products, skill in salting and the use of Portuguese salt (better for preserving than French salt) all combined to procure a ready market for Irish salt beef and butter, and gave the former a maritime and colonial monopoly it held almost to the end of the eighteenth century. In the primitive Irish economy of the seventeenth century, the fact that two of the three principal products (beef, butter, wool) of the island had a non-English market, meant that the continental and colonial trade became the most important branch of Irish foreign trade. But with the rise of the Irish linen industry at the end of the century, which found its only overseas market in England, the relative importance of other branches of Irish foreign trade declined rapidly. Moreover, Irish foreign trade was limited also by high tariff barriers on the continent, and the raising of French tariffs at the end of the century greatly reduced the volume of the trade to France. In particular, the enormous importation of Irish butter to Normandy and French Flanders had already led to a heavy tariff being placed in 1687 and 1688 on Irish butter imported for French home consumption, and considerably lessened the butter trade with France. Throughout the first half of the eighteenth century France remained one of the most important markets for Irish butter, largely because of temporary reductions of the import duties on account of unsatisfactory home production. But from the end of the 1730s when the reduction of the duties was not renewed, the exports to France fell away, and Holland, Portugal, Cadiz and the English West Indies became the main markets.[1] For the rest of the century the principal item in the French trade was salt beef, sent to France for re-shipment to the West Indies or for victualling French colonial and naval shipping. This trade reached its zenith over the years 1716-75 when French colonial development was most rapid. Exports of beef to France were then two to four times their level of the 1680s and accounted for 40 to 60 per cent of total Irish exports of beef.

The Irish trade with the continent and with the colonies thus consisted mainly of the specialist provision trade with its ancillary products, and though this trade increased in volume over the first half of the century, its rate of growth was a good deal less than that of Irish overseas trade as a whole. Apart from the provision trade, prospects in foreign markets for Irish exports were poor and only in Spain, Portugal and the British colonies were there outlets, all of them small, for Irish products other than provisions, tallow and hides. Although the general export trade increased, that to countries other than England was static, or declining, from the mid-century. It recovered for a time in the 1780s, but declined so heavily in the 1790s that whereas total Irish exports in 1800 were 119 per cent above the level of 1750, exports to countries other than Great Britain were now 25 per cent below their 1750 level.

As one would expect, the wine trade in the underdeveloped state of the economy in the seventeenth century occupied an important place in the country's trade and greatly enhanced the importance of imports from France. But as the Irish economy evolved in the eighteenth century, the relative position of this trade diminished and this

[1]See P.R.O., Customs 15 for statistics of the Irish provision trade from 1698 onwards.

change contributed to the reduced importance of Southern Europe in Irish foreign trade. As for other imported commodities it is clear that they became less competitive with English goods on the Irish market. This may be in part attributed to some increase in the margin of tariff preference English goods enjoyed in the Irish market or to their supply not being disrupted by the series of wars that hampered commercial intercourse with the continent. It arises also however from the increase in the relative efficiency of British production. The inclusion of trade with Ireland in the Anglo-French Commercial Treaty of 1786 was for instance only barely reflected in an increase in the quantity and range of imports from France. Moreover, the advantages of direct importation especially of commodities of colonial origin were offset by the capital of British entrepôt merchants. Although in the second half of the century Irish imports as a whole almost trebled, those from countries other than Great Britain only doubled, despite the fact that in 1780 all the restrictions on direct trade between Ireland and the British colonies in the Western Hemisphere had been removed.

The less developed nature of the Irish economy was reflected also in the organization of overseas trade. The capital of Irish merchants was limited, and dealings on their own account were made less profitable by virtue of the fact that the legal rate of interest was 10 per cent in the second half of the seventeenth century and was only reduced finally from 7 per cent to 6 per cent in 1731.[1] Moreover, the demand on Irish merchants was for cash in their purchases and, in their sales of imported goods, for long terms of credit to customers whose reliability was often in doubt.[2] The assistance afforded to the merchant by the Irish banking system was limited, for even in the second half of the eighteenth century when it was most developed Irish banking was built around the discounting of bills with not more than two months to run. As a result of these difficulties the greater part of Anglo-Irish trade was transacted on the account of English merchants whose capital was generally greater and who enjoyed access to more highly developed credit institutions and a lower rate of interest. Some

---

[1]The rate was reduced to 8 per cent in 1703 and to 7 per cent in 1722.

[2]Dobbs in 1729 complained that, 'many now take up goods from merchants and other industrious traders without any view or design of payment, but only to have a show of business that they may, with more ease, gain credit and impose upon others in order to blaze a little with a borrowed light'. Arthur Dobbs, *An essay on the trade and improvement of Ireland* (Dublin, 1729), in *A collection of tracts and treatises illustrative . . . of Ireland* (Dublin, 1861) vol. 2, p. 440.

even of the trade with France, Holland, Spain and the Mediterranean was effected with English finance, while the great bulk of the provision trade with the English colonies was carried on on English or colonial account. While, in the direct exports of linen to England by Irish bleachers, much of the trade was on Irish account, it was associated to a large extent with the advances to the bleachers by linen importers in England either at the time of importing or of selling the linens. A great part of the trade with the continent was itself effected on commissions from abroad, but in contrast to Anglo-Irish trade, much of the continental trade was on Irish account, or on the joint account of merchants in Ireland and members of the Irish merchant colonies on the continent. This contrast in the main arises from the presence in Irish trade with the continent of institutional factors absent for the most part from Anglo-Irish trade, and from the fact that the economies of Southern Europe were themselves relatively primitive.

The limitations of the Irish merchant community are also clearly seen in the small amount of Irish-owned shipping. While the trade with France, Spain and Portugal was mainly carried in Irish-owned ships, few engaged in Anglo-Irish trade were registered in Ireland. Over the century as a whole, as the relative importance of the trade with Southern Europe declined, the percentage of Irish-owned shipping 'invoiced' to total tonnage 'invoiced' fell heavily. In absolute terms, the tonnage of Irish shipping increased steadily over the century, apart from some sharp decline, real or apparent, during war years, but its proportion to total tonnage 'invoiced' declined from 26 per cent in 1700 to 13.5 per cent in 1800.

Table 1: Tonnage of shipping invoiced in the ports of Ireland[1]

Year	Irish-registered	British-registered	Total tonnage
1700	31,755	77,680	121,096
1730	39,997	132,343	191,637
1750	42,678	173,522	252,997
1770	64,156	310,819	401,363
1800	92,767	502,067	688,273

The percentage of British shipping 'invoiced' on the other hand increased from 64 per cent in 1700 to 73 per cent in 1800. Total Irish-registered shipping reached its maximum in 1791 with 1176 vessels of 69,231 registered tons, employing 6,638 seamen. But much of this

[1]P.R.O., Customs 15.

tonnage was employed solely in the coastal trade or in fishing and there were never more than 70 or 80 Irish vessels of a tonnage of 140 tons or upwards. In 1789 there were only 16 vessels exceeding 200 tons, almost all belonging to Dublin or Cork.[1] It would appear that as a result of the centralization of trade on the larger ports and the decay of local exports especially, a greatly increased tonnage of shipping 'invoiced' in the smaller ports was by the end of the century carrying a much decreased volume of imports per ton of shipping with still more sharply reduced prospects of obtaining export freights. This was true certainly of Galway,[2] and probably of many lesser ports. Apart from possible outlets that may have offered in other business, developments of this nature made ship-owning uneconomic for the local merchants; and with the decline of the French trade and slow growth of the Spanish and Portuguese trades, in which conditions appear to have been most favourable to Irish shipowners, probably account for the relative decline in the tonnage of Irish shipping invoiced in the Irish ports. Moreover, the capital cost of Irish-owned ships was likely to be higher than that of English, because of higher construction costs and the higher rates of interest, and this in conjunction with probable higher operating costs, is the reason for the almost complete absence of Irish-owned shipping from the coal trade, in which profits were negligible.[3]

IV

The rising prices of agricultural produce from the middle of the century and the great expansion of the linen industry suggest a general increase of prosperity in Ireland over the century as a whole. In fact, the volume of exports increased three to four-fold during the century.[4] As population growth was substantially less rapid—the population apparently doubling in the course of the century[5]—this suggests a fairly substantial rise in the standard of living. Figures for imports

[1]P.R.O., Customs 17. (Statistics of Shipping registered in Ireland from 1789).

[2]See L. M. Cullen, 'Tráchtáil is Baincéaracht . . .' (Trade and banking . . .) loc. cit., pp. 55-6.

[3]Opposition by the masters and owners of vessels in the English coal ports appears to have been another reason, though probably not a fundamental one. On profits in the coal trade, see chapter XI, pp. 210-11.

[4]As calculated from the ledgers of Irish exports and imports, assuming the rise in official valuations over the century to amount to 50 per cent.

[5]See K. H. Connell, *The population of Ireland, 1750-1845* (Oxford, 1950) p. 25.

appear to corroborate this. The volume of imports appears, roughly, to have quadrupled,[1] and the increase in the import of many individual consumer goods was even sharper. The import of tobacco, already a widespread luxury among the common people in the 1660s,[2] doubled between the beginning and the end of the eighteenth century. Of course, the standard of living was affected by the distribution of wealth. In this respect both the land system and the incidence of the 'Penal Laws' or 'Popery Acts'[3] are said to have resulted in a redistribution of income. The 'Penal Laws', directed against Catholics forming the vast majority of the population, aimed at excluding them from the ownership of land and from the professions, and were only repealed in 1778 and subsequently. Catholics were not excluded by statute from business and commerce, but the laws preventing them from purchasing lands, lending money on mortgages; and the exactions and privileges of the Protestant corporations of the towns, were of themselves a handicap to Catholic enterprise. These measures certainly had an adverse effect on the Catholic wealth-holding classes, though more by depressing their relative share than by keeping them at absolutely low levels. While there were many Catholic merchants, few of them, apart from the Dillons, were among the more prominent members of the business community in the first half of the century. In the second half of the century the Catholic merchant community appears to have improved its position.[4] The firm of the Dublin Catholic, Edward Byrne, was said to be the most extensive in Ireland. While Catholics subscribed only £60,000,[5] or one-tenth of the capital of the Bank of Ireland, Catholic subscribers were to be found in the

[1]Assuming official valuations to have risen only slightly over the century as a whole.

[2]Petty, *Political anatomy . . .*, in Hull, op. cit., vol. I, pp. 191–2.

[3]Generic terms to describe the anti-Catholic legislation of the Irish Parliament in the seventeenth and, more especially, in the eighteenth century.

[4]Some contemporary writers, over-zealous in the Protestant interest, greatly exaggerated the wealth of the Catholic merchants. For an account of the Catholic merchant community see M. Wall, 'The rise of a Catholic middle class in eighteenth-century Ireland', *Irish Historical Studies,* vol. xi, September, 1958. However, the number and wealth of non-Catholic merchants rose rapidly in the course of the eighteenth century and it is far from obvious that the increase in the relative position of the Catholic business community was very great.

[5]*Irish Parliamentary Register,* vol. 15, p. 350; vol. 17, p. 95. In so far as Catholics were excluded from the Court of Governors of the Bank, there may possibly have been some reluctance on the part of some merchants to invest in the Bank. There is, however, no evidence that such a reluctance did in fact exist.

merchant class rather than in the landed class in contrast to non-catholic subscribers, among whom the landed classes were prominent.

The land system of the eighteenth century (allowing for the fact that at the outset only 14 per cent of the land[1] was in Catholic hands and that Catholics were not free to purchase land until 1782) was not as potent a factor in aggravating the existing maldistribution of wealth as has been generally suggested. Population pressures far from existing throughout the century emerged only in the second half of the century. Food deficiencies themselves were a result of harvest failure or inadequacies, not the sign of a perpetual imbalance between demand and supply. It is only in the second half of the century that competition for land sharpened seriously. The early stages of the changes culminating in the Great Famine were by then apparent: firstly, the number of cottiers began to multiply disproportionately, emphasizing the changing balance between cottier and tenant, and secondly, potato culture and diet spread *pari passu* with this development. Rents in these circumstances rose sharply, but the move from a land system in which rents were determined by purely economic considerations to one in which the decisive factor was the peasant demand for land was still far from complete at the end of the eighteenth century. Thus, while the growing numbers of cottiers could hardly hope to fare very well, the existence of a still substantial degree of balance in rural society meant that the precarious position of the cottiers had to have offset against it the possibilities of gains by tenants during the long period of rising prices, broken only at the end of the Napoleonic Wars.

It is of course true that apart from some probable fall in rents on lands leased at the end of the 1720s and at the beginning of the 1730s, when because of bad conditions slow payment and arrears were very common,[2] rents were already rising sharply after the first decade of the century[3]. About 1717 and 1718 in particular the leases for much land which had been let for low rents while the country lay waste after the Williamite Wars began to fall in and the rents were doubled

[1]J. G. Simms, *The Williamite confiscation in Ireland, 1690–1703* (London, 1956) p. 160.

[2]e.g. P.R.O. London, C 110/46, St. George *v.* St. George, bundle P, no. 6, George Westgate, Dungannon, 21 March 1729; Irish MSS. Commission, *Kenmare MSS.* (ed. E. MacLysaght), pp. 49, 141 and note.

[3]See R. J. Dickson, *Ulster emigration to colonial America, 1718–1775* (London, 1966), pp. 10–11, 70, 72; National Library of Ireland, Ainsworth Reports on MSS. in private keeping, vol. 5, p. 1206, vol. 9, p. 2094.

and trebled[1]. But the full sharpness of the increase was only in appearances. Rents were now being adjusted to more realistic levels than the artificially low ones of the early 1690s. It is true that rents rose sharply again between the 1720s and the 1750s. This again is misleading because even where rents were raised in the 1720s it is unlikely that in the difficult circumstances of that decade the increase brought rents up to a level reflecting long-term equilibrium. Rents continued to rise in the second half of the century, in Young's opinion doubling since the 1750s. There is no doubt that an increase of these proportions reflected greater competition for land as well as the substantial increase in prices of cattle, beef, dairy produce since the 1750s. Conditions for the cottier who paid a rising rent out of labour services, or by selling his labour on a market on which wage rates were becoming rigid, can scarcely have improved much except to the extent that the economies associated with the potato enabled him to use some land for market crops or for feeding a pig. For the tenant farmer the difficulties were much less as the increased rent on a long lease was in time offset by rising prices realized by his market crops and cattle. Large rent arrears were uncommon, except in the late 1770s,[2] the swollen rents were paid promptly, and there is no evidence from the estate papers of this period to parallel the primitive condition and acute suffering of the tenantry in many of the years of low prices in the early decades of the century. Young's impression on his tours through Ireland in 1776, 1777 and 1778 was that the condition of the people had improved over the previous thirty years. Complaints of poverty and depression, though not unvoiced, were less common in the last two decades of the century, and contemporaries referred to a growth of wealth and prosperity generally. Standards remained low in Ireland, of course; in the opinion of visitors from England, much lower than on the other side of the Irish Sea. Moreover, one must always bear in mind the growing contrast between the condition of the cottier, whose plight had been noted in some instances as deteriorating as early as the third quarter of the century, and the tenant. Acute distress in the towns, migrant labour in the countryside, and to some extent emigration, were all common; but there were also improvements for many which in retrospect in the

[1]W. E. H. Lecky, *A history of Ireland in the 18th century* (London, 1892) vol. I, pp. 245–6.
[2]i.e. in late 1777 and in 1778. But compare Young's remark that 'rents are not paid as well as they ought, and that tenants and agents make a pretence of bad times to an extent far beyond the fact'. *Tour in Ireland,* op. cit., part II, p. 149.

3

darker days of the nineteenth century were to give to the last days of the Irish Parliament a deceptive brightness.

In general, seventeenth- and eighteenth-century economic policy towards Ireland was resented more on constitutional than economic grounds. Subsequent controversy inevitably dwelt on these alleged adverse effects, and many who wrote on Irish economic questions were better versed in constitutional matters than in economics. These writers tended to attribute to English policy, or to its unconstitutional restrictions on Irish trade, Ireland's failure to share fully in the progress of the eighteenth century. But this overlooked the fact that Ireland was primarily an agricultural country with limited natural resources. Want of capital and a shortage of essential raw materials, more than the restraints on Irish trade, however numerous, arbitrary or irritating, prevented Ireland from emulating the industrial and commercial feats of her sister island. The prohibition on the export of woollen goods to foreign countries, the most famous of the 'restraints' on Irish trade and to many contemporaries the most burning of Ireland's economic wrongs, was in fact of relatively little consequence, and Irish trade and revenue remained buoyant for two years after the industry's 'repression', thus belying the views of contemporaries, who saw in it the cause of the acute depression that Ireland suffered in the first three decades of the eighteenth century. The real reasons for the poverty in Ireland in these decades were low agricultural prices, a poorly regulated monetary system, and stagnant or only slowly rising markets in England and on the continent. The Navigation Acts, though they certainly had some adverse effect on Irish trade and probably denied Cork some share in the tobacco trade with Glasgow, were not as important as contemporaries alleged. Even after 1780, when the colonial trade was almost wholly open to Irish merchants, their lack of capital and the limited domestic market prevented them from making much use of their freedom.

Yet, despite these disadvantages there is every evidence of rising prosperity in Ireland in the second half of the century. The maritime and colonial demand for salt beef and butter, and the growing industrialization of Britain both contributed to the strong demand for Irish commodities in the second half of the century, and the terms of trade moved in Ireland's favour. Only in the nineteenth century did conditions alter. The demographic explosion was of itself the most decisive factor. But there were other sources of weakness as well. The livestock and dairying industries were faced by a change from an environment favourable to growth to one less favourable. In the eighteenth century the low state of animal husbandry throughout western Europe had combined with the intense development of an Atlantic community built around the slave trade, plantation sugar and tobacco and the use of salted provisions to give a distinct advantage to the Irish economy which alone of European countries had a surplus of beef and butter. But there were already abundant signs in the late eighteenth and early nineteenth centuries within the agricultural economy of Europe and within the intra-trade of the western hemisphere that the supply of livestock and dairy products, as the supply of grain previously, was becoming less unstable, and that the inadequate and precarious balance between demand and supply, which had favoured Ireland as the only region with a significant, permanent and reliable surplus, was being righted. While the output of dairy products and livestock in Ireland continued to expand in the nineteenth century—and more rapidly after the Famine and emigration released land for export production—Ireland had to contend with an easing in the internal supply in other countries, with significant new export surpluses both within and without Europe and with the decay of the ageing transport system built around salt provisions in transatlantic trade. Even the linen industry, though after faltering in the first decade it continued to expand in the course of the century, was in a much less favourable environment than previously. The growth of the industry in the second half of the century is associated with a very sharp contraction of the industry in Scotland and England. In this instance the forces of industrial localization which in other cases were drawing industry out of Ireland reinforced the progress of the Irish linen industry. However, the overall rate of growth of the industry was slower; tendencies to depression more powerful and prolonged; and the industry, formerly widespread in the north, by gravitating towards Belfast and its environs was no longer the powerful agent of rural improvement and development that it had been in the eighteenth century.

While the Famine and subsequent emigration eased population pressures (although later in the more remote and backward areas than in the rest of the country), they added the difficulties of a falling population to the country's growing industrial diseconomies. In this way they helped to ensure that outside a narrow and sharply defined industrial base in the north-east industrial development fell increasingly behind. The existence of an Irish Parliament could have served only to mitigate not to prevent the impoverishment of nineteenth-century Ireland. As it was, Ireland suffered under the mutually con-tradictory policies of British rule and laissez-faire and the contrast between Ireland's relative decline in the nineteenth century and ab-solute decline in population, and its relative prosperity in the last decades of the old Irish Parliament, contributed the economic basis of the thought that helped to bring about an independent Irish state in 1922.

CHAPTER II

ANGLO-IRISH TRADE, 1660–1700

THE volume and trends of Anglo-Irish trade prior to 1660 are obscure. However, it is quite clear that most Irish commodity trade was with England. Cattle and wool were the principal exports, and Ireland relied on England for its supply of manufactured commodities and essential raw materials, and for much of its tobacco, the country's largest import. Irish trade with the Continent was less important, comprising mainly the import of wine, once the principal Irish import and still in the 1660's the second most important commodity entering the Irish ports. The returns in the continental trade consisted of hides, skins, tallow, salt beef or butter, but the chief items among the Irish exports, cattle and wool, had an exclusively English market apart of course from wool illegally sent to the continent despite the bonds to land it in England. Trade with England was effected principally from the ports of the east and south-east. Dublin however had close connections with the continental ports and the harbours of the south-west were dependent upon this branch of the overseas trade. The English ports most concerned in dealings with Ireland were Bristol and Chester, which thus retained their supremacy of medieval times, and by the late 1650s there was also substantial business in live cattle and sheep with Minehead.

The wars and devastations of the 1640s and 1650s with their attendant evils of famine and depopulation reduced Ireland to a state of desolation, the import of food and livestock from England and Wales being necessary in the early 'fifties. Irish overseas trade must have fallen well below its normal volume at this time. However, recovery gradually set in and despite a great 'mortality' of livestock in 1660 Irish trade had again attained a substantial volume by 1665. Figures for exports, available only for two isolated years, ending 25 March 1641 and 25 December 1665, reflect the probable expansion of Irish overseas trade despite the set-backs of the 'forties[1] and early 'fifties. Exports of cattle were 57,545 head in 1665, compared with 45,605 in 1641, and the export of sheep had risen more sharply still from 34,845 in 1641 to 99,564 in 1665. As exports of beef were twice

---

[1] The troubles in Ireland began in October 1641. The figures for the year ending 25 March 1641 are thus free from distortion occasioned by the political or military situation in Ireland.

as great in 1665 as in 1641 the figures point to a very considerable increase in the number of cattle in the country. Assuming two barrels of beef to equal one ox or cow (the barrel containing 2½ cwt of beef), the combined exports of cattle and beef in 1665 were the equivalent of 72,177 head of cattle, which represents an increase of 36 per cent over the corresponding total, for 1641, of 53,212. The growth in volume of exports was fairly general though most pronounced for sheep and cattle;[1] but the extremely lively export trade in sheep, conducted mainly with Minehead, reduced the supply of wool; exports in 1665 amounting to 131,013 stone, 20,000 stone less than had been exported twenty years previously.[2]

These figures as a whole suggest that Irish trade had fully recovered by the mid-1660s, and it appears probable that Irish trade just before the passing of the Great Cattle Act in 1666 had attained a record volume. The total value of Irish exports in the year ending 25 December 1665 was £402,389, of which £295,833 represented exports to England, and only £106,500 exports to all other parts.[3] Exports were predominantly pastoral, sheep and cattle and products thereof amounting to 75 per cent of the total.

Table 2: Principal export categories

	£	%
Cattle and cattle products	220,685	54·8
Sheep and sheep products	79,325	19·7
Fish	24,107	6·0
Horses	20,010	5·0
Other items	58,262	14·5
	402,389	100

[1]Irish exports in 1641, 1665 and 1669 are given in *Calendar of State Papers, Ireland, 1669-70*, pp. 54-5. The export of cattle in 1665 is given inaccurately as 37,544 head instead of 57,545. (See *Calendar of State Papers, Ireland, 1663-5*, p. 694 for correct figure. See also below page 31 note 1.)

[2]Exports of wool between 25 March and 29 September 1662, a period which covers much of the exporting season, were only 67,342 stone. Shaftesbury Papers, P.R.O., 30/24/50, part 2, no. 8. For figures of wool exports in 1632-40 see H. F. Kearney, *Strafford in Ireland, 1633-41* (Manchester, 1959) p. 152.

[3]Totals as given in extant copies of the statistics. Some minor discrepancies occur, including some in individual copies due to seventeenth-century errors in transcription, in these documents. In particular, it should be pointed out that some 'rounding' of figures meant that totals are not numerically precise, although the differences caused by rounding are too insignificant to be of consequence. Precise figures for exports to England are £295,778 7s. 11d., to other parts £106,753 15s. 6d. and to all parts £402,532 3s. 5d. as against the rounded totals of £295,833, £106,500 and £402,389 respectively. See above note 1 and page 31 note 1 for details of statistical sources.

Three-quarters of the total were exported to England, of which oxen, sheep, wool, tallow and hides between them represented 70 per cent.

Table 3: Irish exports to England, 1665

		£	%
Oxen	57,545 head	100,703	34·0
Sheep	99,564 head	24,891	8·4
Wool	131,013 great stone	49,130	16·6
Tallow	14,000 cwt	19,600	6·6
Hides	43,318	12,995	4·4
Other items		88,514	29·9
		295,833	100

Imports from England amounted to £200,450, compared with £135,987 from all other parts.[1] The principal imports from England were in order of importance, woollen or worsted cloth, tobacco, coal, haberdashery, grocery, ironware, silk manufacture, linen and hops, which between them amounted to 68.7 per cent of total imports from England.

Table 4: Imports from England in 1665

	£		£
Cloth (woollen and worsted)	27,560[2]	Ironware	10,976
Tobacco	26,000	Silk manufacture	9,850
Coal	18,350	Linen	9,526
Haberdashery	14,225	Hops	8,400
Grocery	12,790	Other items	62,773
			200,450

Woollen cloth and tobacco were easily the most important imports from England, though as the Navigation Laws had not yet forbidden the direct import of English colonial goods to Ireland, tobacco imports from England were at this time a good deal less substantial than they became later. Coal was the third commodity in Anglo-Irish trade; and its importance is due primarily to the growth of the

[1]*Calendar of the State Papers, Ireland, 1663–5*, p. 698. Some of the figures in the copies printed in the Calendar are obviously inaccurate, and can be checked by comparison with the copy in the Shaftesbury Papers (P.R.O., 30/24/50, part 2, nos. 2 and 11) or from the internal evidence of the figures themselves. The total imports from England add up to £200,450 and not the round figures of £200,000 as indicated in the copies cited in the *Calendar of State Papers,* and imports from other parts amount to £135,987 and not £136,000. Excluding very minor discrepancies arising from the 'rounding' of figures in these documents, the total from all parts should be £336,437 instead of £386,540.

[2]Comprising new drapery or 'stuff'—£16,733 and old drapery or 'cloth'—£10,827.

Dublin market. At least as early as 1667 shiploads of 40 or 50 tons were arriving daily in Dublin from Liverpool and Whitehaven.[1] Goods shipped to Ireland were purchased on credit terms said to be six months, followed by a bill of exchange.[2] But some, at least, of the trade may still have been effected on a barter basis; as even as late as the 1650s, Irish merchants shipping wool to England were said to give credit or, instead, to accept goods.[3]

The export trade was highly seasonal, lasting from late spring to autumn, and once the season was over Irish trade remained stagnant till it picked up again in the following spring. Few of the cattle exported were fat stock, the bulk consisting of lean cattle for fattening in the English feeding counties. The trade was carried on principally with the ports of Cumberland, with Beaumaris in Wales, and with Chester and the Severn port of Minehead. In the summer months whole fleets of cattle boats, or 'cow carriers', sailed from the Irish ports. As many as 20 vessels with cattle and sheep might arrive in Minehead in a single day.[4] 300 or 400 sail of ships were said to be kept in constant employment in the cattle trade,[5] and landed small mixed cargoes of 50 or so cattle and 200 sheep in the English ports.[6]

Some of the cattle undoubtedly were fattened in the immediate hinterland of the ports. This was particularly true of Minehead, from which Somerset was supplied with feeding stock. The demand for lean Irish cattle extended, however, as far as Yorkshire[7] and even to Norfolk and Suffolk.[8] Carlisle was one of the principal centres for the disposal of Irish stock: in the year 1 August 1662–1 August 1963, 26,440 head of Irish and Scottish cattle were imported into Cumberland.[9] Much of the trade was apparently transacted by 'drovers' or dealers, who took the cattle across to England and disposed of them at the fairs and markets. The journeys of these drovers were very

[1]Import and Export Book 1667 (Public Record Office of Ireland) quoted in D. A. Chart, *Economic history of Ireland* (Dublin, 1920) p. 84. The original MS was destroyed in 1922.
[2]*Calendar of State Papers, Ireland, 1666–9*, p. 186.
[3]Ibid., *1660–2*, pp. 151–2.
[4]*Calendar of State Papers, Domestic, 1666–7*, p. 226.
[5]B.M., Add. MSS. 4761, f. 210, *Reasons for taking off the prohibition . . . of Irish Cattel.*
[6]Only the Minehead Port Books remain to illustrate the Restoration cattle trade. P.R.O., E. 190, 1090/3; 1090/5.
[7]*Calendar of State Papers, Domestic, 1664–5*, p. 580.
[8]Ibid., 1667–8, p. 46.
[9]Ibid., 1663–4, p. 245.

extensive. In 1665, for example, some Irish drovers, having failed to sell their cattle in Carlisle, went on to Norwich in the hope of disposing of them there.[1] Under favourable circumstances the cattle would no doubt have been disposed of at Carlisle to English dealers, who in turn would distribute them to the English fattening areas.

The pattern and structure of Irish trade as it stood in the 1660s were to change radically with the passing of the Cattle Acts. Falling rents in England had focussed attention on the Irish cattle trade and the acts of 1663 and 1666 were passed in the belief that the elimination of Irish cattle imports would protect the home breeder. The total prohibition in 1666 and subsequently of the import of cattle, sheep, beef, butter or pork from Ireland caused considerable hardship in Ireland, though the fall of prices which had already been set in operation by the earlier act was somewhat checked as a result of another 'mortality' of cattle in 1666. The impact of the cattle acts was, however, exaggerated at the time because of the political agitation for their removal and much of the suffering in Ireland was due rather to the war with France which affected Ireland's trade with the continent. It was of course only natural that in the heat of the controversy the various interests in Ireland and England affected by the acts attributed the distress to the controversial legislative measures rather than to any other factor. But in reality many of the great Irish landowners had not been utterly opposed to the passing of the acts, seeing in them an opportunity 'of knocking off that beggarly trade of transporting our cattle', and had determined, in anticipation of the closing of the cattle trade, to improve their cattle breeds.[2] The growth of the Irish provision trade with foreign countries was far from being a result solely of the Cattle Acts as contemporaries and later writers opposed to the Acts claimed. The provision trade already existed on a substantial and increasing scale,[3] and the Irish landlords, some of whom were to be directly concerned in the export trade, saw in the Cattle Acts the prospect of enlarging the growing exports of salt beef to France and to the West Indian plantations.

[1]Linen Hall Library, Belfast: Letter Book of George Macartney, 1660–67. See various letters in 1665 and 1666.
[2]See H.M.C., *Hastings MSS.*, vol. II, pp. 374–5; *Calendar of State Papers, Ireland, 1663–5*, p. 658; H.M.C., *Ormonde MSS*, new series, vol. 3, pp. 64, 72.
[3]See L. M. Cullen, 'An Ceangal Tráchtála idir Éire agus an Fhrainc 1660–1800' (Franco-Irish trade, 1660–1800), unpublished M.A. thesis, National University of Ireland, 1956, pp. 107–8; Linen Hall Library, Belfast, Letter Book of George Macartney, 1660–67.

The war did not wholly cut off Ireland's foreign trade, even with
France itself, and with the re-establishment of peace in the autumn
of 1667 there was a strong foreign demand for Irish commodities.[1]
However, the capacity of the foreign market was not large enough,
even in the years of peace, to absorb at profitable prices all the Irish
production of salt beef, the demand for which was limited by the
relatively slow rate of development of the French and English plantations in the West Indies at this time. The result was that the prices of
beef and cattle which had fallen most sharply in 1666–7 recovered
less than those of butter and wool in the years of peace that followed.
The prices of beef and cattle remained extremely low and unremunerative during the next two decades,[2] and contrasted with
relatively buoyant prices for butter in ready demand at low import
tariffs for home consumption in Flanders, France and Spain;[3] and

[1] *Calendar of State Papers, Ireland, 1666–9*, p. 479.

[2] In December 1664 beef had been 18/– a barrel, 19/6 clear aboard in January
1665, and 20/– clear aboard in July of the same year (Linen Hall Library, Belfast,
Letter Book of George Macartney, 1660–7: 20 December 1664, 26 January, 8,
15 and 28 July 1665). The valuation of beef for the estimates of Irish exports in
1665 was 18/– a barrel (*Calendar of State Papers, Ireland, 1663–5*, pp. 694–5).
But in June 1668, despite the fact that hostilities both with the Dutch and the
French were long over, beef cost at most only 16/8 a barrel (*Calendar of State
Papers, Ireland, 1666–9*, p. 609), and prices appear to have deteriorated even
further subsequently. It was said that foreigners could victual in Ireland at 12/–
per 2½ cwt barrel (B.M., Add. MSS. 4761.f.210, *Reasons for taking off the
prohibition . . . of Irish Cattel*), and that the French and Dutch had Irish beef
at 6/– or 7/– a cwt (B.M., Harl. MS. 4706, f. 39. The minutes of two arguments
made in the House of Commons against the bill for continuing the Prohibition
of Irish Cattel). In September and October 1679, in the course of the beef
slaughtering season, the price of beef which had been 16/– and 17/– in June and
July declined to 14/–. In September 1680 prices were also at the level of 14/– and
15/– and in December, beef was 14/–. (Linen Hall Library, Belfast, Letter Book
of George Macartney, 1679–81). In the estimates of Irish exports in 1683,
beef and mutton were valued at 15/– a barrel (B.M. Add. MSS. 4759, Exports
and Imports of Ireland, 1683–6). Even in 1689 beef was only 8 French livres for a
barrel of 2 cwt (Irish Manuscripts Commission, *Négociations de M. Le Comte
d'Avaux en Irlande*, ed. J. Hogan, 1934, p. 211). This would correspond to 10
livres or 15/6 approximately, for a barrel containing 2½cwt of beef. In 1673 Sir
William Temple had noted that 'beef is a drug, finding no constant vent abroad
therefore yielding no rate at home' (Temple, *Essay upon the advancement of
trade in Ireland, 1673* in *Miscellanea* (London, 1697), pt. 1, p. 119).

[3] According to Temple in 1673 'hide, tallow, butter . . . are certain commodities
and yield the readiest money of any that are turned in this kingdom, because they
never fail of a price abroad' (Temple, op. cit., pt. 1, p. 119). In Belfast, butter had
been 24/– a cwt in November 1661, 24/– and 25/– in August 1662, 24/– in December 1663, 27/– and 28/– in September and October 1664, and 23/– and 24/–
throughout the second half of 1665. In the calculations of Irish exports in 1665,
butter was valued at 25/– (*Calendar of State Papers, Ireland, 1663–5*, pp. 694–5).

for wool shipped to England for the expanding English woollen manufacture.[1] As a consequence, the price trends led to a large-scale change from cattle-raising and beef production to dairying and sheep farming. The few figures available to illustrate Irish overseas trade in this period appear to bear out the trends suggested by other evidence. Irish exports of beef in 1669 were less than half the equivalent figure for beef and cattle in 1665 (assuming a conversion ratio of 2½ barrels of beef to equal one ox or cow); and even in 1683 were still well below the level of 1665. On the other hand, exports of butter and wool increased very sharply, and butter became the most important item in the export trade. Exports rose from 26,413 cwt in 1665 to 58,041 cwt in 1669, and by contemporary standards to the large total of 146,966 cwt in 1686.[2] Wool exports to England jumped from 131,013 great stone in 1665 to 254,760 in 1669, and to 352,306 stone in 1671.[3] Though they declined somewhat after that, they amounted over the next few decades to the substantial amount of 200,000 to 250,000 stone per annum.[4] Wool prices were subject at times to sudden fluctuation,[5] but on the whole wool appears to have been the most remunerative commodity among the Irish exports.[6]

The effect of war with France was seen in the fall of prices to 20/–, and later to 19/–, in 1666. After peace came in the autumn of 1667, prices recovered to 22/– and 22/6 (Linen Hall Library, Belfast, Letter book of George Macartney, 1660–67). The invoice prices of a shipment to France in April 1668 averaged £1/4/6 a cwt (*Calendar of State Papers, Ireland, 1666–9*, p. 615). In a boom in butter exports in 1679, prices rose in September to 26/– and 27/– in Belfast, and to 30/– and 31/– in Dublin. In 1680 prices were 22/– to 24 shillings in Belfast, falling in the course of September as low as 18/– and 19/–. In July of the following year, prices were 20/– to 21/– (Linen Hall Library, Belfast, Letter book of George Macartney, 1679–81). In the statistics of Irish exports in 1683, butter was valued at £1/2/6 a cwt (B.M., Add. MSS. 4759, Exports and Imports of Ireland, 1683–86). In June 1689, butter cost 15 to 16 French livres (*Analecta Hibernica*, no. 21, p. 126) which would correspond to a price of 23/– to 24/8.

[1]See below, n. 6.

[2]Figures for 1665 and 1669 from *Calendar of State Papers, Ireland, 1669–70*, pp. 54–5; for 1686 from B.M., Add. MSS. 4759, Exports and Imports of Ireland, 1683–6.

[3]Year ending 29 September 1671. *Calendar of State Papers, Domestic, 1671*, p. 507.

[4]B.M., Add. MSS. 4759, 1683–6. Some other figures cited in J. O'Donovan, op. cit., pp. 82–3.

[5]Ir. MSS. Comm., *Analecta Hibernica*, no. 15, p. 347.

[6]The valuation of wool in the estimates of Irish exports for 1665 was 7/6 a stone (*Calendar of State Papers, Ireland, 1663–5*, pp. 694–5). Although a writer in 1673 stated that wool prices had fallen two shillings at least since the Cattle Acts (*A letter sent to Mr. Garway a member of the Rt. Hon. the House of Commons of England by an English Gentleman*, 1673), actual wool prices in Ireland in 1673

In 1688, for instance, an Irish farmer wrote that 'nothing now bears a price but wool, cattle being extremely cheap'.[1]

The Cattle Acts certainly reduced the volume of Anglo-Irish trade. Exports of cattle were brought to an end, and Irish exports of beef and especially butter to the continent rose rapidly. Exports to England which had been valued at £295,833 in 1665 had in 1683 dwindled to £171,191.[2] The only substantial items were wool, tallow, lamb skins and linen yarn, which between them amounted to 72 per cent of the total.

Table 5: Exports to England, 1683

		£	%
Wool	191,832 great stone	71,937	42·0
Tallow	23,508 cwt	29,385	17·2
Linen Yarn	3,670 cwt	11,011	6·4
Lamb skins	1,766 hundred	10,596	6·2
Other items		48,262	28·2
		171,191	100

Exports to England would have fallen much more sharply but for the growth of wool shipments, which, despite a decline from an apparent peak in the early 1670s, were 46 per cent higher in 1683 than in 1665. The value of exports to England in 1683 contrasts with exports to France valued at £242,766 for the same year and total Irish

---

and 1674 ranged from under 6/– to 8/– (H.M.C., *Ormonde MSS.*, new series, vol. 3, pp. 333, 347; Irish Manuscripts Commission, *Calendar of Orrery Papers,* ed. E. MacLysaght, p. 117). This suggests a measure of stability in wool prices, and would appear to bear out Temple's remark that 'there is in a manner no vent for any commodity but of wooll' (Temple, op. cit., pt. 1, p. 107). The relative prices of wool were of course enhanced at this time by the war with Holland, which would have less direct effect on wool prices than on prices of beef and butter, whose main markets were continental. In the estimates of Irish exports in 1683, wool was again valued at 7/6 a stone (B.M., Add. MSS. 4759, Exports and Imports of Ireland, 1683–6). D'Avaux, the French Ambassador to King James' Court in Ireland noted in February 1690 that although wool prices in Ireland had fallen to 7/– a stone since the outbreak of war, the common price had never been above 8/– to 9/– in peace time (Irish Manuscripts Commission, *Négociations de M. le Comte d'Avaux en Irlande*, ed. J. Hogan, op. cit., p. 668). Earlier in June 1689, he noted that the prices at that time of wool were 6/–, sometimes 8/–, 9/– or 10/– or even up to 12/– a stone, and that the average price was 7/– to 9/– (ibid., p. 292. See also ibid., pp. 121, 211, 285, 625–6). These figures, although admittedly somewhat isolated, point to a firm trend in wool prices over the period as a whole.

[1]Ir. MSS. Comm., *Orrery Papers,* ed. E. MacLysaght, p. 352. See also H.M.C., *Ormonde MSS.*, old series, vol. 2, p. 307.

[2]*Calendar of State Papers, Ireland, 1663–5*, pp. 694–7; Add. MSS. 4759.

exports to all parts of £570,343. Between 1665 and 1683 Irish exports generally increased by 42 per cent and exports to England declined by 42 per cent. As a result exports to England which were 74 per cent of the total in 1665 formed only 30 per cent in 1683.

The increased volume of Irish exports is reflected in a growth of imports as well. Contemporary interests affected by the Cattle Acts alleged that the decline in exports to England consequent on the Cattle Acts brought about a sharp decrease in imports from England. But the claim is not borne out in the evidence. England was in a better position to provide such items as coal or woollen goods than was the continent. In addition the Irish tariff system generally favoured imports from England. English goods all entered at lower rates than foreign; and in woollens, for example, the extent of discrimination was utterly prohibitive. English colonial produce also entered at substantially more favourable rates than that of foreign colonies, and to counteract the effect of the incomplete drawback of duties on re-exports from England colonial produce entered from England was charged a lower duty than if imported directly from the colonies. As a result, England remained the chief supplier of the Irish market after, as before, the passing of the Cattle Acts. Imports of wine, brandy and salt alone from the continent rose sharply, though much less so than Irish exports in that direction. But otherwise England continued to supply the Irish market apart, to some extent, from the ports of the west and south-west. Sugar, woollens, silks, linen, hops, mainly came from England and in the statistics for 1683–6 compiled from the customs books of the Irish ports, a large miscellaneous category described as 'Smallwares vizt. grocery, haberdashery, ironware, millinery, etc.' was supplied principally by England.

Table 6: 'Smallwares, vizt. grocery, haberdashery, ironware, millinery, etc.'
1683–1686[1]

Date	Imported from England £	Total imported £	England as % of total
1683	105,397	119,582	88·1
1684	116,072	131,275	88·4
1685	88,938	101,794	87·4
1686	85,390	105,156	81·2

The dependence on England was further reinforced as a result of the Navigation Act of 1671 which forbade the direct importation of

[1]B.M. Add. MSS. 4759, Imports and Exports of Ireland, 1683–6.

colonial produce from the English colonies to Ireland. The greater part of Ireland's tobacco had hitherto been imported directly from America to the Irish ports of Cork, Galway and Belfast, but Ireland now became dependent on England for all its supply.[1] On the expiry of this act in 1680 the Irish merchants resumed the direct importation of tobacco mainly to the more western ports. But a further act of the English Parliament in 1685 terminated this trade, and in 1686, 3,058,007 lb. of tobacco out of a total of 3,312,451 was imported from England. There was, of course, considerable laxity in the enforcement of the Navigation Laws in Ireland at this time,[2] but even allowing for this it is quite clear that despite the Cattle Acts dependence on England as a source of supply became probably more complete even than it had been on the eve of the Great Cattle Act of 1666.

The imports at this time reflect an increase in prosperity. Imports of tobacco rose from 1,817,775 lb. in 1665 to 2,834,926 lb. in 1683, and coal imports rose from 24,467 tons in 1665 to 42,727 tons in 1683. Admittedly there are no figures for the intervening years, but evidence of a growing volume of trade is also afforded by the revenue from the customs and excise duties on exports and imports. The figures rose from £80,666 in 1664, £85,672 in 1668 and £93,825 in 1676, to £121,391 in 1680, £117,539 in 1683 and £138,857 in 1686, declining slightly to £124,779 in 1688.[3] In the early 'eighties the country was, even in the opinion of contemporaries, relatively prosperous; trade was on the increase and rents were rising. The growing prosperity was not due to any special profitability of the provisions trade, but was a result of a growing volume of trade in general, the most profitable single sector being that in wool which, apart from a limited clandestine trade with France, was conducted exclusively with England.

[1] See *Calendar of State Papers, Colonial, 1685-8*, p. 167, for some estimate of the size of this traffic for three years to 1680. The Irish Revenue Commissioners claimed that the revenue from the ½d. per lb. not drawn back on re-exports of tobacco to Ireland had never exceeded £5,000 (ibid., p. 175), which suggests that re-exports of tobacco to Ireland from England had been less than 2,400,000 lb. per year.

[2] See *Calendar of Treasury Books*, vols. iii, iv, v, vi, vii, viii, x; Public Record Office of Ireland, *Wyche Documents*, 1st series, iv/2, 26 Jan, 1676; Irish MSS. Comm., *Orrery Papers*, ed. E. MacLysaght, p. 167.

[3] *Calendar of State Papers, Ireland, 1663-5*, pp. 460-1; ibid., 1666-9, pp. 672-3; Petty, *Treatise of Ireland* (1687) in Hull, *Economic writings of Sir William Petty* (Cambridge, 1899) vol. 2, p. 584; B.M., Add. MSS. 18022, ff. 49, 51, 52.

Apart from the trade with England, there was also some commerce with Scotland.[1] But the Scottish economy at this time was even more primitive than the Irish, and the trade between the two countries was therefore of a very rudimentary character. It was principally effected from the ports of the Clyde and Ayr coast, for the most part in tiny open boats, which crossed to and from the adjacent Irish coast; vessels from the Scottish ports rarely venturing as far south as Dublin.[2] The imports from Scotland were mainly coal, salt, herrings and kentings (linen). Much timber was carried back from Ireland, and there was also a demand in Scotland for Irish horses and tanned hides.[3] The most important Irish export to Scotland had been cattle, but in 1667 and 1668 the Scottish Privy Council in an ambitious attempt forbade the import of corn, horses and cattle from Ireland. In the primitive condition of the Scottish economy these measures proved difficult to enforce: relaxation was frequently necessary, and smuggling was at all times rife.[4] Irish exports to Scotland were worth only £16,010 in 1683, in 1698 they were worth £23,774 and imports were £11,255. The minute coal trade of the 1660s had also developed somewhat. Imports were 1,864 tons in 1683 and 2,795 tons in 1698.[5]

Irish prosperity in the 1680s was, however, brittle. It was heavily dependent on two commodities, wool and butter, and was at times adversely affected by slumps on the markets abroad or destruction of animal stocks at home through disease. The first general set-back however came only in 1687, when James II's reforming zeal made the Protestant merchants of the Irish ports uneasy about their safety. The rates of exchange became unfavourable and there was a strong outflow of specie. The uneasiness among the merchant community resulted in an exodus of merchants together with their effects to England, which reached a climax amid the turmoils of 1689. Nevertheless, there appears to have been little or no decline in the volume

[1]See Smout, T.C., *Scottish trade on the eve of the Union, 1660-1707* (Edinburgh and London, 1963) pp. 175–82 and passim.

[2]Scottish Record Office, General Register House, Edinburgh. Port Import and Export Books, boxes 3, 9, 13, 28–30, 31.

[3]B.M., Add. MSS. 4759, Exports and Imports of Ireland 1683–6; P.R.O. of Northern Ireland, T. 552, p. 59, an acct. of Timber, barrell staves, etc., shipt off in the ports of Belfast and Coleraine 1683–95. For a brief description of Irish trade with Scotland, see also T. Keith, *Commercial relations of England and Scotland,* p. 110.

[4]*Registers of the Privy Council of Scotland,* passim; Scottish Record Office, Edinburgh, Customs Account of bounty money paid out of the customs to importers of victuals 1699 (2 portfolios).

[5]B.M., Add. MSS. 4759; P.R.O. Customs 15/1.

of trade before 1688. In 1689 the normal pattern of Irish trade was completely disrupted by the opening of the Jacobite and Williamite campaigns in Ireland, which lasted two years and utterly impoverished the country. Trade with England was at least partially blocked by the Irish Jacobites, and the English government for its part embargoed trade with those parts of the country under the control of the French and Jacobite forces. Once the country was deprived of the English market on which it was normally dependent for its supplies, shortages of goods became acute, and because of a want of shipping, risks at sea and the reluctance of James to yield to French commercial policy, imports from France were very inadequate. The Irish revenues fell heavily, and after the peace recovery was slow and painful. The export trade especially was affected, the customs collected on exports being in some years four or five times less than the corresponding amounts collected in the 1680s.[1] So complete had been the destruction of cattle and sheep during the campaigns that it was necessary in September, 1691, to prohibit for six months the export of beef, pork and butter.[2] The volume of exports particularly was small, imports being much larger because of the necessity to compensate for the shortages and devastations of the war years.

Table 7: England: exports to and imports from Ireland[3]

Year ending Christmas	Exports to Ireland £	Imports from Ireland £
1693	152,392	49,915
1694	146,567	114,905
1695	189,114	83,876

Recovery, uncertain at first, quickened from 1696: imports of wool from Ireland, for example, rose to 86,625 stone in 1696 and 204,594 stone in 1697.[4] By 1698 recovery in the Irish export trade was complete. Exports from England to Ireland also expanded; tobacco exports which were 1,851,993 lb. in 1693 rose to 2,866,991 lb. in 1695, and the Irish figures for imports of tobacco were higher in 1698 than

[1]B.M., Add. MSS. 18022, ff. 52-5. Cf. B.M., Add. MSS. 4761, ff. 1, 11-12.
[2]By January 1692, depletion of animal stocks was so serious that the Privy Council of Ireland petitioned the Treasury, desiring leave for some time to transport horses, mares, cows, hogs and sheep from England and Scotland into Ireland duty free. Calendar of Treasury Books, vol. ix, pt. 4, pp. 1456-7, 1547.
[3]B.M., Add. MSS. 20,710. Imports from and exports to Ireland, 1692-7.
[4]B.M., Slo. MSS. 2902, ff. 134, 293. The figure for 1697, as estimated in P.R.O. Customs 2, is 150,878 stone.

in any previously recorded year, though the imports of many other commodities were still below the level of the early 1680s. Anglo-Irish trade, and Irish trade generally, had now overcome the set-back of the early 1690s, and the last years of the century in Ireland as in England were boom years, though the appearance of prosperity in Ireland was heightened by the substantial depreciation of the Irish coinage and by a speculative rise in commodity prices and in real estate values through purchases made in the expectation of a currency revaluation, which was not effected finally until 1701.

As trade revived, so also did the prices of Irish commodities. In the early years the rise of wool prices was sharpest, and wool prices in 1696 were well above those of the 1660s and early 1670s[1] in contrast to the prices of beef and butter[2] which, despite the depreciation of the Irish currency since 1689, were scarcely above the level of the early 1660s. The consequence was a pronounced movement towards sheep rearing and in 1698, despite the growing volume of yarn exported, exports of raw wool were 75 per cent above the level of 1683, whereas exports of beef remained stagnant at their former level, and butter exports actually declined. Though wool prices fell in 1696 and seem to have remained low in the following year[3] also, the rise in the prices of beef and especially of butter in the peace years following 1697[4] was offset by a recovery in wool prices towards the end of the

[1] In May 1696, wool was 11/- to 14/- a stone in Ireland, and prices rose even to 16/- and 17/- (P.R.O., Chancery Masters Exhibits, C 104/12, Letter book), one merchant Abraham Smith of Waterford stating that 'as for wool it hath this season solt for a greater rate than ever I knew it' (ibid., Letter book, 20 May).
[2] In 1696 butter was about 23/- to 26/- a cwt, and beef 4/- to 6/- a cwt, or 16/- a barrel (ibid., Letterbook). Although the barrel at this time would appear to contain only 2 cwt of beef in contrast to 2½ cwt in earlier decades, the extent of the depreciation of the currency was such that the price per cwt must have been, if anything, lower than in the early 1660s.
[3] Wool prices in Ireland fell sharply at the end of May 1696, and for the rest of the year were only 10/- and 11/- a stone. In England, prices which were 18/- to 21/- a stone in 1695 and early 1696, declined towards the middle of the year, and were only 12/- to 14/- a stone in 1697, and 1698. A wool importer from Ireland voiced the opinion in May 1697 that the trade was 'now . . . a little flatt' (P.R.O., Chancery Masters Exhibits, C. 104/12, Cleek v. Calpine, letter book; C. 110/181. On the trend of prices in wool imported from Ireland, see also Chester City Record Office C/MC/402, 403, 22 June, 2 July 1696). Prices in the summer of 1697 were said to be as low as 5/- and 7/6 a stone in Ireland (*A discourse concerning Ireland and the different interests thereof* (London, 1698) p. 70).
[4] The official valuation of butter in the Irish Export and Import ledgers for 1698 and 1699 was 35/- declining in 1700 to 22/- (P.R.O. Customs 15). A contemporary in 1699 noted that 'our butter was likewise much couched abroad, which raised that 26/- or 28/- per cwt to 45/- which at last fell so abroad that by

century[1]. The effects of a fall in wool prices in the early years of the eighteenth century were partially deflected by the general decline in agricultural prices, and no actual decrease in wool exports took place until 1705. The greatly increased export of wool taken in conjunction with the growing export of woollen and worsted yarn formed the largest component of Irish overseas trade at the end of the century. Principally because of this trend exports to England were, for the first time since the Cattle Acts, the largest single branch of the Irish export trade. Whereas the total value of exports had increased from £570,343 in 1683 to £996,305 in 1698 or by 74 per cent, exports to England rose from £171,191 to £364,588 or by 113 per cent. The exports to England as a percentage of the whole had moved from 30 per cent to 37 per cent.

Table 8: Exports to England 1698[2]

		£	%
Wool	335,574 stone	167,787	46·0
Woollen yarn	3,938 stone	3,446	·9
Worsted yarn	12,849 stone	17,346	4·8
Linen yarn	8,917 cwt	44,585	12·2
Linen	23,176 pieces	40,558	11·1
Tallow	26,996 cwt	40,494	11·1
Other items		50,372	13·8
		364,588	100

---

all ye later deare bought butter ye marchants lost some 50 per cent and others more; and altho' we abound in that comodity now they do not bring it in judging by the last year's success that they that can keep their goods longest will meet with the highest prices'. (B.M., Add. MSS. 21133, ff. 45-7, Dublin, 7 Sept., 1699) However, it was not possible for producers to hold prices at the inflated level of the previous few years and in November 1699 butter was only 23/6 to 25/- a cwt (Liverpool Record Office, Norris Papers, 16 November 1699). Over the interval between the ending of the War of the League of Augsburg and the advent of the War of the Spanish Succession as a whole, beef prices were better maintained. In November 1699 beef was 16/- to 18/- a barrel (Liverpool Record Office, Norris Papers, 16 November 1699). The official valuations in the Customs ledgers rose from 18/- in 1698 and 1699 to 20/- in 1700 and 1701.

[1]See B.M., Add. MSS. 21133, ff. 45-7; Extract to Lord Weymouth in answer to queries sent touching the high rates of wool, there, etc . . . Dublin, 7 September 1699. 'As to ye present rise of wool altho our flocks increase (if yr Ldp will be at ys paines to enquire about May next) I doubt not but you will find not so much wool by ⅓th part imported into England as hath been for ye yeare past, very little of ye laste shearing is unsold; and the general cry is that ye markets of England doe not encorage ye prices that are here given. However if ye people of England did not encorage the giving these prices I presume it would fall. . . . I do not yet perceive any occasion for lessening our flocks, for by experience I can say if these will not support us, tillage never will'.

[2]P.R.O., Customs 15, vol. 1.

Despite the fact that London dominated English overseas commodity trade in general by the middle of the seventeenth century, it had a very small share in commodity trade with Ireland in the second half of the century. This is, of course, somewhat deceptive. A portion of Irish trade with the outports and some of the shipments from Ireland even to places as far away as the Mediterranean were financed by the capital of London merchants, who already dominated the English side of the exchange business between the two islands. Nevertheless, the bulk of the commodity trade between Ireland and England passed in 1660 through Chester and Bristol, since medieval times the most important ports in Anglo-Irish trade. The balance was, however, now changing. Bristol's relative importance declined in this period, and there was a movement of the plantation trade, and hence of re-exports to Ireland, north to Liverpool and Whitehaven.[1] Chester, which still had an extensive trade with Ireland in the early 'sixties,[2] was affected by the rapid growth of Liverpool whose trade, though small in the 1650s, increased rapidly in the following decades.[3] In addition, Chester, one of the principal centres for the importation of Irish cattle, suffered from the Cattle Acts. The relatively high number of entries and clearances of vessels to and from Ireland in Chester in the 1680s is deceptive in that they relate mainly to the packet service and passenger traffic between the two countries. In absolute terms the volume of commodity traffic passing through Chester had become very small, and the port had no share in the growing commerce in colonial produce effected from Bristol and latterly from Liverpool and Whitehaven as well.

Wool was mainly imported through the ports of Devonshire and Somerset.[4] Although Bideford, Barnstaple and Minehead were the principal ports for this trade, Exeter, despite the fact that it appears

[1] See *Calendar of State Papers, Colonial, 1685–8*, p. 177. For some statistics of Bristol's Irish trade, see P. McGrath, *Merchants and merchandise in seventeenth-century Bristol* (Bristol, 1955), pp. 279–94. For the number of vessels sailing to and from Ireland in English ports in 1686, see R. Davis, *The rise of the English shipping industry* (London, 1962), p. 211.

[2] Chester City Record Office, C/B/166, Protested bills, etc., 1639–65. See also Custom House Library, London, Selections from Record Offices, Dublin and Edinburgh, 1533–1781 (compiled by H. Atton, 1911), p. 25.

[3] By the 1680s, 110 out of 310 English vessels 'constantly employed to and from Ireland' were said by Harris to belong to Liverpool. Harris, W., *Remarks on the affairs and trade of England and Ireland* (London, 1691), pp. 18–19.

[4] P. J. Bowden, *The wool trade in Tudor and Stuart England* (London, 1962) p. 62.

to have imported only one-fifth of total wool imports from Ireland,[1] was the main centre for distributing the supply to the manufacturing districts: in 1673, for example, the Duke of Ormonde discussed the question of sending a cargo of wool into 'Barnstaple or rather into Bideford or Exeter, the last being the place to which that commodity must be brought to be taken off'.[2] The quality of wool in demand varied somewhat from port to port. In 1673 Colonel Richard Laurence advised Captain Geo. Mathew: 'What you ship to Minehead let it be most combing wool; at Taunton, serge makers give the best rates; for Bristol some combing, but most clothing; at Bideford both sorts usually do well'.[3] From the beginning of the next century, Devonshire's relative place in the wool trade declined, and by the 'twenties its share was greatly reduced. The bulk of the wool and yarn trade had moved north to Bristol and Liverpool. The development of Anglo-Irish trade in the eighteenth century is associated with a re-orientation of the channels of communication between the two countries.

[1]Statistics of wool imports at Exeter, compiled from the Port Books are given in W. B. Stephens, *Seventeenth-century Exeter* (Exeter, 1958) pp. 36, 123, 170; E. A. G. Clark, *The ports of the Exe estuary, 1660–1860* (Exeter, 1960) pp. 139, 153. Wool imports from Ireland to Exeter were said to have been worth £40,000 a year. *Journals of the English House of Commons,* vol. xi, p. 467; H.M.C., *House of Lords MSS.,* new series, vol. 2, p. 247.

[2]H.M.C., *Ormonde MSS.,* new series, vol. 3, p. 329.

[3]Ibid., p. 336.

CHAPTER III

ANGLO-IRISH TRADE IN THE EIGHTEENTH CENTURY

I. VOLUME AND GROWTH

THE English trade was now of growing importance to the Irish economy, and at the end of the seventeenth century though the increase in wool exports was most noticeable there were also sharp increases in exports of linen and linen yarn to England. These trends

Table 9: Exports from Ireland

Year ending 25 March	(1) to Great Britain £	(2) to all parts £	(3) Great Britain as % of total %	(4) %
1700*	372,585	814,746	45·7	(42·2)
1710	361,152	712,497	50·7	(48·8)
1720	461,350	1,038,382	44·4	(43·1)
1730	430,520	992,832	43·4	(42·6)
1740	677,738	1,259,853	53·8	
1750	1,069,864	1,862,834	57·4	
1760	1,450,757	2,139,388	67·8	
1770	2,408,839	3,159,587	76·2	
1780	2,384,899	3,012,179	79·2	
1790	3,695,670	4,855,319	76·1	(66·6)
1800	3,482,691	4,079,272	85·4	(80·9)

*Year ending 25 Dec.

Table 10: Imports into Ireland

Year ending 25 March	(1) from Great Britain £	(2) from all parts £	(3) Great Britain as % of total %	(4) %
1700*	427,603	792,473	53·9	(51·5)
1710	309,709	554,248	55·9	(52·8)
1720	514,057	891,678	57·7	(53·4)
1730	457,302	929,896	49·2	(46·4)
1740	499,480	849,678	58·8	
1750	920,341	1,531,654	60·1	
1760	1,094,753	1,647,592	66·4	
1770	1,878,599	2,566,845	73·2	
1780	1,576,636	2,127,579	74·1	
1790	2,663,448	3,829,914	69·5	(62·3)
1800	4,862,626	6,183,457	78·6	(73·2)

*Year ending 25 Dec.

For the sake of uniformity the figures for Great Britain only are given. But where separate figures for England exist, the percentage English trade formed of total Irish trade is indicated in parentheses in the fourth column.

were to continue throughout the eighteenth century, and exports to
Great Britain which were only half, or less than half, of the total Irish
exports in the first three decades of the century, rose to 85.4 per
cent of Irish exports in 1800. Similarly, imports from Great Britain
which were only 53.9 per cent of total imports in 1700 had risen to
78.6 per cent in 1800.[1] The most striking feature of Irish overseas
trade in the eighteenth century is therefore the growing dependence
on England, which provided a much bigger outlet for Irish exports
than the limited markets on the European mainland. Moreover, as
English home production was far from adequate for the domestic
demand, concessions were made to the Irish linen industry and provision trade despite the fact that England was prepared to make no
general relaxation in favour of Irish exports. As a result the relative
importance of the Irish trade in the general pattern of English overseas trade increased sharply. In the second half of the seventeenth
century and in the early years of the following century the Irish trade
was a very small fraction of English foreign trade. In 1700, for example, exports to Ireland were only 4.2 per cent of total English
exports and imports from Ireland 3.9 per cent of total imports. The
relative importance of the trade expanded as linen imports increased
in volume; and increased especially when both the linen trade and
the provision trade grew rapidly in the second half of the century. In
this period exports to Ireland and imports from Ireland accounted
for more than 10 per cent of England's foreign trade.[2] It was, there-

Table 11: Imports into England

Year ending 25 Dec.	from Ireland £	from all parts £	Ireland as % of total %
1700	233,853	5,970,175	3·9
1710	310,846	4,011,341	7·7
1720	282,812	6,090,084	4·6
1730	294,156	7,780,020	3·8
1740	390,565	6,703,779	5·8
1750	612,808	7,772,040	7·9
5 Jan.			
1761	904,181	9,832,803	9·2
1771	1,214,398	12,216,938	9·9
1781	1,549,388	10,812,240	14·3
1791	2,203,099	17,442,549	12·6
1800	2,445,079	24,483,840	10·0

[1]See tables 9 and 10.
[2]See tables 11 and 12. For published tables of Anglo-Irish trade statistics, see
E. B. Schumpeter, *English overseas trade statistics, 1697–1808* (Oxford, 1960);
B. R. Mitchell and P. Deane, *Abstract of British historical statistics* (Cambridge,
1962).

fore, one of the most important branches of English overseas trade, and the trade with Ireland was greater than that with any other European country.

Irish plain linens were exempt from duty in England from 1696, and from 1743 also benefited by bounties on re-export; and from 1758–9, Irish beef, butter, pork and cattle were re-admitted to the English market, and the duty on tallow removed. On the continent Irish commodities had to face high tariff barriers. They enjoyed a clear advantage only in re-exports of salt beef to the West Indies, a trade in which Irish beef had a European monopoly; and to a lesser extent in salt butter whose production in Southern Europe especially was very inadequate either for home consumption or for re-export to colonial possessions. The Irish linen industry, however, had no expanding market outside England to rely on, and after 1760 even the Irish provision trade began to develop a dependence on the English market. The importance of England now became very marked, as high prices there attracted Irish provisions and as linen exports continued to expand steadily. The effect of the numerous French wars and of a declining use of salt beef in the colonies and in the French navy also served to bring about a decline in this once extensive branch of Irish foreign trade. As a consequence of these factors dependence on the English market by 1800 was nearly complete.

Ireland's dependence on English imports was always very considerable. This was due partly to the fact that in many commodities England was the country best suited to supply Ireland's needs, and partly to Irish tariffs and Irish economic policy, which were subservient to England's interests. The Navigation Laws, which

Table 12: Exports from England

Year ending 25 Dec.	to Ireland £	to all parts £	Ireland as % of total %
1700	271,641	6,469,146	4·2
1710	285,424	6,295,208	4·5
1720	328,584	6,910,899	4·8
1730	532,699	8,548,983	6·2
1740	628,288	8,197,789	7·7
1750	1,316,600	12,699,081	10·4
5 Jan.			
1761	1,050,401	14,694,910	7·1
1771	2,125,467	14,267,655	14·9
1781	1,930,338*	12,597,138	15·3
1791	1,937,538	18,884,716	10·3
1800	3,786,085	34,074,699	11·1

*From P.R.O. Customs 17. £1,888,055 in Customs 3.

prohibited the direct importation of many commodities from the colonies, and a lack of capital which limited direct foreign trading from Ireland, helped to maintain this dependence. But even the removal of these restrictions in 1779–80, in so far as they related to Ireland, had little effect in making Ireland economically more independent of England. Only in the case of tobacco did a substantial share of Ireland's supply come directly from the former colonies in America, and even then probably to a large extent on English account. Sugar and many other colonial commodities continued to be imported mainly through England. The Irish merchants were able to purchase these commodities on credit in England whereas direct imports from the West Indies were financed by outward shipments on Irish account of linen and provisions. As this trade was limited and the Irish merchants' resources were too small to finance large-scale direct imports from the West Indies, these commodities continued to be supplied to Ireland on credit terms by merchants in England.[1] The legal dependence had indeed been removed, but the economic dependence remained.

Irish exports to England increased from £307,048 in 1701 to £3,497,550 in the year ending 25 March 1797, and within the same period imports from England rose from £385,307 to £3,088,962. The value of Irish exports to England therefore rose by 1040 per cent approximately, and the value of imports by 700 per cent. In the case of exports, however, the rate of growth is boosted by some fairly substantial upward adjustments in valuations; in imports, on the other hand, there is little change over the century as a whole, a downward trend in valuations in the first half of the century being roughly equalled by an upward one in the second half. The statistics of the English Inspector General are in some respects a better measure of the growth of the trade as apart from the first years of compilation stable valuations were with few exceptions employed throughout.[2] According to these figures, imports from Ireland rose from £285,391

[1]P.R.O. of Ireland, Customs and Excise Administration Papers, 1A/43/5, No. 4. John Beresford, Custom House, Dublin, 1 April 1792.

[2]But certain commodities were entered at value. Though these values themselves tended to become formalised they do reflect in some degree the trend of prices; and two of them, salt and tea, were important items in Anglo-Irish trade. Adjustment of valuations after the first years of compilation were negligible, apart from adjustments before 1714 to the important category of woollens (see Professor Ashton's introduction to Schumpeter, *English overseas trade statistics, 1697–1808*, p. 4). Woollens were, however, a very minor component of English exports to Ireland in the early eighteenth century.

in 1701 to £2,383,149 in the year ending 5 January 1797 i.e. by 735 per cent, and exports to Ireland from £305,418 to £2,653,959 i.e. an increase of 770 per cent.

The sustained growth in the volume of imports from Ireland dates from the beginning of the 1730s. Before that, growing imports of linen and linen yarn had been offset by the decline in the Irish wool trade. But there was a steady increase of imports over the 1730s and 1740s, mainly as a result of the expanding Irish linen industry. Imports from Ireland further increased sharply in the second half of the 1750s and again in the second half of the 1760s. They increased over the 1770s as a whole, and by a further 50 per cent in the 1780s. Exports to Ireland had already been growing rapidly in the 1710s and 1720s, and over the rest of the century the rise was particularly pronounced in the decade 1740–50, when their volume doubled, in the second half of the 1760s, and in the late 1790s.

The variety of Irish exports to England was exceptionally limited, and the trade depended almost exclusively on two or three commodities or categories of commodities. This was true, of course, of Irish trade with other countries as well. Wool in its raw state formed 42 per cent of Irish exports to England in 1683, and this percentage had increased to 46 per cent in 1698. The declining importance of the trade in wool, woollen and worsted yarn from the early eighteenth century was offset by expanding exports of linen and linen yarn. In 1683 exports of linen and linen yarn to England were only 6.7 per cent of total exports to England, but in 1698 amounted to 23.3 per cent of the total. Thereafter, the rise in their prominence was impressive (see Table 14, p. 51).

The relative importance of linen declined somewhat in the last four decades of the century as a result of the growth of the trade in cattle and provisions with Britain after 1758-9. The basis of the export trade with Britain broadened significantly in this period. Whereas linen, linen yarn, wool, woollen and worsted yarn had amounted to 90.7 per cent of Irish exports to Britain in 1738, the same commodities, even with the addition of salted provisions, amounted to only 82.7 per cent of the total in 1798. This change is due to the growing trade in grain and flour with Britain in the last three decades of the century. Exports of grain, flour and oatmeal to Britain were valued at £72,211 in 1778; by 1798 the corresponding exports to England alone were worth £291,010. Foster's celebrated corn law of 1784 simply fitted into a changing market pattern.

Table 13: Principal exports to England (Great Britain)* expressed as percentages of total exports to England (Great Britain)*

	1698 %	1709 %	1718 %	1728 %	1738 %	1748 %	1758 %	1768 %	1778 %	1788 %	1798 %
Wool	46·0	15·5	9·4	5·3	3·7	2·8	0·2	0·7	0·04	—	—
Woollen yarn	0·9	2·9	3·3	1·7	2·4	1·0	0·3	0·3	—	0·6	—
Worsted yarn	4·8	6·6	23·7	11·1	12·7	13·7	8·8	10·2	7·5	0·3	·5
(1)	51·7	25·0	36·4	18·1	18·8	17·5	9·3	11·2	7·5	0·9	·5
Linen cloth	11·1	30·5	19·3	49·3	55·6	58·9	67·1	58·5	56·8	66·3	56·0
Linen yarn	12·2	16·0	25·1	13·8	16·3	13·0	13·1	8·4	6·2	4·3	2·2
(2)	23·3	46·5	44·4	63·1	71·9	71·9	80·2	66·9	63·0	70·6	58·2
Beef								1·7	5·3	2·4	4·0
Butter								6·9	11·1	12·9	14·2
Pork								0·9	1·9	1·9	5·8
(3)								9·5	18·3	17·2	24·0
(1)+(2)+(3)	75·0	71·5	80·8	81·2	90·7	89·4	89·5	87·6	88·8	88·7	82·7

*Based on Irish valuations of exports to England for 1698–1728, 1788, 1798; to Great Britain, 1738–78.

Table 14: Percentage of total exports to Great Britain*

Year ending 25 March	Wool, woollen yarn, worsted	Linen cloth and yarn
1698†	51·7	23·3
1718	36·4	44·4
1728	18·1	63·1
1738	18·8	71·9
1748	17·5	71·9
1758	9·3	80·2

*England, 1698, 1718, 1728; Great Britain, 1738, 1748, 1758.
†Year ending 25 December 1698.

The only other important items in Irish exports to Britain were also typical of an agricultural country, especially tallow, raw cow-hides, and calf skins. There were also fairly substantial exports of sheepskins, rabbit skins, coney skins and some other animal hides or skins. Apart from these items, exports were negligible, the only other commodities entering permanently into the trade in quantities valued at £1,000 or more per annum being soap, kelp, frieze, glue and copper ore. Even these commodities, with the exception of copper ore, were primarily agricultural products. Exports of manufactures to England, even of such goods as candles, tanned hides or shoes, in which Ireland was likely to enjoy a substantial price advantage, remained very small, primarily because of high English tariffs.

In contrast to Irish exports, Irish imports were very varied and their variety emphasises the great degree of dependence on England. Eight of the principal commodities imported from England accounted, on an average, for only 50 to 60 per cent of total imports, and exceptionally—in 1798—69.2 per cent. Moreover, there were many other items in Irish imports from England whose value frequently exceeded that of the staple goods. The English commodity in most constant demand was coal: throughout the century coal imports grew at roughly the same rate as total imports from Britain. The other items of importance were drapery, muscovado sugar, and tea. But the relative importance of drapery is exaggerated by the fact that the import valuations greatly exceeded the real prices. However, even if prices are adjusted to a more reasonable level,[1] drapery still re-

[1] The altered percentages have been calculated on the basis of old drapery, 9s. 3d. per yard, and new drapery 1s. 4½d. per yard, which were computed as 'the rate of real or current value' of imports on the average of three years ending 25 March 1799. See *Account presented to the House of Commons respecting the official and the real or current value of the imports and exports of Ireland,* 8 May 1804. P.P. 1803–4, vii, 93.

Table 15: Principal imports from England (Great Britain)* expressed as percentages of total imports from England (Great Britain)*

	1698 %	1709 %	1718 %	1728 %	1738 %	1748 %	1758 %	1768 %	1778 %	1788 %	1798 %
Coal	9·1	10·2	6·9	8·4	6·7	6·1	9·6	7·9	8·0	9·4	9·5
Old and new drapery	1·7	1·7	3·9	5·3	2·5	5·2	8·9	11·4	17·2	22·1	23·6
Muscovado sugar	2·3	4·3	7·4	4·8	12·9	10·2	10·3	15·2	10·1	12·5	13·7
Hops	5·2	8·5	15·2	9·7	11·0	9·4	6·1	3·2	2·6	2·2	4·8
Tea	—	—	1·7	2·8	8·0	4·6	3·2	4·5	8·5	12·8	10·5
Tobacco	26·0	20·7	11·6	7·2	4·0	3·6	3·8	2·3	2·2	1·0	5·0
Silk manufactures	4·7	3·7	3·0	5·1	3·8	4·4	4·7	4·4	3·9	1·4	·5
Silk, raw and thrown undyed	4·1	4·2	9·5	9·6	5·9	8·0	7·4	5·2	4·9	1·2	1·6
	53·1	53·3	59·2	52·9	54·8	51·5	54·0	54·1	57·4	62·6	69·2

*Based on Irish valuations of imports from England, 1698–1728, 1788, 1798; from Great Britain, 1738–78.

presents 15.5 per cent in 1788 and 16.8 per cent in 1798 of total imports from England. Tobacco was easily the most important import in the early years of the century, but its relative importance fell as prices dropped and also as the tobacco trade, well developed already at the end of the seventeenth century, grew much less rapidly than Anglo-Irish trade in general. English industrial progress is reflected in the growing variety of imports, and imports of hardware, steelware, etc., and of textiles including cottons from Lancashire increased sharply in the latter half of the century.

II. EXPORTS FROM IRELAND

Wool was the chief export to England from the time of the passing of the Cattle Acts to the early eighteenth century. The demand for it came principally from the wool combing and manufacturing districts of Devon and Somerset and the bulk of the wool trade was effected with ports south of the Bristol Channel or with Exeter. The volume of wool shipments increased sharply after the Cattle Acts. By 1688 Irish wool was a 'vital necessity'[1] in Devonshire. Allegations that much of the Irish supply was shipped, in violation of the wool acts, to the continent under pretext of shipment to England were frequent. These claims were, however, generally exaggerated. The trade with England was very brisk. The patentees of the office for registering wool bonds claimed that the amount fraudulently exported was never thought to have exceeded one-quarter of the total exports.[2] While the patentees had an interest in minimizing the extent of smuggling in order to protect their office, the available evidence would suggest that it is nevertheless probably an acceptable estimate. Contemporaries overrated the necessity for Irish wool in France and the excessive attention devoted by the authorities to the question arose from their mercantilist principles rather than from any evidence of widespread smuggling. Even in a remote port like Galway where customs administration was very lax, and wool shipments to the continent not uncommon, much of the wool was actually carried to England. In

[1]Hoskins, *Industry, trade and people in Exeter, 1688–1800*, p. 30.
[2]'Une narrative de nostre affaire d'Irlande' in *Analecta Hibernica*, vol. 2, pp. 68–70 (n.d., probably 1677). Some extravagant contemporary estimates put the total smuggled as high as half the total export of wool (*Calendar of State Papers, Domestic, 1677–8*, p. 71; *Journals of the British House of Commons*, vol. xviii, p. 714).

1683, for example, 11,790 stone of wool were shipped,[1] of which 7,520 stone arrived at Barnstaple and Bideford alone.[2]

In the early eighteenth century wool prices in Ireland fell more heavily than other prices, and exports of Irish wool began to fall steadily from 1705 onwards. This decline is registered in the Irish and English statistics, both of which maintain a close correspondence. The fall in legal exports, which was quite evident to contemporaries, was attributed to an increase of smuggling, especially in the peace years following the Treaty of Utrecht, which it was believed offset, in whole or in great part, the decline expressed in the statistics. The more extravagant evidence all comes, however, from very doubtful sources. Despite the fact that there were many allegations of smuggling from Ireland during the War of the Spanish Succession, the French themselves were not prepared to grant passports for wool from Ireland in the years 1704-8, and as a consequence wool smuggling ceased despite an otherwise flourishing illegal trade. The decline in exports to England was a very real one at that time. It was accentuated in the following years, as prices of beef and butter recovered more rapidly from the effects of depression and war than wool prices. The post-war decline in shipments should be regarded as part of a lessening production of wool (which was temporarily reversed in the 1730s, the late 1740s and again in the early 1760s) and of a gradual switch, within the declining supply, to the preparation of worsted yarn for the English market, rather than the result of a revival of a large-scale smuggling trade. Admittedly the methods of wool smuggling had altered meanwhile, and the smuggling was no longer effected under the guise of shipment to England, as an improved correspondence between the customs administrations in the two countries had made frauds in the way of false certificates of wool having been landed in England more readily detectable.[3] As a result of this, the English and Irish statistics for the wool and yarn trade tally very closely. In fact, as there was a tendency for merchants to try to underestimate exports of wool or yarn to avoid the fairly heavy export duties and fees, the English statistics at times appear to exceed the Irish. The smuggling trade was of significance only in a number of years in the 1730s after a recovery in Irish wool production had been followed by a break in prices. Subsequently the rising demand

[1] B.M., Add. MSS. 4759.
[2] P.R.O., E. 190/961/7/1.
[3] See Chapter VIII, pp. 140-3

of the Irish combers, spinning for the English market, raised prices to the smugglers who by 1756 had virtually abandoned their wool trade.

Prices of wool in Ireland had been as much as 30 per cent or more lower than prices in England in the second half of the seventeenth century.[1] The fall in wool prices[2] in Ireland at the opening of the eighteenth century, sharper than that of other commodities, was the first step in a decline of production. Wool was also diverted to yarn spinning in which, as labour was cheaper in Ireland than in England, the Irish producer enjoyed the more considerable advantage on the English market.[3] Exports of woollen yarn to England were already 20,000 stone at the beginning of the century and remained fairly stable at that level till the middle of the century, when they fell away rapidly. Worsted yarn exports amounted to 12,849 stone in 1698 and grew rapidly in the following years, reaching 57,562 stone in 1717. Exports remained fairly stable at 60,000 to 70,000 stone till 1747 when annual exports reached 100,000 stone, and in the 1760s exports of worsted yarn reached 150,000 stone a year. As early as 1731 Irish wool prices exceeded English.[4] But this was a temporary phenomenon at the height of a short-lived boom. The subsequent slump in wool prices was severe. But with the significant expansion in wool combing in Ireland in the 1740s prices became firmer. From the 'sixties especially, the prices of wool soared sharply in Ireland and they were now well above the level of English prices.[5] As a result of

[1] H.M.C., *Ormonde MSS.*, new series, vol. 3, p. 347; *Calendar of State Papers, Ireland, 1669–70*, p. 104; Davenant, Balance of trade, B.M., Slo. MSS. 2902, f. 16.

[2] According to the valuations of wool exports in the ledgers of Irish exports and imports, wool rose from 10/- a stone in 1699 to 11/- in 1700, fell to 9/- in 1701, 7/- in 1702, 6/6 in 1703, 6/- in 1704, 5/- in 1706.

[3] *Analecta Hibernica*, vol. 2, p. 80; P.R.O. of Ireland, Private Letters on Irish affairs: Letters to and from Lord Townshend in 1779, letter from John Beresford, n.d., *Journals of the British House of Commons*, vol. xv, p. 553; vol. xvi, p. 137.

[4] *Journals of the British House of Commons*, vol. xxi, p. 691. The official valuations of Irish exports recovered from 5/3 to 8/- a stone in 1714, and from then to end of the 1720s were generally from 7/- to 8/-. In 1731 however, they rose from 8/- to 9/- and in 1732 to 10/-. From 1735 to 1742, prices declined, but rose in 1743 to 8/6 and 1744 to 12/-. The high prices of the early 1730s and 1744 are confirmed in other evidence (e.g. *Faulkner's Dublin Journal*, 5 September, 7 and 28 October 1732; Young, *Tour in Ireland*, pt. 1, p. 230). The overall trend from the mid-1740s was also upwards (e.g. see *Faulkner's Dublin Journal* 1749; ibid., 28 June 1748, 25 September 1750, 10 July 1753; *Cork Evening Post*, 1757–8).

[5] e.g. prices of Irish (Ballinasloe fair) and Lincolnshire wool, 1770–84, *Report of the Lords of the Committee of Council appointed for the consideration of all matters relating to trade and foreign plantations*, 1785, p. 28.

this price trend exports of wool fell rapidly away, and exports were concentrated almost exclusively on the worsted yarn trade. The great advantage of Irish yarn was its cheapness: despite the sharp rise of wool prices in Ireland in the second half of the century, the low costs of labour in spinning in Ireland still left the yarn competitive on the English market into the middle of the 1790s. Labour in spinning in Ireland was said to be one-third cheaper, and despite the fact that wool cost 10½d. a pound in Ireland, compared with 6½d. a pound in England, Irish yarn was 20 per cent cheaper than English. Even when all costs of importing it were included, it was still as cheap as English yarn in Norwich, sometimes 6 per cent cheaper.[1]

The change in the composition of the wool trade was evident from the very beginning of the century, and frequent complaints were made by the woolcombers and spinners of the south west of the importation of cheap Irish worsted yarn.[2] But the woollen industry in Devonshire was now in a state of decline, and imports of wool and yarn in the ports of Bideford, Barnstaple and Minehead fell off rapidly. Apart from some trade with Minehead, Irish exports of wool and yarn were now directed almost exclusively to Bristol and Liverpool.[3] Liverpool, whose share in the Irish wool trade had been growing from the end of the seventeenth century, almost monopolized the trade in raw wool and supplied the growing woollen industries of Lancashire and Yorkshire. Bristol became the chief centre of yarn imports,[4] which was now easily the more important branch of the wool trade. As early as 1734 a bill to remove the import duties from Irish yarn was considered likely to pass the House of Commons, 'because the Bristol people who chiefly take it [Irish yarn] off desire it should [pass].'[5]

[1]P.R.O., B.T. 6/109, 29 January 1785, Evidence of the representatives of the Manufacturers of Norwich; Paper delivered by Messrs. Walker and Richardson of Manchester, 21 Feb. 1785 (Evidence printed in *Report of the Lords of the Committee of Council*, 1785, pp. 16-17, 40).
[2]See numerous petitions in *Journals of the British House of Commons;* Hoskins, *Industry, trade and people in Exeter*, pp. 31, 52.
[3]*Journals of the British House of Commons*, vol. XXIII, p. 341; Custom House, Liverpool, Register of Wool vessels 1739-92; P.R.O., T. 64/281 (i), (ii), Account of wool bonds, 1739-43.
[4]Between Michaelmas and 24 November 1707, 1,381 packs of yarn in all were imported through Bristol, and within apparently the same period, only 1,580 packs to Bristol, and 'other western ports' together. (*Journals of the British House of Commons*, vol. XV, pp. 475-6, 553).
[5]H.M.C., *Egmont Diary*, vol. II, p. 69.

The imports through Bristol were primarily for the supply of the expanding worsted industries of Norwich and Colchester, and had their origin in the fact that, because of the fear of wool smuggling, imports of Irish yarn and wool had been prohibited through any of the ports beyond Lands End. This overland method of supply was cumbersome and expensive: the charges on carrying a pack of Irish wool between Bristol and Colchester or Norwich were computed at 15 per cent of the prime cost, and for yarn at 5 per cent;[1] or according to another estimate, the charges by importing the goods overland were 17 per cent higher for wool, and 6 per cent for worsted yarn, than if imported directly by sea to London or Yarmouth.[2] Much of the Irish yarn appears to have been sent by land carriage first to London and then shipped coastwise to Yarmouth. In 1732-3, for instance, the port of Great Yarmouth received 479,510 lb. of Irish worsted yarn from London.[3] The difficulties involved in these round-about methods of trade appear to have had some effect in discouraging Irish merchants from dealing in yarn on their own account to be sent any farther than Bristol. In 1734 the Youghal merchant, Gabriel Clarke, wrote that he could 'find none inclinable to send any [worsted yarn] on com[mission] farther than Bristol.'[4] The restriction on shipping Irish wool and yarn to Exeter and the other ports beyond Lands End was finally removed in 1752 and 1753.[5] But despite the fact that Exeter had campaigned for 60 years against the restriction, the pattern of the wool trade had so altered that a free commerce did not bring back the wool trade to Exeter. The merchants and manufacturers of Norwich, Yarmouth and Colchester had also agitated for a free trade,[6] and after 1753 a direct yarn trade developed between Dublin and Cork and Yarmouth. A sharp decline in what remained of the export trade in raw wool coincides with the removal of the restriction.

The demand for Irish yarn was considerable in Norwich, and the various manufacturers required specific kinds or qualities for use in their manufactures. Even as late as the 1780s, 3,500 packs of Irish yarn, valued at about £87,500, were used at Norwich each year, and

[1]B.M., Add. MSS. 33344, f. 67. Commissioners for Trade and Plantations, 25 Feb. 1731-32.

[2]*Journals of the British House of Commons*, vol. XXI, p. 693, 23 March 1730-31.

[3]T. S. Willan, *The English Coasting Trade, 1600-1750* (Manchester, 1938) pp. 93-4. Cf. P.R.O., C. 105/15, Gabriel Clarke, Youghal, 25 November 1733.

[4]P.R.O., C. 105/15, 1 February 1733-4, Youghal.

[5]See chapter VIII, p. 142, n. 5.

[6]*Journals of the British House of Commons*, vol. XII, p. 79; vol. XVIII, p. 718, 721, 727; vol. XXI, p. 693.

amounted to one-fifth of the total quantity used.[1] The demand for
Irish worsted yarn was smaller in Manchester, where it was said to
be used in the smallware trade, but not at all in the cotton manufacture.[2] 1,052 packs (at 270 lb per pack) were used in Manchester
in 1781; 1,359 in 1782; 1,332 in 1783, and 2,088 in 1784.[3] Considerable quantities were also said to be sent to Exeter, Coventry, Kidder-
minster, Wilton, Kendal, Glasgow and 'several other parts of Great
Britain'.[4] But it is doubtful if the amount of Irish yarn used in these
centres was very large. In Devizes, for example, no Irish yarn was
used; in Gloucestershire the quantities were small, and the Hampshire manufacturers used little or no Irish worsted in their stuffs.[5]
Comparing the above estimates with the Irish exports of wool, it
would appear that about 60 per cent of total Irish exports of yarn
(or of the corresponding English figures for imports) was used in
Norwich; 25 per cent in Manchester, and the remaining 15 per cent
was for the most part probably taken by Yorkshire. The merchants
and manufacturers of Halifax claimed that they made a great use
of Irish worsted yarn, and stated that though it was not 'absolutely
necessary so far as related to [the] quality of their manufactures,
[they] could not carry them on to their present extent without it.'[6]

By 1709 linen and linen yarn had become the principal Irish exports
to England, linen cloth remaining the largest single item in Anglo-
Irish trade throughout the century. The rise of the Irish linen industry
has been attributed largely to the presence in Ireland of Huguenot
immigrants, but the industry was growing before their arrival. Exports of linen cloth to England rose from 11,376 yards in 1683 to
131,568 yards in 1686 and 556,224 yards in 1698. Yarn exports
amounted to 3,670 cwt in 1683, 5,992 cwt in 1686 and 8,917 cwt
by 1698. Undoubtedly, favourable climatic factors, the skill and
capitals of the Huguenot refugees, and the founding of the Linen
Board in 1711 are of significance in the rise of the Irish linen industry.

---

[1]P.R.O., B.T. 6/109, 29 Jan. 1785. Evidence printed in *Report of the Lords of
the Committee of Council appointed for the consideration of all matters relating to
trade and foreign plantations*, 1785, p. 16.
[2]P.R.O., B.T. 6/109, 31 Jan. 1785. Evidence printed, loc. cit., p. 34.
[3]Ibid., 21 Feb. 1785. Evidence printed, loc. cit., p. 40.
[4]Ibid., 21 Feb. 1785. Evidence printed, loc. cit., p. 40.
[5]*Report of the Lords of the Committee of Council*, p. 27; *Minutes of Evidence
before the Committee of Lords*, p. 280.
[6]P.R.O., B.T. 6/109, 8 Feb. 1785. Evidence printed in *Report of the Lords of
the Committee of Council*, 1785, p. 25.

But the real reason was the growing English market and the advantage from the end of the seventeenth century of duty-free entry for Irish linens. Additional duties in 1742 enhanced this advantage. As the duties on foreign linens imported to England amounted for instance by 1780 to 20 or 25 per cent of their value, the margin of preference enabled Irish linens to capture much of the English market from the German exporters. At the end of the seventeenth century exports of linen yarn were still worth more than exports of cloth, but from 1706 onwards cloth became the main export. The growth of the industry in the eighteenth century is remarkable and transformed Ulster from being with Connaught the most backward of the four provinces to the most progressive. Exports of linen to England were less than half a million yards in 1700, but in 1800 imports of Irish linen into Great Britain had increased to over 38,000,000 yards, and several million yards were also exported from Ireland to other parts, principally to the West Indies.

The Irish statistics for linen exports must, however, be accepted with some caution. Irish linens were duty-free on export and exporting merchants, therefore, tended to make over-entries to suit their convenience or out of vanity. Irish figures for exports, probably for this reason, tend to exceed the corresponding English figures for imports. Though the divergence between the two sets of statistics is small, normally about 5 to 10 per cent, this is probably because Irish merchants made under-entries of linens shipped to Chester, Bristol and Liverpool to avoid the payment there of local duties,[1] which were apparently levied on the basis of the merchant's cocquet.

[1]*Journals of the Irish House of Commons*, vol. 10, App. ccccxvii, ccccxxviii; B.M., Add. MSS. 33119, ff. 293–7; *Report on the circulating paper, the specie and the current coin of Ireland*, 1804, reprinted 1826, p. 109. These under-entries seem to have been numerous enough to balance the over-entries; but the size of the latter may perhaps be gauged from the fact that in the 'eighties and early 'nineties, the official figures for Irish exports of linen to Scotland, where no local duties were levied on linens, were sometimes twice or three times greater than the corresponding Scottish figure for imports. On the other hand, laxity in ascertaining the precise quantities of linen shipped in each entry spread among the Irish customs officers towards the end of the century to such a degree that the figures for the export of Irish linens to England were less than the corresponding English figures for imports from Ireland by 1800 to the extent of about 15 per cent, and even the former exceptionally wide disparity between Scottish and Irish figures had disappeared. Another discrepancy in the Irish statistics can be detected in the case of canvas, Irish exports to England amounting to only 4,000 yards, whereas English imports from Ireland in the second quarter of the century were as high as 60,000 yards. The divergence arose from the fact that in Ireland only such linens as were exported at the time of claiming the production premium on

England was easily the main market for Irish linens. Though Irish attempts to enter other markets, especially the coveted Spanish market, were not infrequent, they met with very little success till after 1780.

Table 16: Linen: Exports from Ireland[1] (in yards)

Year ending 25 March	To Great Britain	To all parts
1700*	298,992	305,160
1710	1,528,185	1,688,574
1720	2,560,114	2,637,984
1730	3,821,189	4,136,204
1740	6,403,569	6,627,772
1750	10,856,713	11,200,460
1760	13,093,592	13,375,456
1770	19,671,435	20,560,754
1780	18,298,815	18,746,902
1790	33,361,190	37,322,126
1800	32,912,500	35,676,908

*Year ending 25 December.

The English demand was primarily for home consumption, a good indication of this being the importance the Chester fairs held in the trade.[2] The competition of Irish linen was very severe and was acutely felt by the foreign suppliers of the English market.[3] Apparently, even as early as the 1730s, London drapers had begun to substitute Irish linens for German (although only to a limited extent as yet, as imports of German linens were still rising). In 1735, Egmont, who was in-

---

canvas at the Custom House were entered for export as canvas. The rest of the canvas receiving the bounty was entered for home consumption, and if exported later, was entered simply as linen. (See B.M., Add. MSS. 21134, ff. 27-8, 66, 68, 74, 77-86). In England on the other hand a more exact account was kept and this is the cause of the apparent discrepancy.

[1] P.R.O., Customs 15. Ledgers of Irish Exports and Imports.

[2] In the period 10 April-14 July 1775 of 520,669 pieces entered at the Dublin Customs House 209,399 were for London, and 127,520 for Chester (Chester Chronicle, 31 July 1775). Sales of Irish linens at a single Chester fair were estimated at £75,000 (Reasons for and against lowering the gold and silver of this kingdom (Dublin, 1760) p. 10). In the 1770s peace-time exports of linen from Dublin to Chester amounted apparently to 1,200 packages, about 3,000,000, yards a year, one-third of which were not endorsed on the customs certificates. (Journals of the Irish House of Commons, vol. 10, app. ccccxxviii). Parkinson states, without indication of source, that imports of linen through Chester reached a peak of 5,000,000 yards in 1786 (Parkinson, The rise of the port of Liverpool (Liverpool, 1952) p. 142).

[3] For its impact on the Dutch suppliers, see C. H. Wilson, Anglo-Dutch commerce and finance in the eighteenth century (Cambridge 1941) pp. 56-62.

terested in establishing the linen industry on his own estates in County Cork, wrote from London that 'our kingdom will infallibly loose its trade with England for coarse linnens unlesse we keep to ye old price and raise them not as we have done of late in so much as ye linnen drapers are resolving to send again to Hamburg.'[1] The Dutch linen industry based on the bleaching of German linens suffered especially, and the turnover of the bleaching business at Haarlem declined from a total of 80,000 to 110,000 pieces in the early years of the eighteenth century to less than half that figure by 1800.[2]

The decline of the Dutch bleaching industry was, however, only partially due to Irish competition. It was also caused by an increasing tendency towards direct exports of bleached linens from Germany to England. But the direct exports also suffered severely from the competition of the Irish linens. In the first half of the century imports to England of German narrow linens, which were the closest in quality and breadth to the Irish linens, fluctuated between 10 and 23 million yards per annum, whereas imports from Ireland exceeded 9 million yards only from the end of the 1740s. The success of the Irish linens was, however, already quite apparent. Whereas imports of German narrow linens rose only from 13,330,950 yards in 1700 to 17,103,876 yards in 1750, imports from Ireland in the same years rose from a mere 318,364 yards to 9,072,239 yards. Imports of German narrow linen began to decline sharply from the mid-1750s, and from the mid-1760s were exceeded by imports from Ireland. By the end of the 1770s narrow linens from Germany amounted only to about 8 million yards, whereas imports from Ireland were now 20 million. In 1795, narrow German cloth had fallen to 4 million yards, and the figures for Irish linens had climbed to 38 million yards.[3] German narrow linens had been easily the most important foreign linens on the English market, and in the first half of the century amounted to about 50 per cent or more of total imports of foreign canvas and linen, excluding Irish. In the first 70 years of the century imports of foreign linen as a whole appear to have remained fairly stable, though with some tendency to decline from the early 1750s. Total imports, however, probably fell considerably after the sharp decline in imports

---

[1]Egmont Papers, B.M., Add. MSS. 47000, p. 87. 31 July 1735.
[2]Wilson, op. cit., p. 61.
[3]Figures for 1795 are for *Great Britain,* but imports to Scotland being much smaller, they do not seriously affect comparisons with earlier figures for *England.*

of narrow German linens in the mid-1770s.[1] An increasing proportion of the growing English market was being supplied by an expanding Irish and home linen industry.[2] The Scottish linen industry
expanded at an only slightly slower rate than the Irish. Before the
Union, imports from Scotland had amounted, for example, in 1700,
to 2,137,045 yards. Progress was rapid throughout the eighteenth
century, the quantity of linens stamped in Scotland growing from
3,755,622 yards in 1730 to 24,506,007 yards in 1799.[3] There was also
a substantial English production of pure linen cloth. England imported a considerable amount of linen yarn from Ireland, and even
larger quantities from the continent. Though much of this was used
in the manufacture of mixed cotton and linen goods, it also suggests
a large production of pure linens, and in 1780 the Board of Trade
reported that 'this kingdom . . . is at present supposed to manufacture
more linens than are exported from Ireland.'[4] By 1795 exports of
British plain bounty linens at 9,311,880 yards compared with re-
exports of Irish bounty linens at 6,741,633 yards, whereas prior to
1764 re-exports of Irish linen had generally exceeded the corresponding British exports.

Irish linens were, on the whole, too expensive for the colonial

---

[1]In 1785, Lord Sheffield wrote that the value of foreign linens, exclusive of
Irish linens, imported into England used to be computed at one million and a
half and at the time of writing at about one million. *Observations on the manufactures, trade and present state of Ireland* (London, 1785) p. 61. The percentage
of total linen imports supplied by Ireland as a result rose very sharply. Ireland's
share in imports of linen rose from under 1 per cent in 1700 to 18 per cent in
1750, 46 per cent in 1772 and 70 per cent in 1800 (Professor Ashton's introduction
to Schumpeter, op. cit., p. 12).

[2]At the beginning of the 1730s the Scots and the Irish were said to supply only
between one-quarter and one-third of British home consumption. B.M., Add.
MSS. 21134, ff. 50–51.

[3]See J. Horner, *The linen trade of Europe during the spinning-wheel age* (Belfast,
1920) p. 299, for statistics of linen goods stamped in Scotland 1728–1822.

[4]*Report of Board of Trade to the Rt. Hon. the Lords of the Committee of Council
appointed to consider the Irish Bills,* 1780 in A. Anderson: *An Historical and
Chronological Deduction of the Origin of Commerce* (London, 1801) vol. iv., p.
392. See also Sheffield, *Observations on the manufactures, trade and present state
of Ireland* (London, 1785) p. 62; and for some account of the English linen industry, Horner, op. cit., pp. 222–37. But for a different view, see *Minutes of the
Evidence taken before a Committee of the House of Commons . . ./on/the adjustment
of the commercial intercourse with Ireland,* 1785, pp. 12, 34–5. On the level of
output in the English industry in 1770 and its probable decline subsequently, see
also, P. Deane and W.A. Cole, *British economic growth, 1688–1959* (Cambridge,
1962) pp. 53, 202–3.

market.[1] Plain Irish linens were, however, entitled to the same bounties as British linens on re-export from Britain from 1743, and one or two million yards of Irish linen were thus shipped every year.[2] But this figure represents only a very small proportion of the total imported from Ireland. The quantities shipped under bounty increased, however, towards the end of the eighteenth century, amounting in 1795, for example, to nearly seven million yards. Even at this relatively high level they represented less than one-fifth of the total quantity landed from Ireland. Direct exports from Ireland were still smaller. The planters had their linens directly from England in exchange for their sugar and rum.[3]

The Irish linens appear to have been particularly suitable for the requirements of the English market. According to the evidence of James Huey, a North of Ireland man who had settled in London in the linen trade, 'the Irish linens are cheaper than the foreign for home consumption, he having been informed by several retail drapers that they get better profit by the sale of them than Hamboro' linens.'[4] Exports of linen from Ireland to England were 'chiefly for the wear of the common people',[5] and Irish linens were in demand in inland districts as well as in the vicinity of the importing centres. In 1773, for instance, Henry Hindley of Mere in Wiltshire ordered two pieces of 'stout' Irish seven-eighth wide linen at about 1s/4d a yard, 'fit for making school boys shirts'.[6] Irish production of linens was therefore mainly in the middle grades, the output of both the coarser and finer linens being relatively small. However, the range of Irish linens was gradually widened, and by 1738 there was already some production of the coarser linens for shipment to the West Indies from Whitehaven and Liverpool.[7] Towards the end of the century there was also a large demand in Lancashire for unbleached linens for shirting. The unbleached Drogheda linens, for example, 26 to 28 inches wide and

[1]B.M., Add. MSS. 21134, ff. 50–1; New York Historical Society, Letter Book of Greg and Cunningham, 1756–7.

[2]Horner, op. cit., pp. 231–2, Statistics of the Export from England of British and Irish bounty linens, 1743–71; P.R.O., Customs 3.

[3]*Reports from Committees of the House of Commons*, vol. II, p. 71, 11 March 1744.

[4]*Journals of the British House of Commons*, vol. XXIII, p. 81. (Report from the Committee on the manufacture of linen thread and tape in Great Britain and Ireland, 1738.)

[5]B.M., Add. MSS. 21134, ff. 1, 2, 19 Jan. 1722.

[6]Wiltshire Record Office, Trowbridge, Hindley MSS., 27 Feb. 1773.

[7]*Journals of the British House of Commons*, vol. XXIII, p. 78.

costing 5d to 13½d per yard, were for shirting, though in the opinion of a witness before an Irish Parliamentary committee of 1781 'the making the better sort of [Drogheda] linens wider would better answer the English market, as they are principally used for shirting for the colliers and working people, and 28 inches is too narrow for the body of a shirt'.[1] Production of the finer linens although not unimportant formed a relatively small proportion of total output. In 1738 there was already some export of these from Ireland, said to undersell the lower priced Dutch linens at 3/– and 3s/6d an ell.[2] In 1742 some cambric was being exported to London.[3] As late as 1770 the invoice prices of Irish linen shipped to England rarely reached 3/– to 4/– a yard. The invoice prices of a Belfast bleacher, James Ferguson, averaged around 2/–,[4] and another northern bleaching firm were exporting linens in 1780 in the price range of 13d to 3/–, mainly middle-priced linens at 13d to 19d.[5] In the ledgers of Irish exports and imports, linens exported are valued at 1s/4d in the final decades of the eighteenth century although this price of course was regarded as being less than their true value. The range of prices for individual cloths was wide, and a Bristol merchant in 1788 for example, bought Irish linens from the Bristol firm of Parsons Studley and Hurles at prices ranging from ¾ wides as low as 8d to yard wides as high as 3s/8d.[6]

The secular trend of prices is somewhat difficult to measure not only because of inadequate data but because of the great variety of widths and qualities of cloth. Moreover, while the long-term trend was favourable, the growth of the trade was uneven.[7] Rapid growth was often followed by periods of stagnation. The swings in the direction of trade correspond to the shifts in the fortunes of its participants. The rise in output was particularly sharp in the early 1720s,

[1]*Journals of the Irish House of Commons*, vol. 10, App. ccccxviii.
[2]*Journals of the British House of Commons*, vol. XXIII, p. 78.
[3]*Faulkner's Dublin Journal*, 30 Jan. 1742. The manufacture of cambric in Ireland dates back at least to 1731. See item no. 4197 in L.W. Hanson, *Contemporary printed sources for British and Irish economic history, 1701–50* (Cambridge, 1963).
[4]P.R.O. of Northern Ireland, D.468. Invoices and ledger of James Ferguson, linen bleacher, Belfast, 1771–84.
[5]Andrews MSS. Messrs John Andrews to George Miller, Glasgow, 14 Sept. 1780.
[6]P.R.O., C.107/1. Brig *Martin* to Tortola, 1788.
[7]Witnesses before the 1738 Committee claimed that prices had fallen 15 per cent in 15 years, and 10 per cent in the last 7 or 8 years, but this information is suspect. *Journals of the British House of Commons*, vol. XXIII, pp. 78, 79.

the mid-thirties, the late 1740s, the 1760s, the 1780s, and early 1790s. Output contracted in the late 1720s and early 1730s, in some years in the early 1740s, the early 1750s, the early 1770s and again in some years in the late 1770s and early 1780s. Emigration from the north was most marked in these periods (except in the last when it was cut off by the war in the American colonies). Bad harvests in the 1720s, the early 1740s, early 1750s and early 1770s, encouraged all the more the emigration, which was most pronounced in these four periods.

While the general trend of prices is difficult to measure, comparisons between the prices per box do, however, over a period reflect in some degree the movement in prices. The box generally contained 48 to 50 pieces of cloth ranging from the inferior varieties to the more expensive, although it must be pointed out, of course, that the contents of a box reflect the range of business of the individual bleacher or draper rather than of the industry as a whole. The price per box in the early 'thirties, in which some years were very active, was about £75 to £90[1] and twenty years later, in the early 'fifties, about £100 to £130.[2] In the 'seventies boxes of Irish linen were fetching prices of £125 to £150 on the London market.[3] By 1796–7 English merchants were purchasing linens from an Irish bleacher for £150 to £175 per box of 54 to 60 pieces.[4] The movement of linen prices, therefore, appears to have been on the whole favourable to the Irish producer and indeed the volume of production could hardly have increased to the extent it did in the eighteenth century had the trend been otherwise. In 1799 prices were very high. In October a bleaching firm in the North informed a London factor that 'what we have now to send you stands us exhorbitantly high and we are buying the brown at a very considerable advance'.[5] A month later the captain of an English vessel, instructed by his London employer to purchase linens, wrote to him from Dublin that 'linings in Dublin is not quite so cheap as might be expected'.[6] The increase in the trade however depressed the

[1]P.R.O., C.105/15, Letters from Ireland received by a London linen draper, 1731–4.

[2]P.R.O. of Northern Ireland, T.1044, Accounts of a Ballycastle merchant, 1751–4.

[3]P.R.O. of Northern Ireland, D.468. Invoices and ledger of James Ferguson, bleacher, Belfast, 1771–84.

[4]P.R.O. of Northern Ireland. Copies of invoices and of accompanying letters of a Belfast bleacher, William McCance.

[5]Isaac Andrews & Son Ltd., Belfast. JJA to Robert Jameson, London. 30 Oct. 1799.

[6]P.R.O., C. 114/52, Wm. Vollum, Dublin, 9 Nov. 1799.

London market, and white linen sales were very inactive in 1800 and 1801, although this was not fully reflected in the brown linen markets in Ireland. Signs of recovery appeared again in 1802. The progress of the Irish linen industry was indeed not yet at an end. But the forces of expansion were no longer comparable with those of the eighteenth century. Within the first two decades of the century there was little overall change in exports. And while the industry expanded in the remainder of the century it was in no small measure due to the contraction of the industry in the rest of the British Isles.

Despite the expansion of linen weaving, there was a growing export trade in yarn to England.[1] The yarn was exported principally from the ports of the north-east from Drogheda to Londonderry which drew their supply not only from the immediate hinterland but from districts as far away as Connaught. At their peak exports of yarn were valued at over £200,000 per annum, being Ireland's most important export after linen, butter, beef and pork. Exports were 10 to 20,000 cwt in the first half of the century, but increased to 30,000 and up to 40,000 cwt in the second half. These quantities were taken mainly by Manchester, but some yarn was also imported to other centres in Lancashire. The amounts of Irish linen yarn imported in Manchester were:

in 1781—2,764,872 lb.
1782—3,164,832 lb.
1783—3,590,136 lb.
1784—2,806,056 lb.[2]

As Irish exports to England at this period amounted to 30,000 cwt these figures suggest that over 70 per cent of the total was taken by Manchester. The yarn was used principally in the manufacture of sheetings, checks, smallwares, printed cottons, printed and check handkerchiefs and low- and middle-priced fustians.[3] After 1780 exports of yarn began to fall. This arose partly from the increased consumption of yarn in the Irish industry, but also from a lessening demand for it in Lancashire because of the growing production of pure cotton goods.[4]

[1] Ireland also imported linen yarn. But being of different qualities, imports and exports did not compete with each other.
[2] P.R.O., B.T. 6/109, Paper delivered in by Messrs. Walker and Richardson of Manchester, 21 Feb. 1785 (printed in *Report of the Lords of the Committee of Council*, 1785, p. 41).
[3] Ibid.
[4] C. Gill, *Rise of the Irish linen industry*, p. 40.

Beef, butter and pork were, after linen, the principal Irish exports
to England and Scotland in the last 40 years of the eighteenth century. Irish cattle, beef and butter had been excluded from the English
market in 1666–7 because they were cheaper than English commodities,
and were, therefore, believed to contribute to a fall in English agricultural rents. In the course of the eighteenth century Irish production
of beef, butter and pork grew rapidly in response to favourable price
trends. By contrast, rising prices for livestock and livestock products
in England reflected a growing imbalance between demand and
supply there.

By and large the Cattle Acts were a success in excluding Irish produce from the English market. In the years immediately after their
enactment there was some smuggling of livestock which was counten-
anced by the Irish authorities, but it was small in volume[1] and soon
fell off. Only in Scotland, where home agriculture was very weak and
the demand for Irish stock therefore more pressing, did smuggling
continue.[2] This trade probably continued in Scotland into the eighteenth century; although it was by then of small proportions, with
the exception of horse smuggling, which was especially active as the
time of the Ayr horse fairs approached.[3] There was also some smuggling of Irish beef and butter into Britain in defiance of the Cattle
Acts. In 1704, for instance, the Customs Commissioners admonished
the Collector of Whitehaven that 'the country about Whitehaven is
in great measure supplied with beefe and other provisions from
Ireland which posebly could not happen without the connivance of
some of the officers of the customs'.[4] The Scottish Board employed
an Officer called the 'Surveyor General of the Riding Officers for
preventing ye importation of victualls and cattle from Ireland'.[5] At
times seizures of Irish beef in Scotland were associated with riotous
mobs.[6]

Large seizures were rare, and much of the beef and butter was in

[1] J. O'Donovan, op. cit., pp. 60–1.
[2] *Registers of the Privy Council,* Scotland, 3rd series, passim.
[3] Custom House, London. Selections from Scottish outport records, southern
Scotland, 1928, pp. 164, 192–3. Cf. Dobbs. *Essay upon the trade of Ireland,* 1729
in *A collection of tracts and treatises illustrative of Ireland* (Dublin, 1861) vol. 2,
pp. 524–5.
[4] Custom House, Whitehaven. Letter Books, Board to Collector, 1703–10, 26
October 1704.
[5] Custom House Library, London. Selections from Scottish outport records,
southern Scotland, 1928, p. 85. Cf. H.M.C. *Supplementary report on the MSS. of
the Duke of Hamilton,* p. 163.   [6] Ibid., p. 194.

fact irregularly imported for trans-shipment.[1] The ledgers of Irish exports and imports sometimes record annual shipments of several thousand barrels of beef or hundredweights of butter with no corresponding entries in the English Inspector General's ledgers. But as these exports tended to occur in periods of war, it is probable that they relate to shipments under licence or other exceptional conditions and are not entered on the English side either because of difference in procedure as to entry on both sides, or because of the particular nature of the transactions, which in the last analysis were on Government account.[2]

Again some of the quantities entered in the Irish statistics may reflect victualling by English ships in Irish ports. English ships trading to Ireland frequently provisioned in Ireland, and some of the exports to England may consist of amounts regarded by the Irish customs officers as being in excess of victualling requirements, which latter were in accordance with usual practice not taken into account for the purpose of compiling statistical returns. On the English side, vessels were permitted to retain these quantities for use, even during the period of prohibition of Irish provisions, provided that English duty was paid in respect of the salt contained in the provisions.[3]

Smuggling of the by-products of the cattle industry was more common. The high import duties on Irish tallow, soap and candles, coupled with the high excise on English soap and candles, encouraged a widespread smuggling trade. Irish soap and candles were imported all along the west coast of England, and seizures were very frequent. The amounts seized in individual cases were generally very small, the smuggling ventures consisting of small parcels brought back by individual sailors or passengers. The coal vessels returning from Ireland especially bore the name of being concerned in this business. Many of the contemporary assessments of this traffic are extravagant.[4] The

[1]Custom House, Bristol. Letter Books, Barnstaple, Bd. to Collector, 1717-28, London, 19 June 1722.

[2]In October 1740, for instance, a Dublin newspaper reported that 'Mr. Wilton, a very eminent butcher of this city, has an order from the Lords of the Admiralty for slaughtering 1,000 choice oxen, for H.M. Fleet. We hear the commissions to Cork and Waterford are much larger' (*Faulkner's Dublin Journal*, 28 October 1740).

[3]Custom House Greenock. Letter Books: Port Glasgow, Collr. to Bd., 1749-52, 12 Jan. 1751.

[4]For example, the soap-boilers and tallow-chandlers of Liverpool, Lancaster, Warrington, Preston and Chester computed the extent of the traffic at '2,000 tons of soap or upwards' each year. *Journals of the British House of Commons*, vol. XXV, p. 1002.

soap-boilers and tallow-chandlers greatly exaggerated the volume of this activity. In Devonshire, for example, much soap and candles were legally brought in from Wales, 'which the dealers here in these commodities allways imagine to be run from Ireland, being detrimental to their trade'.[1]

Despite the high duties the exportation of tallow to England was very considerable, and the figures for exports tally fairly well with those for imports. Exports to England in the first thirty years were 20 to 30,000 cwt but thereafter declined principally because of the attractions of the French and Dutch markets. After the removal of the duties in 1759 exports to England recovered amounting to as much as 40,000 or 50,000 cwt a year. Total Irish exports of tallow declined sharply in the last twenty years of the century, falling to 15,000 cwt. The continental markets had by this time all fallen away, and little tallow was now shipped except to England. The English demand was primarily from the outports especially from Bristol and Liverpool. Little was sent to London, which was largely supplied from Russia. Some of the Irish tallow was used in the Navy, and had been imported for that purpose since 1661.[2] The rest of the imports from Ireland was probably used by the tallow-chandlers and soap-boilers of the west coast. A petition to Parliament from the soap-boilers and tallow-chandlers of Bristol alleged that 'English tallow [was] very unfit' for the purpose of making candles for the export trade,[3] but it is doubtful whether Irish tallow had any decided advantage over English apart from its relative cheapness.

The prices of cattle and cattle products rose sharply at the end of the 'fifties and Parliament was petitioned from all over England for the repeal of the Cattle Acts. Once Irish cattle, beef and butter were re-admitted, exports to England increased. But a sharp decline of the continental provision trade began only in the 1780s and would suggest that the continental and colonial demand for these commodities was slackening at the same time as the English demand was intensified.[4]

[1]Custom House, Bristol. Letter Books, Barnstaple, Collr. to Bd., 1727–36, 18 March 1728–9.

[2]W. Beveridge: *Prices and wages in England,* vol. i, *Price Tables: Mercantile Era,* (London, 1939) p. 632; *Calendar of State Papers Domestic, 1665–6,* pp. 324, 347, 348, 352, 363.

[3]*Journals of the British House of Commons,* vol. xxv, p. 1020.

[4]On England's growing dependence on imports of cattle and cattle products, especially from Ireland, see A.H. John, 'The course of agricultural change, 1660–1760', in *Studies in the industrial revolution* (London, 1960) ed. L.S. Pressnell, pp. 152–5; Deane and Cole, op. cit., pp. 74–5.

Table 17: Beef, butter and pork: Irish exports[1]

Year ending 25 March	Beef (barrels)*		Butter (cwt)		Pork (barrels)*	
	to Great Britain	to all parts	to Great Britain	to all parts	to Great Britain	to all parts
1760	24,072	164,903	35,162	229,227	13,293	54,401
1765	20,108	199,999	38,026	301,109	7,383	44,361
1770	31,275	208,269	114,363	262,717	12,089	43,947
1775	36,455	192,452	115,100	264,140	17,199	50,367
1780	89,698	187,756	135,465	244,185	49,302	96,554
1785	43,024	136,651	159,526	282,802	21,539	58,446
1790	51,203	126,994	194,748	300,669	46,067	100,266
1795	95,475	124,607	214,962	276,403	88,304	129,922
1800	123,947	149,857	208,683	263,290	98,348	114,745

*The barrel containing 2 cwt approx.

[1] Figures for the provision trade require to be handled with caution. Large variations occur between the trade figures in the two countries. Salt provisions because of the official nature of much of the demand, or their importation expressly for the purpose of transhipment, appear in certain cases to have been governed by different rules relating to entry than were other commodities. On the Irish side, certainly, provisions bought by the Agent for victualling the navy were exempt from entry, and during the War of American Independence provisions shipped for the British forces in America were also exempt (Details of the purchases in Cork of provisions for His Majesty's Service in the years 1779–84, though unfortunately without differentiation between the different kinds of provisions purchased survive in P.R.O., Adm. 112/39). Large official purchases might therefore explain why the English figures frequently exceed the Irish figures in the last twenty years of the century. But explanation is necessarily complex as before 1780 entries on the Irish side appear to have been larger than the corresponding entries on the English side, in contrast to the larger entries on the English side between 1780 and the end of the century for beef and pork and between 1780 and 1795 for butter. That differences in the methods of entry are at the root of the divergence is suggested by the fact that other pastoral products such as tallow and hides bear a fairly close correspondence in both countries and that in the small provision trade with Scotland the Irish and Scottish figures tally reasonably well. But as far as Anglo-Irish trade is concerned the evidence on both sides is clearly at variance: for example by 1800 English imports of pork from Ireland exceeded Irish exports of pork to all parts. The most plausible explanation of the inconsistency before and after 1780 of the divergence of trade figures in the two countries is that the handling of official purchases itself changed in the course of the last four decades. The growing importance of the victualling agency of the British Government in Ireland may have resulted to an increasing extent in purchases on direct government account in Ireland, which before 1780 were commonly handled by Irish merchants commissioned for the purpose. Shipments before 1780 thus generally were entered for export in accordance with normal procedures for exports but were not necessarily entered in British ports. From 1780 a growing portion of Irish exports were exempt from normal entry procedure on the grounds of being entered by a government agency for export, while on the English side they were accounted for trade purposes because government purchases were often consigned from Ireland on merchant vessels and the official nature of the purchase may not as a result have affected entry in the normal fashion in English ports.

The degree of the change over in these years is quite striking, and by 1800 the English market had become the principal one in all cases. Between 1770 and 1800, exports of beef to Britain quadrupled, exports of butter doubled, and exports of pork increased eight-fold. By 1800 the only important overseas market was the English colonial one; the continental markets had practically disappeared with the exception of the Portuguese.

The principal English centre for Irish salt beef, butter and pork was London, which normally took as much as 60 per cent or more of the provisions imported from Ireland. But salt provisions from Ireland were imported in all the larger ports of the south-west, and in many of the smaller ones. Butter was the largest single item, and at the current wholesale prices in the Irish ports exports to England were worth over £700,000 a year at the end of the century. London was the largest single market, but Irish butter was also imported in large quantities in many of the ports on the south coast and through Bristol and Liverpool. In the year 1791-2 the Waterford provision merchants, Courtenay and Ridgway, consigned goods—mainly butter shipped along with some pork—to 52 merchants in London, 18 in Bristol and on or near the Bristol Channel, 36 on the south coast of England, and 1 in Liverpool.[1] Much of this butter was for inland consumption. In Kent, for example, wagons bringing hops to London were loaded back with Irish butter.[2] The heavily-salted Irish butter was probably relatively little in demand in the London area itself, and in the early nineteenth century certainly much of it was distributed by the cheesemongers to country shop-keepers and merchants who in turn disposed of it to the lower classes.

Much of the butter was in fact imported from Ireland on the account of inland merchants themselves. Some of the butter shipped through Bristol was on the account of merchants in Bath and Devizes, and inland merchants in Wiltshire and Hampshire imported a good deal of Irish butter through Portsmouth. Irish butter was also designed for shipment to the colonial markets. This was packed in tight firkin barrels containing 56 lbs of butter and heavily pickled with

[1]Ledger of Courtenay and Ridgway, in the possession of Mrs. Olive Ridgway, Rossmore, Mallow, Co. Cork. See L.M. Cullen 'The overseas trade of Waterford as seen from a ledger of Courtenay and Ridgway', *Journal of the Royal Society of Antiquaries of Ireland*, vol. LXXXVIII, Pt. 2 (1958) p. 168.

[2]G.E. Fussell and Constance Goodman: 'The eighteenth-century traffic in milk products', *Economic History* (Supplement to the *Economic Journal*) vol. 3, No. 12, Feb. 1937, p. 386.

Portuguese salt. Butter for the English and European home markets was packed in heavier barrels, called casks, weighing a cwt or more, and less heavily salted. Its good preserving qualities were the chief characteristic of Irish butter; otherwise, it was not a very distinguished commodity. But the influence of the English market with its demand for a fresher and less heavily salted butter, had some effect in improving the quality of Irish butter in the second half of the century.[1] The most popular Irish butter in the trade to London was the Carlow butter. This came from the prosperous agricultural region north of Carlow in the Barrow valley, was less heavily salted, and in London fetched the highest prices of all the Irish butter. It was exported from Waterford and Dublin, and gave to those two ports the reputation of exporting the best butter in Ireland. A fairly large amount of butter was also sent to England from the north of Ireland ports. Cork, despite its more heavily salted butter, shipped more to England than Waterford did. Butter from these latter two ports was sent to the ports in the west of England, and some of it was for re-shipment to the West Indies. Some Irish butter was also used for industrial purposes. In Bristol butter was used in the manufacture of baize. The Society of Merchant Venturers in that port on one occasion applied for leave to import butter that had been rendered inedible by the admixture of dirt.[2] In the ledgers of Scottish imports and exports separate figures are given for the quantities of 'foul butter' imported from Ireland. But the quantities are very small. In England, too, it would appear that the quantity of Irish butter imported for industrial purposes was but a small proportion of total imports.

Irish salt beef was also prized for its good preserving qualities. The large quantities imported to England from 1760 onwards were almost exclusively for use as ship's provisions (mess beef) or cargo beef for re-shipment to the West Indies. Some of the salt beef and pork from Ireland was also used in victualling vessels engaged in the coastwise trade. Irish beef was imported to London and to all the ports of the south and west, and in Liverpool was also taken as provision by the vessels engaged in the slave trade. Again, much of the beef was taken by the Navy. The Navy had always employed victualling agents at Cork and Kinsale where vessels frequently called. From

[1] J. Rutty, *Essay towards a natural history of the county of Dublin,* vol. i, p. 266; S. Ní Chinnéide, 'A Frenchman's impressions of Limerick . . .', loc. cit., p. 99.
[2] J. Latimer, *The history of the Society of Merchant Venturers of the City of Bristol* (Bristol, 1903) p. 193.

the time of the suspension of the acts in 1758, Irish salt beef and pork
began to be imported to Deptford, Portsmouth and Plymouth, and
were used in increasing quantities from that date, gradually replacing
the English beef and pork which had hitherto been purchased at the
victualling ports for salting.[1] Total Irish exports of beef declined in
the last 20 years of the century. This is partly due to internal conditions in Ireland, but is also a reflection of a declining global demand
for salt beef.[2] Salt pork was in fact proving a more satisfactory product and was being widely substituted for salt beef. This is also reflected in Irish exports to England. Over the 40 years from 1760
exports of pork grew much more rapidly than exports of beef, and by
1800 were little short of beef exports. A good deal of bacon was also
exported. This was sent almost exclusively to England, principally
from Waterford. Exports rose from 20,729 flitches in 1768 to 52,822
flitches, valued at £39,617, in 1798.

Despite the fact that Irish cattle could freely be imported into
England since 1759 exports grew very slowly. Prior to 1800, they
exceeded 20,000 head only in a few years, and were mainly for
Scotland. In 1798 only 14,898 out of 30,670 cattle shipped were for
England. Exports were mainly through Donaghadee and some of the
other smaller ports in the north-east,[3] although in the south Wexford
also had some share in the trade;[4] and Portpatrick[5] in Scotland,
Chester, and later Parkgate, were the principal ports of import. There
was some intake of Irish cattle for fattening in Yorkshire and the
Midlands[6] but in view of the low level of imports it must have been
very limited. The revival of the export trade in livestock was opposed
by the merchant communities of the Irish towns, and was not favoured
by the Irish Parliament itself. The trade was considered detrimental

[1]W. Beveridge, *Prices and wages in England,* vol. 1 (London, 1939) pp. 529, 549.
[2]The apparent decline is probably also partially the result of the non-entry of
official purchases of provisions made in Cork in the course of the Revolutionary
Wars.
[3]Some reference to the Cattle trade from Donaghadee in the Downshire
Papers, P.R.O. of Northern Ireland, D.607, nos. 892, 915, 23 Nov., 4 Dec.
1796. See also *Journals of the Irish House of Commons,* vol. 6, app. cclxvii–cclxxiv.
[4]Cattle Exports, Wexford, 14 June–5 Oct. 1792; P.R.O. of Ireland (Dublin)
Customs & Excise Administration Papers, 1A/43/5, No. 79.
[5]Scottish Record Office, General Register House, Edinburgh, Customs Accounts: Portpatrick. A.R.B. Haldane, *The drove roads of Scotland* (London and
Edinburgh 1952) p. 163. E. Wakefield, *An account of Ireland, statistical and
political* (London, 1812) vol. ii, p. 32.
[6]G.E. Fussell, 'Eighteenth-century traffic in livestock', *Economic History*
(Supplement to the *Economic Journal*) vol. 3, No. 11, p. 220.

to Irish interests, and on one occasion the popular excitement was so great that a whole boat-load of cattle for England were destroyed by a mob.[1] The trade took root only in a few of the smaller ports, like Donaghadee and on a much smaller scale, Wexford, which were removed from the principal centres of the beef trade, and where young stock, as a result, might not be as easily disposed of as in the districts near the principal centres of the trade. But even in Wexford the merchant community was opposed to the trade and petitioned the Lord Lieutenant against it.[2] High prices in the victualling ports for beef for salting made the export trade in livestock not a very profitable one in this period, and it was re-established on a large scale only in the following century, when the demand for salt beef had dwindled. The large export of calf skins during the eighteenth century also suggests that some livestock exports could take place without making serious inroads on the source of supply for the dead meat trade.

[1]*Journals of the Irish House of Commons,* vol. 6, app. cclxxi.
[2]P.R.O. of Ireland, Official Papers, 511/40/40.

CHAPTER IV

ENGLISH EXPORTS TO IRELAND

I. EXPORTS FROM ENGLAND AND SCOTLAND

THE principal group of commodities in British exports to Ireland were goods of foreign origin. Thus, whereas goods of English origin invariably exceeded re-exports in the case of English exports to all parts, the reverse generally held in English exports to Ireland.

Table 18: Exports from England[1]

Year ending 25 Dec.	Exports of domestic origin to Ireland	to all parts	Re-exports to Ireland	to all parts
	£	£	£	£
1700	131,042	4,337,049	140,598	2,132,137
1710	101,525	4,728,783	183,899	1,566,425
1720	181,695	4,611,247	146,888	2,299,652
1730	240,072	5,326,143	292,626	3,222,840
1740	241,954	5,111,297	386,334	3,086,491
1750	666,015	9,473,791	650,585	3,225,289
5 Jan.				
1761	692,072	10,980,758	358,330	3,714,214
1771	1,003,432	9,503,227	1,122,038	4,764,428
1781	890,163	8,032,692	997,892	4,319,362
1791	1,114,393	14,056,633	823,145	4,828,083
1800	2,195,391	22,465,458	1,590,696	11,609,241

Table 19: Exports from Scotland to Ireland[2]

Year ending 5 Jan.	Exports of domestic origin to Ireland	to all parts	Re-exports to Ireland	to all parts
	£	£	£	£
1761	33,142	437,237	62,877	644,490
1766	75,874	400,928	200,436	779,694
1771	115,172	510,577	330,708	1,217,049
1776	98,338	352,484	184,726	770,698
1781	175,653	767,412	122,394	233,361
1786	150,346	659,546	135,740	346,890
1791	213,996	864,831	114,235	370,574
1796	119,782	848,462	52,401	128,530
1800	210,600	1,618,755	90,291	297,876

[1] P.R.O., Customs, 3, 17.
[2] P.R.O., Customs, 14.

The importance of this re-export trade explains why the merchant communities of the English sea-ports were so hostile to trade concessions to Ireland. In the long run their fears were proved ungrounded. Despite the repeal of the restrictions on direct importation from the colonies to Ireland, the re-export trade continued in the last two decades to form a higher percentage of exports to Ireland than of English exports generally.

Scottish trade with Ireland also consisted to a large extent, from the middle of the century, of re-exports of colonial produce. At the beginning of the century Irish imports from Scotland were small, consisting largely of coal. But Scotland was already developing a colonial trade, and by the 1720s Glasgow's trade had expanded sufficiently to affect Whitehaven's interest in the tobacco trade. From the mid-1750s Scotland began to find substantial markets in Ireland for some of its re-exports. As early as 1756 the values of foreign goods re-exported to Ireland from Scotland exceeded the values of goods of Scottish manufacture exported to Ireland. By 1770 this trade had greatly expanded: re-exports to Ireland doubled between 1759 and 1764 and doubled again by 1770. In 1770 they amounted roughly to one-fifth of total re-exports of foreign goods to Ireland from Great Britain. Scottish re-exports to Ireland consisted mainly of three commodities, sugar, tobacco and rum, and the sharp increase in re-exports to Ireland at this time was largely due to the sudden increase in rum exports. This trade originated in the early 1760s and between 1764 and 1771 re-exports of rum to Ireland increased 400 per cent.[1] But much of this trade cannot be considered strictly as re-exports, as it consisted largely of rum on Irish account, entered in the Scotland ports, and for which the duties were secured there, to effect a fictitious landing and thereby obtain a drawback on re-export to Ireland a few days later. The rum trade through the Scottish ports reached its peak in 1770, when rum exports were valued at £211,840 out of total exports of foreign goods to Ireland valued at £330,708. In 1772 the anomaly in the Irish customs duty on rum was removed by the Irish Parliament, and the entrepot rum trade was practically annihilated, exports of rum falling from 759,621 gallons in 1771 to 68,808 gallons in 1772. Total re-exports to Ireland also fell sharply as a result of the reduction of this trade, in 1772 amounting only to £117,215. They never recovered substantially again. However, Glasgow's place in

[1]Details of the shipments made in these years are available in P.R.O., T. 64/180.

the colonial trade as a whole was now beginning to wane. Tobacco exports from Scotland to Ireland had risen from 872,730 lb. in 1755 to 4,333,850 lb. in 1773. Over much of this period the Clyde supplied more tobacco to the Irish market than all the English ports combined. The trade began to decline however after 1773. Sugar re-exports fell less rapidly. The export of muscovado sugar to Ireland had risen from 5,777 cwt in 1755 to 62,939 cwt in 1778, and in peak years Scotland was, therefore, a substantial supplier of the Irish market. By the 1780s Scotland's trade in colonial goods with Ireland was a small one, and its wane contrasted with a growth in exports of goods of domestic origin to Ireland.

Irish imports were numerous and very varied. Growing population and consumption standards are reflected in the increasing imports of commodities like tobacco, sugar and tea. The limitations of Irish industry can be seen in the rapidly increasing imports of earthenware, ironware, hardware, haberdashery, and textiles (woollen, linen, cotton, pure and mixed). But at the same time note should be made of the substantial imports of raw materials, especially for the textile industry or food-processing industries. The largest industry in the ports was sugar refining, and with the aid of a moderate degree of protection it proved more than a match in the Irish market for the refineries of the English ports. The large imports of hops point to a fairly extensive and prosperous Irish brewing industry. But this industry received a set-back early in the second half of the century. Imports of porter from London became very substantial and the imports of hops declined.[1] In the last decade of the century imports

[1]Between the years 1720 and 1780 very large discrepancies exist between the Irish and English statistics for trade in hops between the two islands, the English statistics showing quantities shipped for Ireland which are greatly in excess of the corresponding Irish imports from England. In the years prior to 1720 and after 1780 on the other hand, when the inland duty on hops was drawn back on exports to Ireland, the divergence between the statistics is much reduced and its direction reversed, i.e. Irish figures for imports exceed the English figures for export to Ireland. The fact that the range of fluctuation is much smaller for the Irish statistics than for the English suggests that the Irish figures for the industry's requirements of hops are much nearer to the truth than the English. The latter, if used as a basis for illustrating the development of the Irish brewing industry, would suggest a marked rise in production from 1720 and a particularly sharp decline in the final two decades, both of which would contradict what we know of likely production trends in Ireland. As the divergence between the statistics on both sides of the Irish Sea is least pronounced during the period when a drawback of inland duty was accorded, it is likely that the statistical control of the trade was firmest, while drawbacks were in operation—which is in fact what one would expect. The apparent large excess of exports from England

of beer declined sharply in contrast to relatively stable imports of hops, and to a presumptive rise in the proportion of the home market supplied by the Irish breweries, which favoured by several factors were now laying the foundation of their rapid early nineteenth-century expansion.[1] Dublin was also the centre of a fairly prosperous silk industry in this century, and imports of raw silks were almost invariably worth more than imports of manufactured silks. In the last three decades of the century an Irish cotton industry was established, and fairly large amounts of cotton and cotton yarn were imported from Manchester. There was little else in Ireland in the way of large-scale industry. Moreover, not only was the range of Irish industry comparatively limited, but it was also dependent on England for many of its most essential raw materials: sugar for the refineries, hops and some of the malt for brewing, iron for ironworking, yarn and silk for the cotton and silk industries, and even bark for tanning. Furthermore, the inadequacy of Irish fuel supplies and growing urbanisation in the ports made Ireland dependent on English coal. In no commodity was Ireland's dependence on England more evident to contemporaries than in coal, and much contemporary economic discussion was devoted to the methods of freeing Ireland from this dependence.

Yet the coal trade is worthy of notice not merely as the most striking example of Irish dependence on England, but also because by its nature it was in tonnage of shipping employed easily the largest single branch of Anglo-Irish trade. In the early eighteenth century roughly one-third of the tonnage entering the Irish ports consisted of vessels

---

over the corresponding figures for Irish imports between 1720 and 1780 would appear to suggest that large quantities were entered for Ireland at the time of payment of duty and were not subsequently either in whole or in part shipped for Ireland. The excess of imports to Ireland during the period in which the drawback was in force (which is in contrast to the general tendency for statistics of exports to exceed the corresponding figures for imports) might plausibly be explained by assuming that the statistics for exports to Ireland may cover only hops on which drawback was claimed at the time the quantities were declared to the inland excise authorities, and do not include hops on which inland duty was paid and a drawback only subsequently claimed. Some function by the inland excise officers in the initial recording of the export trade does not appear unlikely where the duty was an inland one and would explain why during the period in which no drawback was granted it may have been impossible to check quantities nominally declared for Ireland against the amounts actually shipped.

[1] On the Irish brewing industry, see P. Mathias, *Brewing industry in England 1700-1830* (Cambridge, 1959) pp. 151-70; P. Lynch and J. Vaizey, *Guinness's brewery in the Irish economy* (Cambridge, 1960) pp. 37-102.

carrying coal, a proportion which at the end of the century had risen to about a half.[1] Again, in contrast to the other branches of Anglo-Irish trade, in which there was a two-way flow of commodities, most of the colliers departed from the Irish ports in ballast. In the year ending 24 June 1790, for example, a total of 1,481 coal ships with a combined tonnage of 148,480 tons cleared Dublin in ballast.[2]

The coal trade developed rapidly in the second half of the seventeenth century, and imports rose from 24,467 tons in 1665 to 42,727 tons in 1683. It appears to have declined over the remainder of the century, but recovered in 1699 to 49,786 tons. The growth of the trade was fairly continuous through the eighteenth century, apart from depressed conditions during the first decade, and between 1700 and 1800 imports increased eight-fold.

Table 20: Coal: exports and imports[3]

Year ending 25 March	Imports into Ireland (in Irish tons)			Year ending 25 December	Exports to Ireland (in Chaldrons, Winchester M'sure)		
	England	from Scotland	Gt. Britain		England	from Scotland	Gt. Britain
1700*	42,048	4,471	46,519	1700	26,782	—	—
1710	35,287	9,706	44,993	1709	26,966	—	—
1720	49,899	10,236	60,135	1719	38,834	—	—
1730	54,929	13,096	68,025	1729	53,410	—	—
1740	—	—	77,903	1739	63,773	—	—
1750	—	—	99,837	1749	66,444	—	—
				5 Jan.			
1760	—	—	138,682	1760	66,886	3,992	70,878
1770	—	—	197,136	1770	121,391	9,888†	[131,279]
1780	—	—	211,570	1780	150,322	8,591	158,913
1790	311,473	40,921	352,394	1790	225,796	25,346	251,142
1800	330,627	42,328	372,955	1800	272,813	28,398	301,211

*Year ending 25 December. †Year ending 5 January, 1771

Because coals were shipped for Ireland under more favourable duties than were levied either in the foreign trade or in the coastwise

[1] This statement is based on a comparison between the tonnage of shipping invoiced in Irish ports, and the quantity of coals imported in tons. A few separate and discontinuous figures also exist of the tonnage of colliers entering Ireland. In the year ending 25 March 1799, the number of coal ships entering the Irish ports was 3,758, of a total tonnage of 344,564 tons (*Journals of the Irish House of Commons,* vol. 19, app. dcciv), and figures for the tonnage of colliers entering Dublin are available from 1789 in *Accounts of the Dublin Port and Docks Board for the year 1932,* p. 72.

[2] *Journals of the Irish House of Commons,* vol. 14, app. cclxxxi.

[3] Irish figures include imports of culm, but English figures exclude exports of culm, which rarely exceeded 2,000 chaldrons, except in the last decade of the century, when they reached 8,000 or 9,000 chaldrons in some years.

trade, a system of bonds was necessary to prevent abuse, and these bonds were cancelled only on presentment by the merchant of a certificate from the Irish customs signifying the amount of coal landed. By and large, this system worked satisfactorily, and enabled the customs to levy the extra duty in cases where masters either by choice or by force of circumstances went to another market. The certificates returned from Ireland signified the tonnage of coals landed, the rate of conversion varying from $1\frac{1}{3}$ to $1\frac{1}{2}$ Irish tons to the chaldron, Winchester measure,[1] though in the later years some of the certificates appear to have expressed the quantities landed either in terms of chaldrons or of the ton used in the English ports. The English officers do not appear as a rule to have tallied shipments unless the master's entry failed to accord with the ship's full capacity by reference to previous shipments, to a tally at an earlier date, or to ad-measurement of the ship. Even had the officers been able to supervise very strictly the coal trade, the use of the certificates as a means of checking abuses was rather limited, as the methods of computing shipments and the coal measures were not standardized. Moreover the officers on both sides were not always quite sure of the proper rate of conversion between weights or measures in the two countries. The certificates were therefore of very limited use in checking abuses in the actual amounts of coal shipped in the English and Scottish ports. Because of the great volume of business and the low Irish duties, the officers in Ireland were generally content to accept either the master's cocquet or his own entry as to the size of his cargo, and in this manner more coals were landed in Ireland than had duty paid on them in either country. The certificates returned from Ireland were generally—at any rate in Ayr in the 1760s—for lesser quantities than had been shipped, though in some cases they were for a greater quantity. In the opinion of the Collector at Ayr, the lower quantities resulted from the Irish officers accepting the master's entries, and the occasional greater quantities from the fact that the Irish officers, piqued at not being bribed by a master, returned an exact account of the cargo, thus exposing the abuses which existed at the Ayr side.[2]

[1]The Irish ton, despite its name, was a measure, not a weight. The chaldron, Winchester measure, weighed 26 to 33 cwt, with an average weight of about 28 cwt, the Dublin ton weighed 21 to 22 cwt, the Whitehaven ton 14 cwt, and the Scottish colliery ton about the same as the Dublin ton. The ton occasionally used by the Scottish customs, however, appears to have been the ton of 14 cwt, common in the ports of the west of England.

[2]Custom House, Ayr. Letter Books, Collector to Board, 1764-6, 27 Feb. 1766.

In the seventeenth century, and in the first half of the eighteenth, the coal trade was dependent almost exclusively on the Dublin market. Even as late as 1717 only 70 ships sailed from Whitehaven to Irish ports other than Dublin,[1] and as late as 1740 only 2,151 chaldrons out of a total of 51,079 shipped to foreign parts were entered for ports other than Dublin.[2] The small Swansea trade was principally with Waterford and Cork, but Milford, and Tenby, centre of culm exports, were dependent on the Dublin market. This dependence on the Dublin coal trade was a serious drawback in the early decades of the century when Dublin's growth was stagnant, as the experience of the expanding Whitehaven collieries showed.

In the second half of the century, the demand for coals outside Dublin increased at a greater rate than it did in the capital. Dublin's percentage of coal imports from Britain, which had been 78 per cent in 1683, 72 per cent in 1700, 74 per cent in 1740 and 78 per cent in 1760, had fallen to 64 per cent in 1780 and 49 per cent in 1800. Dublin, of course, remained easily the largest centre of import. Coal was almost exclusively the domestic fuel of the capital and large quantities were also required for the city's industries: its glass-houses, sugar houses, breweries and salt works. But Cork, and to a lesser extent, Waterford and Belfast, also became the centres of a large coal trade. As the limitations of Irish fuel resources became more evident, rising quantities of coal were imported to the outports. The demand was not solely from the urban areas, It came also from the countryside: many of the cargoes of coals were in fact landed on the coast outside the legal quays by arrangement with the officers, and the masters had sometimes to travel long distances to the nearest Custom House to enter their vessels. In some places local prejudice against the use of coal survived right up to the end of the century.[3] But, at the end of the century even in centres where peat was readily available, coal was being imported in increasing quantities. However, the two most populous towns on the west coast, Galway and Limerick, were still largely dependent on peat. Galway at the end of the century was still importing less than 1,000 tons of coal a year, and Limerick, although the third most populous town in the island, was importing only 2 to 3,000 tons.

[1]P.R.O., C.O. 390/8B.
[2]Statistics of coal exports from Whitehaven and other ports, taken from the port books are given in W.H. Makey, 'The place of Whitehaven in the Irish coal Trade,' unpublished M.A. Thesis, 1952, London University, App. B. pp. 301–6.
[3]Dubourdieu, J., Statistical account of county Down (1802) pp. 216–17.

In the middle of the seventeenth century the bulk of Ireland's supply of coal appears to have come from South Wales, Chester and Liverpool. But shipments from Whitehaven began to expand rapidly from about 1660, and by 1677 it was estimated that half of the coals used in Dublin, or about 13,000 tons, came from Whitehaven.[1] Shipments from other areas around this time were smaller, the total shipments from Chester, Liverpool, Swansea and Milford in 1681 amounting only to 10,334 chaldrons,[2] about 14,000 Irish tons. As total imports of coal to Ireland from England amounted to 40,863 tons in 1683, it is probable that Whitehaven was now supplying more than half the Irish market. In the first half of 1688, at a time when coal imports into Ireland may have declined somewhat, 6,165 chaldrons of coal were shipped overseas from Whitehaven,[3] a figure which would approximate to 17,000 Irish tons for the whole year.[4] In the opening decade of the eighteenth century, because of depressed conditions in the coal trade, output did not greatly exceed this level, but from 1712 exports rose steadily till they reached a peak for the first half of the century in 1750 at 111,769 Whitehaven tons[5] or 74,512 Dublin tons. Shipments of coals from Whitehaven in this period represented between 70 and 80 per cent of total exports of coals from England to Ireland.

Whitehaven had practically no outlets outside the Irish market for its coals. Placed on a narrow and thinly populated strip between the Irish Sea and the Cumberland hills, its home market was small; far removed from the principal English centres of consumption its coastwise traffic was negligible, and for geographical reasons it was precluded from sharing in coal exports to the continent.[6] Lowther, the owner of the Whitehaven collieries, had made some efforts to develop

[1]*The Petty-Southwell correspondence 1676-87*, ed. Marquis of Lansdowne (London, 1928) p. 26-7.

[2]W.H. Makey, op. cit., app. B., pp. 301-6.

[3]J.U. Nef., *The rise of the British coal industry*, vol. ii, app. D. iii.

[4]W. Harris in *Remarks on the affairs and trade of England and Ireland*, 1691, p. 19, on the basis of some dubious calculations, gave a total export from Whitehaven of 38,400 tons in 1685. According to Harris, 180 sail were employed in the coal trade between Ireland and England, 60 of them from Whitehaven and Workington.

[5]Record Office, The Castle, Carlisle. Abstract Colliery Accounts, 1701-50.

[6]In 1728 the Collector of Whitehaven estimated that 3,600 chaldrons of coal were consumed in the town, 900 in the neighbourhood and 500 shipped coastwise. Custom House, Whitehaven, Letter Books, Collr. to Bd. (1703-10, 1724-35), 7 Feb. 1727-8.

a foreign or coastwise traffic.[1] In connection with the continental
trade, he had in 1748-9 entered into relations with George Fitzgerald,
an Irish merchant in London, and Fitzgerald's Waterford correspondent, Martin Murphy, in the hope of establishing a trade in tranship-
ping Whitehaven coals from the ports in the south of Ireland to
France, Portugal and Spain. But there was little real prospect of establishing a trade of this nature and Ireland remained Whitehaven's only
significant market for coals throughout the century. Lowther made
efforts to develop the trade with Irish ports other than Dublin; and
at times a system was enforced in Whitehaven whereby ships taking
in coals for ports other than Dublin were loaded out of turn. Lowther
also had his own vessels employed to some extent in developing new
markets in Ireland. By the middle of the century there was a growing
demand for coals in many of the smaller Irish ports, though this is
a reflection of local conditions in Ireland rather than a result of
Lowther's efforts to re-direct the coal trade.

Shipments from the other collieries were small in the first half of
the century, and appear to have shown little tendency to rise. Exports
from Chester and Liverpool were declining. Exports of culm from
Tenby remained stable at about 2,000 chaldrons a year. Only in
Swansea were coal exports to Ireland rising. But Swansea's exports
to Ireland were modest. In 1713 the total tonnage of shipping clearing
for Ireland amounted only to 6,236 tons,[2] though this was apparently
a brisk year in Swansea's trade with Ireland. Whitehaven's only rivals
in the Irish coal trade in the early eighteenth century were the Scottish
ports. Imports of coal from Scotland, which were only 1,864 tons in
1683, had risen to 4,471 tons in 1700, and in 1731 to 14,804 tons.
The Scottish collieries, especially at Saltcoats, were therefore expanding shipments to Ireland at a much faster rate than the Whitehaven collieries, and in 1731 were supplying 22 per cent of total Irish

[1]Record Office, The Castle, Carlisle. Sir James Lowther's Letters to his agent
at Whitehaven.

[2]P.R.O., C.O. 388/18. In 1728 Sir James Lowther of Whitehaven, writing
about the coal trade, remarked that 'the Welsh [who] say they have little or no
trade to Ireland and absolutely refuse to concern themselves in these disputes'
(Record Office, The Castle, Carlisle, Sir James Lowther, London, 4 April, 1728
(nᵒ 4)). 23 years later, however, he wrote to Whitehaven from London that 'Mr.
Macilworth tells me at the house they send a good deal of coals from Wales
both to Ireland and to Cornwall and Devon' (ibid; London, 28 Nov., 1751 (nᵒ
68)). But the trade with Ireland must still have remained a modest one, as imports
from South Wales to Dublin in the 1770s were small (*Journals of the Irish House
of Commons*, vol. 9, app. dcxliv–dcxlv).

coal imports. The success of the Scottish collieries was a cause of great apprehension to Sir James Lowther in Whitehaven, who feared that Saltcoats would ultimately oust Whitehaven from the Irish coal trade. Indeed, one of his motives in expanding output at Whitehaven was the hope that the subsequent glutting of the Dublin market would ultimately make the coal trade unprofitable and force the Scottish colliery owners out of the Irish trade. Lowther's fears were not subsequently justified. Saltcoats failed to maintain its rate of development, and indeed by the time figures for trade between Ireland and Scotland again became available in the mid-1750s shipments had actually declined heavily.

Shipments from Cumberland continued to expand in the second half of the century. The exports from Lowther's great collieries at Whitehaven itself which had reached 111,769 Whitehaven tons in 1750, grew further and in 1785 reached their maximum at 227,637 Whitehaven tons.[1] Yet Whitehaven's relative importance in the Cumberland coalfields was now declining. Exports from the other Cumberland ports whose share in the coal trade was, apart from Workington, very small in the first half of the century, were now expanding rapidly and by 1790 the total exports from Whitehaven were exceeded by the combined exports of Workington, Maryport and Harrington.[2] From the end of the 1780s shipments from Whitehaven had been falling, and by 1793 coals from Whitehaven formed only about a quarter of the total imported at Dublin from Cumberland.[3]

Cumberland still remained dominant in the Irish coal trade at the end of the century. But its relative importance had declined, and in 1799 coal exports from Cumberland formed only 65 per cent of total exports of coal from England to Ireland. The decline is due principally to the growth of exports from Swansea and Liverpool. Exports from Swansea amounted to 20,073 chaldrons in 1790, and by 1799 had increased 25 per cent. More remarkable still were exports from Liverpool, which were already 31,605 chaldrons in 1790 and doubled by 1799.[4] As late as the 1770s imports of coal from both Swansea and

[1] Record Office, The Castle, Carlisle. Total Account of the number of waggons shipped yearly from Howgill and Whingill Collieries, 1782-1800.
[2] V.C.H. Cumberland, vol. 2, p. 383; Hutchinson, *History of the county of Cumberland,* vol. 2, p. 84.
[3] P.R.O. of Ireland, Committee Books of the Parliamentary Committee on the Dublin Coal Trade, 1 Feb. 1793.
[4] *Report from the Committee on the Coal Trade,* in *Reports from Committees of the House of Commons,* vol. x, app. 42, pp. 612-15. These statistics include negligible quantities of coal shipped to overseas destinations other than Ireland.

Liverpool to Dublin were modest.[1] Their expanding coal trade must therefore have emerged only after the 1770s. It would appear plausible to attribute the growing exports from Liverpool to the tapping of the South Lancashire coalfield by the Liverpool end of the Leeds and Liverpool canal. The exports from Swansea reflect the development of the collieries made possible in the mining valleys by tramways and, from the 1790s, canals.

The best known English coals were, of course, the Cumberland coals, and colliers from Whitehaven and Workington visited ports all around the island. Whitehaven coals were the most popular, selling at 1/- a ton more than the other Cumberland coals. But once they had access to the Irish market Wigan coals proved the most sought after, and on the Dublin market commanded 4/- to 5/- a ton more than even Whitehaven coals.

Scottish coals, as a rule, fetched a lower price than other British coal imported to Ireland, and reached a less widespread market. The Scottish coal trade in the early eighteenth century was centred principally on the port of Irvine, especially at the creek of Saltcoats. But difficulties in mining appear to have been encountered as exports declined heavily by the middle of the century. On the other hand, the mines of Ayr began to expand to a significant degree at this time, and exports from Ayr, which were insignificant in 1742, were as large as Irvine's in 1770,[2] and in the following year the Collector, writing to the Commissioners at Edinburgh, remarked upon the 'increase of the shipping of coals upon each side of the river particularly to Ireland'.[3] There were several small collieries concerned in exports from Ayr, but by 1789 the Blackhouse colliery was estimated to provide nine-tenths of the coal shipped.[4] Coals from the colliery were carried down to the harbour in lighters—at any rate in the 1770s —and in this respect the colliery enjoyed an advantage over the other collieries, from which the coals were brought down to the harbour in

---

[1] *Journals of the Irish House of Commons*, vol. 9, app. dcxliv–dcxlv.

[2] General Register House, Scottish Record Office, Customs Accounts. Figures for imports to Dublin from individual British ports between 1771 and 1777 show imports from Saltcoats and Irvine as being larger than from Ayr (*Journals of the Irish House of Commons*, vol. 9, app. dcxliv–dcxlv) but, as the Scottish customs accounts show, Ayr's Irish trade was more diversified and far less dependent on the Dublin market than that of the Port of Irvine (of which Saltcoats was a creek).

[3] Custom House, Ayr, Letter Books, Officers to Bd., 1771–4, 10 August 1771.

[4] Ibid., Officers to Bd., 1788–90, 31 March 1789.

carts, frequently the carts of local farmers or labourers, which were employed for short periods during the summer months. By comparison with the Cumberland collieries the coal handling in Ayr was very primitive, though of course the small volume of trade there would not have warranted the application of capital on the same scale as in Cumberland.

The Scottish coal trade grew rapidly during the last two decades of the century, doubling between the early 1780s and 1800. Exports from Ayr appear to have increased substantially during the 'eighties, and reached a peak at the opening of the 1790s. But exports from the port of Irvine had recovered quickly, and even in 1790 were double those of Ayr. They remained stable at 18,000 chaldrons for the last decade of the century, whereas exports from Ayr declined; and accounted for about 60 per cent of Scottish exports to Ireland. Little coal reached Ireland from the Lanarkshire coalfields. Shipments grew in the last decades, and appear to have reached a peak in 1793 when the combined exports of Glasgow, Port Glasgow and Greenock amounted to 6,613 chaldrons. They declined sharply thereafter.[1]

II. THE ENGLISH AND SCOTTISH PORTS

If the relative importance of the English ports trading to Ireland is measured in terms of tonnage cleared, the colliery ports were easily the most important. The tonnage of shipping cleared for Ireland in Swansea was greater than that in Bristol, and the tonnage cleared in Whitehaven greatly exceeded the clearances for Ireland in either Liverpool or London. Whitehaven, because of its large coal trade to Ireland, was throughout the century one of the most powerful ports in England in shipping,[2] and even in the years 1711–17 when the coal trade was still on a relatively small scale, the total tonnage cleared for Ireland in Whitehaven was twice the tonnage of vessels cleared to all parts from Liverpool, and about a fourth of total

[1]Report from the Committee on the Coal Trade, in *Reports from Committees of the House of Commons*, vol. x, app. 44, pp. 615–27.

[2]J.E. Williams, 'Whitehaven in the 18th century', *Economic History Review*, 2nd Series, vol. 8 (1955–6), pp. 398–9. In 1728 the Collector of the port of Whitehaven informed the Board of Customs Commissioners in London that 'the vessels belonging to this port concerned in the coal trade to Ireland are near 100 sail from 20 to 190 tons burthen and from three to eighteen hands' (Custom House Library, London, Selections from Customs outport records, Northern England 1924, pp. 18–19).

clearances from London.[1] In terms of value, however, the trade of the coal shipping ports was relatively small, and in particular they imported little from Ireland in return for the great quantities of coal they shipped. For these reasons the coal ports were of relatively little importance in the overall picture of the Irish trade, which, on the English side, was to a large extent dominated by the three great ports, London, Liverpool and Bristol (in that order) and in Scotland by Glasgow.

One of the most striking features of Anglo-Irish trade in the eighteenth century is the growing importance of London.[2] In 1700, a boom year, only 6.9 per cent of imports from Ireland were entered in London, and only 17.2 per cent of the exports cleared from there. During the years of the War of the Spanish Succession, London's trade with Ireland was reduced virtually to nothing, in some years no exports or imports to or from Ireland being recorded at all. In the other wars of the eighteenth century also, London's Irish trade declined sharply. During the War of the Austrian Succession direct trade between London and Ireland was in some years virtually nil, and though the decline was not so sharp in subsequent wars, it nevertheless reflected a 50 per cent reduction on the figures for the trade in the immediate pre-war years. French privateering activities in the waters around the two islands and the consequent high rates of insurance were, of course, the principal cause of the reduction of the volume of direct trade with London. Losses on even the relatively short and remote routes from Chester to Ireland were very heavy, and in the War of the Austrian Succession a very large discrepancy of 30 per cent, probably the result of privateering activities, arises between the statistics for exports of linen to Britain, and the corresponding figures in England. The hazards of direct shipping between the two countries did not, of course, lead to a corresponding reduction in commercial activity between Dublin and London, which continued more or less as in peace time. Instead, goods were consigned overland, and periods of war were boom years for the port and merchants of Chester. However, apart from periods of war, London's trade with Ireland increased steadily over the century.

The growth in London's relative importance was very rapid in the early decades of the century. By 1730 37 per cent of the imports from

[1] P.R.O., C.O. 390/8B; 388/18.
[2] On London's share in English foreign trade generally in this period, see Professor Ashton's introduction to Schumpeter, op. cit., pp. 9, 10.

Ireland entered by London—this was due principally to the import-ance of the London market for Irish linens. London's share of the export market was somewhat slower in growing at first; but in 1715 it was 28 per cent and by 1730 it had risen to 47 per cent. London's share of the export trade to Ireland was larger than its share of the

Table 21: London and the English outports—I

	Exports to Ireland			Imports from Ireland		
	London £	Outports £	England £	London £	Outports £	England £
25 Dec.						
1700	46,699	224,941	271,641	16,227	217,627	233,853
1715	118,627	301,426	420,063	30,567	358,870	389,437
1730	252,424	280,274	532,699	111,147	183,009	294,156
1735	363,532	405,713	769,245	159,924	257,498	417,422
1750	566,670	749,930	1,316,600	187,848	424,960	612,808
5 Jan.						
1766	584,309	1,182,711	1,767,020	357,020	713,514	1,070,534
1771	822,822	1,302,646	2,125,467	559,654	654,745	1,214,398
1776	941,679	1,227,929	2,169,609	846,228	703,934	1,550,162

Table 22: London and the English outports—II

Year ending 25 Dec.	Goods of domestic origin		Re-exports	
	London £	Outports £	London £	Outports £
1700	19,430	111,612	27,269	113,329
1715	46,890	124,419	71,737	177,007
1730	111,142	128,930	141,282	151,344
1735	127,383	241,794	236,149	163,919
1750	290,665	375,350	276,005	374,580
5 Jan.				
1766	223,359	576,691	360,950	606,020
1771	320,855	682,577	501,967	620,069
1776	362,673	770,277	579,006	457,652

import trade of course, although this changed significantly after the readmission to the English market of Irish provisions, more than half of which were taken by London. After 1770 imports through London accounted for over 50 per cent of total imports from Ireland, in 1775 for example, amounting to 54.6 per cent of the total. Beef, and especially butter and linen, were the principal imports through London, the other staple imports, tallow, hides, and yarn being im-ported almost exclusively through the outports. In the case of exports to Ireland, London's share of the trade was largest in re-exports. Apart from London, which from about 1725 had a larger share of Anglo-Irish trade than any other port, Liverpool and Bristol were the chief ports concerned in the trade. The volume of trade effected through Bristol expanded fairly constantly over the century, though as it expanded at a slower rate than the volume of the trade as a whole, its relative share of the trade would appear to have fallen. In the year 25 June 1699–24 June 1700 68 vessels of a total tonnage of 2,228 tons arrived in Bristol from Ireland,[1] and in 1790 198 vessels of a total tonnage of 12,258.[2] Vessels clearing for Ireland were 109, tonnage 4,470 tons, in 1717,[3] and 169 of a tonnage of 10,385 tons in 1790. Liverpool's rate of increase was much faster. Its trade with Ireland had been negligible in the 1650s, but in 1717 the tonnage of shipping clearing for Ireland from Liverpool was more than twice as great as in Bristol. By 1775 entries from Ireland were almost three times as many as in Bristol, and in 1790 over four times.

Table 23: Entries from Ireland[4]

	Liverpool	Bristol
1760	288	79*
1775	287	102
1780	485	87
1790	817	198

*year 1764

Chester's trade with Ireland remained fairly large if measured in numbers or tonnage of ships. These, however, exaggerated its trade as many of the movements were those of the packets. Chester's Irish trade was now in fact very small apart from the large linen imports that occurred around the times of the two fairs.[5] Even the packet traffic in time deserted the port, moving further down the Dee to Parkgate. The growing volume of trade between the inland industrial regions and Ireland in the last decades of the century largely by-passed the port, and at the end of the century Chester lost its importance in the distribution of linens as well. The last linen ships from Ireland apparently came in in 1810,[6] and with their passing

[1]B.M., Add. MSS. 9764, f. 116.
[2]W.E. Minchinton, *The trade of Bristol in the eighteenth century,* (Bristol, 1957) pp. 53–5.
[3]P.R.O., C.O. 390/8B.
[4]Figures for Liverpool from *Williamson's Liverpool Advertiser;* for Bristol, as given in Minchinton, op. cit., pp. 53–5, 181.
[5]In nine months ending 7 March 1776, for example, it exported only 13 cargoes to Ireland apart from 63 shipments of coal. Imports from Ireland amounted only to 47 cargoes, compared with a total of 178 imported in Liverpool in the same period. *Chester Chronicle,* 22 May 1775–7 March 1776.
[6]Guynett M. Haynes-Thomas, 'The port of Chester', *Transactions of the Lancashire and Cheshire Antiquarian Society,* vol. lix (1947) p. 40.

Chester's long history of merchandising with Ireland was virtually at an end.

Other English ports which had a fairly substantial commodity trade with Ireland included Whitehaven, which had entered into the colonial trade from the end of the seventeenth century, and which, though its tobacco trade was sadly reduced in the 1750s, continued to supply tobacco to Ireland up to the end of the 1770s. The Clyde ports of Glasgow, Port Glasgow and Greenock, which may be grouped together, developed an important Irish trade as Whitehaven's tobacco trade decayed, and from the early 1760s to the early 1780s were the main suppliers of tobacco to the Irish market. The port of Lancaster was in the early eighteenth century the fourth English port in the trade to Ireland.[1] The trade in colonial goods was centred mainly on the four ports London, Bristol, Liverpool and Whitehaven. Bideford re-exported some tobacco to Ireland in the second half of the seventeenth century, but this fell off as Bideford and its sister Severn ports declined to a very minor position in Anglo-Irish trade in the early decades of the following century. The ports on the East coast, apart from London, had little connection with Ireland. Yarmouth was the only exception. It was the centre of worsted yarn imports from Ireland, and also exported malt and wheat to Ireland,[2] as did Ipswich and London; and Shoreham, Arundel and Chichester on the south coast.

[1] In 1717 93 vessels of a total tonnage of 3,305 tons cleared for Ireland, and at one of its creeks, Pile of Fowdrey, 225 of a burthen of 6,750 tons cleared for Ireland between Christmas 1758 and midsummer 1764: at Ulverston alone 50 vessels were said to be employed in carrying iron ore and bark to Ireland. B.M., Add. MSS. 9293, ff. 95, 97.

[2] See especially *Journals of the British House of Commons,* vol. xl, p. 783.

CHAPTER V

THE ORGANIZATION OF TRADE

I. THE MERCHANT COMMUNITY

ANGLO-IRISH trade at this time differs from most branches of
British overseas trade in that it was not carried on by more or less
organized 'colonies' of merchants from one or the other island. In
certain respects the trade bears a closer resemblance to the coastal
trade of the period than to the foreign commerce. This is scarcely
surprising. Not only were the two islands adjacent, but they enjoyed
parallel systems of law, followed similar customs and commercial
procedures, and the merchant communities of the Irish seaports
spoke English and were for the most part of English birth or descent.
The difficulties that in an age of imperfect communication required
the presence of colonies in foreign or distant lands did not therefore
arise. This should not, of course, obscure the fact that there was some
movement of merchants between the two countries. English and
Scottish merchants settled in Ireland; and as a result of the emigration of many of the Catholic merchants to the more hospitable shores
of France and Spain, the bulk of Irish overseas trade lay in the hands
of English and Scottish immigrants or their descendants by the opening of the eighteenth century. The English background of the Irish
merchant community is particularly striking in the case of Quaker
merchants who were connected with their English correspondents
not merely by a common religion but frequently by bonds of warm
friendship or close kinship. On the other hand there was also a small
movement of Irish merchants to England. A few Irish names occur
in Whitehaven, Liverpool, Bristol, and especially in London, of which
those of George Fitzgerald[1] and of some of the merchant importers
of Irish linens were most prominent.

Trade in most Irish ports being small, scope for specialization was
restricted. The typical intermediary in the Irish outports was a general
merchant dealing both in exports and imports and trading with
several countries. A good example is Daniel Mussenden, who for
forty years had dealings from Belfast with practically every region

[1] P.R.O., C. 105/24, Power *v.* Fitzgerald, contains some items relating to
Fitzgerald's trade 1737–42 though without relevance to his Irish correspondence.

with which Ireland traded.[1] The position was much the same in the small and decaying port of Galway where the only prominent merchant house was that of the Frenchs, trading with Bristol, Norway, France, Spain and Portugal, and conducting a small inland banking business. Relatively large merchant communities existed in only two Irish ports, Dublin and Cork; and, at the end of the century, in Belfast. Only in Dublin were the volume and variety of trade sufficient for any great degree of specialization to arise and here almost alone among Irish ports were there men who specialized in particular branches of the export and import trade. Many of these were the great wholesalers engaged in the import of raw silks or draperies, etc. Dublin was the main wholesale market in the finer goods and raw materials for the whole country, and the large wholesalers there were almost invariable importers. But even these merchants were not always tied to the one article. The Jaffrays, for instance, though silk importers, also sold 'Vigonia' wools and bought rabbit fur and coney wool on commissions received from a London hat manufacturer.[2] In Cork and the other southern ports the merchant community was built around the provision trade and other business was generally transacted as a sideline. The evolution of the overseas trade merchant to his modern position as a specialist in a particular commodity was even at the end of the eighteenth century only in its early stages. He was frequently concerned with a wide range of commodities, and corresponded with many countries. He might even as a sideline to his commodity trade conduct a banking or a quasi-banking business, or be concerned in manufacturing activities.

It is significant that, in contrast to the position in even the smaller English ports, there appear to have been no elaborate partnerships or companies. This was a consequence not so much of the relatively small size of the business as of the fact that so much of Irish trade was effected on commission and did not therefore require a large capital. Again, there was an absence of a strong mercantile tradition, and Arthur Young, after his travels in Ireland, commented 'on commercial people quitting trade or manufactures when they have made from 5,000 to 10,000 pounds to become gentlemen'. Young excluded from his statement only the 'many quakers who (take them for all in all the most sensible class of people in that kingdom) are exceptions

---

[1]Public Record Office of Northern Ireland, Belfast, Mussenden Papers, uncatalogued collection; and catalogued collection D. 354.
[2]P.R.O., C. 107/104, French v. Davies, Foreign letter-book, 1771–92.

to this folly: and mark the consequence they are the only wealthy traders in the island'.[1] The Quaker community was strong both in the more prosperous agricultural and manufacturing communities, and in the three principal Irish ports Dublin, Cork and Waterford. They were prominent also in the linen industry and appear to have controlled virtually the whole of the woollen and worsted yarn trade. The large merchants like Joshua Pim, who claimed before a parliamentary committee that his father controlled at one time one-third of Irish yarn exports,[2] or George Newenham of Cork, single consignments of whose yarns were worth several thousand pounds, were both Quakers.

The trade of even the most powerful merchants in the larger outports was on a modest scale. Thus, Daniel Mussenden, the most prominent Belfast merchant of his day, though his total assets, exclusive of leases, amounted to £14,206, had only £1,370 in goods. Assets included debts due to him of £6,820 14s. od., but only £134 in cash. Nevertheless, despite the small scale of his business, his interests were widespread, his assets including an investment of £2,000 in a short-lived mercantile bank he had founded, £1,300 in a local wine company, £250 in a salt company, and in partnership with John Bradshaw £742 in linens.[3] The small scale of his business is further evidenced by the fact that his account with his London correspondents, Allen and Marlar, through whom much of his English and foreign exchange was effected, amounted only to £1,896 for the period from 7 February 1755 to 16 March 1756. His commodity dealings with England were also small, his account with his Liverpool correspondent, for instance, totalling only £711 for five years from 15 July 1752 to 29 October 1757. The case of another prominent Belfast merchant of a slightly earlier period suggests a similar picture. James Arbuckle in 1736 had debts due to him in Ireland of above £7,000 sterling and had goods in cellars and warehouses to the value of £1,500. He also had £600 out at interest, was the owner of two ships and had recently purchased shares in vessels to the extent of £800 'moderately computed'. He would, he wrote, also be due £300 once tobacco in hand was sold; and 'excepting a trifle due at White-

---

[1]A. Young, *Tour in Ireland*, part II, p. 140.
[2]*Journals of the Irish House of Commons,* vol. 10, app. cccclxxxix.
[3]Public Record Office of Northern Ireland, Belfast, Uncatalogued Mussenden Papers, an Inventory of debts due to and by Daniel Mussenden, also his goods. stocks, leases etc. 23 June 1756.

haven I do not owe all mankind £20 but what I have above told you of, excepting some ordinary demands in trade, which the current cash in my hands will always discharge'. Arbuckle borrowed £2,000 from John Black, a Belfast merchant settled in Bordeaux, and asked not to be required to liquidate it in one payment, adding 'but if you would be so good as to take it in £500 or £600 in a year in butter, it would be very obliging'.[1]

The resources of the merchants engaged in the provision trade in the southern Irish ports were for the most part no larger. The prominent Waterford firm of Richard and Edward Weeks, reputed 'men of wealth and credit', engaged in trade with Portugal and the West Indies, and enjoying the advantage that their promissory notes were readily accepted in payments, at the time they failed in the 1730s owed only £5,547 to the local bank from which they had been borrowing heavily, and had made over to the bank satisfactory assets valued only at £2,281.[2] In Cork itself, many of the merchants trading on their own account were men of small substance, whose London correspondents were not of good standing,[3] and some of the merchants concerned in the provision trade dealt exclusively on commissions. Even at the end of the century the provision merchants commanded but small resources of their own. The Waterford merchants Courtenay and Ridgway, whose exports of butter alone amounted to the total of £80,000, one-third of Waterford's butter exports, and one-twelfth of the total Irish export, had dealings on their own account of only little more than £3,000 or £4,000.[4] There were of course a few large merchants in the provision ports, George Newenham, for example, whose wealth depended on the yarn trade, and Paul Maylor who was rather exceptional in that he had been prominent by Irish standards in fitting out privateers in 1756–7 and was supported by the credit of his uncle's banking and mercantile firm of Lawton, Carleton and Feray. Maylor failed in 1760 owing

---

[1]Public Record Office of Northern Ireland, Belfast, Black Papers, T. 1073/4/1. James Arbuckle to John Black, 28 August 1736.

[2]*Journals of the Irish House of Commons,* vol. 4, app. cxxii–cxxvi.

[3]See 'Les gens qui tir (*sic*) [de Londres sur Cork] pour l'ordinaire sont de peu de valeur et on court beaucoup de risque avec leurs lettres'. Archives Départementales de la Gironde, Bordeaux 7B 1800. Thomas Thomas to Pelet, merchant in Bordeaux, London, 24 October 1728.

[4]Ledger of Courtenay and Ridgway 1791–2, in the possession of Mrs. Olive Ridgway, Rossmore, Mallow, Co. Cork.

upwards of £30,000, and had effects, at the least, to the value of £15,000.[1]

The drapers in Dublin, through whom the bulk of linen shipments was effected in the early days of the linen industry, also carried on a business of rather modest proportions on their own account. Samuel Watson provides a good example of the medium or large dealer on his own account at the start of the 'thirties.[2] At the time of his decease Watson's goods were valued at the total of £1,206 18s. 7½d. Of this sum £730 10s. 9½d. represented the value of goods in his 'shop'; he also had goods worth £278 15s. 1d. with his London correspondent, Alexander Forbes, while his share of goods in the hands of a factor in Philadelphia was £14 11s. 0½d. A fairly considerable amount (£1,681) was due to Watson, mainly from Irish correspondents, but also £72 from Joseph Hiscox of London, £15 from Joseph Robson in Bristol and £111 by another English correspondent James Hoskins. Sums due by Watson totalled £1,801 16s. 9¾d., the creditors representing in the main the persons from whom he had purchased linens, but there was a total of £192 due to merchants in London, Bristol and Manchester. The extent of Watson's debts suggests that he had obtained credit for his purchases of linen, and the small amounts due by him in England suggest that he dealt in imported fine goods on a small scale, as some other drapers certainly did. Watson's trade was mainly an inland one, and the necessity of carrying this trade on their own account must have been a factor compelling the drapers of the early 'thirties to limit or abandon their English trade on their own account. The Dublin draper, Elijah Chamberlain, however, despite the contraction of credit at the beginning of the 'thirties carried on a trade on his own account equal to an annual turnover of about £1,000, half of which was at the Chester fairs where sales were for cash or liquid bills, and he was dependent upon his London factors disposing of his other goods efficiently to enable him to maintain his purchases.[3]

The rising demand for linens enabled Irish weavers to demand cash instead of credit. In turn, because of the demands on him for cash in buying the linens and in defraying the expenses of bleaching the northern linen dealer also was forced in the early 'thirties to refuse

[1] *Journals of the Irish House of Commons*, vol. 7, pp. 83–4, 100, 102, 105–6, 109, 113, 162.

[2] Friends' Historical Library, Dublin, Collection of Quaker Wills, D. 5. 65.

[3] P.R.O., C. 105/15, Herne *v.* Barber, Letters received by a London linen draper, 1731–4.

credit to the Dublin drapers, except at an exorbitant rate. Because of
this the Dublin drapers abandoned or limited dealings on their own
account, confining them to the home market.[1] However, many of the
Dublin drapers continued to attend the Chester Fair, which was
second only to the London market, with linens of their own. Even
as late as the 1780s when the export trade in linen in Dublin was to
a large extent dominated by linen merchants, Dublin wholesale
drapers or 'shopkeepers' were still crossing to the Chester fairs. The
reasons for this predilection for the Chester market are clear. Sales
at the two annual fairs at Chester were for cash or for short-dated
bills, and this suited merchants trading on their own account under
Irish conditions. Irish merchants also appear to have attended a fair
at Wrexham, and itinerant 'natives of Ireland' often landed in the
ports of Scotland with linens to sell in the countryside.[2] The resources
of the linen merchants in Dublin, who to a large extent replaced the
linen drapers in the export business, appear also to have been very
limited, for relatively little of their business was on their own account.
They acted either as factors to the Northern bleachers, advancing
them sums on a *del credere* basis for short terms of two or three
months, or accepted large buying commissions from England.

The bleachers, who began to emerge as prominent exporters from
the middle of the century, gradually increased the scale of business
on their own account, as opposed to the bleaching they did for
drapers. But even as late as 1763 Andrews of Comber only bleached
500 pieces of linen on their own account, and for twenty-five years
after 1745 the turnover of their combined linen trade and soap and
candle business averaged only about £1,500 a year.[3] In the 1770s, on
the other hand, the cash account of the Belfast bleacher James
Ferguson for irregular accounting periods of up to 18 months, varied
between £2,605 and £5,992.[4] Ferguson's purchases of linen never exceeded 2,000 pieces a year, and his business was therefore on a smaller

[1]Ibid.

[2]Custom House, Ayr. Letter books, Officers to Bd., 1771-4, 23 April 1774.
See also C. Maxwell, *Country and town in Ireland under the Georges* (London,
1940) p. 138. For a similar instance at Liverpool, see R. C. Jarvis, *Customs
letter-books of the port of Liverpool, 1711-1823*, (Manchester, 1954) p. 107, and
in Cumberland, see a letter in Public Record Office of Northern Ireland, D.
1044/370B, Richard Pike, Cockermouth, 2 June 1773.

[3]Sydney Andrews, *Nine generations, a history of the Andrews family, millers
of Comber* (Belfast, 1958) pp. 31, 40.

[4]Public Record Office of Northern Ireland, Belfast, D. 468, Ledger of
James Ferguson, 1771-84.

scale than that of most Belfast bleachers of the day. According to an 1782 estimate the 39 bleach greens in the Belfast area had an annual average output of 4,400 pieces,[1] more than twice Ferguson's output. Some of the bleaching was on a larger scale, and the cash account of the Richardsons of Lisburn during the three years 1785–7, totalled £16,191, £31,948 and £34,788 respectively.[2]

Though much of the exports were on the bleachers' own account, the extent of export dealings on English account, already consider-able, especially in the Dublin market, increased greatly from the 1780s. At the Newry fair in June 1784, one Newry house received commissions of the value of £12,000,[3] and a buyer from England arrived at a Dublin fair in 1793 with 14,000 guineas.[4]

The scale of business in the two principal branches of Irish overseas trade was thus, in general, modest though the size clearly increased over the century. There were, of course, many moderately large merchants, and a few with a very extensive business. But the latter were exceptional. In general, Irish merchants' capitals were slender, and their turnover on their own account limited. Merchants in Dublin were able to provide short-term capital for the bleachers of the North and in Cork, the only other Irish town with an elaborate banking business, for the butter producers of the south-west, but were gener-ally able to undertake only modest commitments in the way of a direct concern on their own account in foreign trade. Importers likewise were an important source of credit for manufacturers and retailers, but held the greater part of their stocks on English account. In 1749 for instance a Dublin woollen draper trading 'for more than his slender stock could admit', failed, owing £3,000 to weavers and others in Dublin, and £4,000 to 'some people' in London.[5] In the second half of the century, the turnover of drapers, whose business was frequently combined with manufacturing, was of course on a larger scale than this. Thus, Dennis Thomas O'Brien had a warehouse for the sale of linen and cotton goods, both English and Irish, was also a manufacturer, and dealt to the amount of £50,000 or £60,000

[1]Gill, *Rise of the Irish linen industry*, pp. 246–7.
[2]Cash Book of J. & J. Richardson of Lisburn, 1785–7, in the possession of Messrs. Richardson, Sons & Owden Ltd., Belfast.
[3]Newry news in *Belfast News Letter*, 29 June 1784.
[4]Public Record Office of Northern Ireland, Belfast, D. 607/485. Downshire Papers, Dublin, 1 November 1793.
[5]Guildhall Library, Radcliffe Papers, MS. 6645/5. Francis Thomé, Dublin, 3 February 1749–50.

a year.[1] But it is quite clear that much of the import business continued to be effected on English credit. A shortage of capital remained a feature of Irish trade. There were a fair number of Irish merchants and manufacturers with sufficient resources to invest £1,000 or £2,000 in a venture; there were few merchants with resources on a princely scale. Subscriptions in the Bank of Ireland founded in 1783 were fixed at a maximum of £10,000, but few merchants subscribed to near that amount.[2]

In Ireland, the smaller and less developed community, merchants were therefore heavily dependent on English credit. In this respect Anglo-Irish trade was similar to that between England and other less well-developed countries. Anglo-Irish trade also contrasts, because of this dependence on English credit, with the other branches of Irish overseas trade, as for example, the trade with France and Spain, or the flax-seed trade from North America, in which much of the business was transacted on Irish account. As a result of the relatively large resources of the English merchant community and their own inadequate capital, Irish merchants concerned in Anglo-Irish trade were much more dependent on buying and selling commissions received from England than on dealings on their own account.[3] No clear division is possible, however, as many merchants combined trading in both manners, and even a cotton manufacturer might be willing to sell yarns on commissions received from his own supplier in Manchester. Some diversity of trade was always desirable, and as the scale of his business was generally small the Irish merchant, even if trading on his own account, readily accepted commissions in business which had little connection with his general line of trade.

The main reason for the importance of commission business was the limited resources of the Irish merchants, which did not enable them to withstand a long lock-up of their capital either in stocks or credits. As a result of this and the general demand for cash, inland bills of longer date or sight than 31 days and foreign bills of more

---

[1] *Journals of the Irish House of Commons*, vol. II, app. cxlix.
[2] For a list of subscribers to the Bank, see F.G. Hall, *The Bank of Ireland 1783-1946* (Dublin, 1949) pp. 508-10.
[3] There were, of course, exceptions. The Dublin merchant, Christopher Bellew, for example, had substantial quantities of oats, beef and bacon in the hands of his Liverpool and London correspondents. But on the other hand, the butter he shipped was on the account of the London cheesemongers 'whose custom I have to sollicit yearly as others are [constantly] applying to them'. National Library of Ireland, Bellew Papers, Dublin, 25 June 1795.

than 21 or 30 days were extremely rare and difficult to discount. There was some improvement in the last decades of the century, bills at 61 or 91 days sight were somewhat more common in the inland trade, but the typical bill in the inland trade remained one at 31 days sight and bills at more than 61 days sight still presented difficulties in discounting. As sales of imported goods for cash, except at a reduced price, were few, and the terms of credit normally granted to customers in different trades varied between 3 and 12 months, the nature of the Irish bill trade with its emphasis on the 'liquid' bill made it difficult for the Irish importer to commit himself on his own account. There were certainly some merchants like the Jaffrays and Francis Thomé who, as well as accepting commissions, were able to deal on their own account even to the extent of importing silks directly from Italy. But in general silks were supplied to the Irish weavers and wholesalers by Irish importers, operating on English account,[1] and conditions in other trades do not appear to have been materially different from those in the silk trade.

Because many branches of trade operated on a commission basis, the directing and financing of business was largely performed by the English importers or exporters, who were often specialized intermediaries. The early wool trade was mainly financed and controlled by specialist importers in the Bristol Channel ports,[2] and the large provision trade of the last three decades of the eighteenth century was almost exclusively effected on the account of cheesemongers, provision merchants and West India traders in London and the English outports. The linen trade is a partial exception in that a fairly considerable quantity of goods was shipped on Irish account. But such business was commonly associated with the insuring of debt and advances by London linen merchants; and with the final supersession of the specialist linen merchant by the wholesaler in the last decades of the century the already considerable proportion of business on English account increased greatly. In the goods imported into Ireland the same pattern of trade held, and business was for the most part directed and financed by English merchants. Tobacco exports, for example, were for the most part financed by the tobacco

[1]Guildhall Library, Radcliffe Papers, MS. 6645/5. Letters from Dublin, 1744-55.
[2]A few of the papers of the Smiths of Bideford survive in P.R.O., C. 110/181, Smith v. Blagden. Imports through Liverpool and Chester were also on English account. See P.J. Bowden, *The wool trade in Tudor and Stuart England* (London, 1962) p. 71.

importers or other English merchants for whom the tobacco merchant acted in the port of import from America.[1]

The major exceptions to this pattern of business were, among exports, the trade in worsted yarn; and in imports, that in sugar and rum. The trade in worsted yarn is only a partial exception, as consignments were also made on English account. The prominence of export dealings on Irish account was due to the organization of the trade. The necessity to purchase yarn from distant areas for the combing districts had led to the emergence of a number of highly capitalized merchants, who distributed wool to thousands of combers and spinners. There were, of course, many small master-combers as well, but the larger ones held a high proportion of the business and were able to forego an immediate return on their capital. Returns were for Irish conditions exceptionally slow in the yarn trade; the Norwich wholesalers, taking commission from the Irish master-combers, granted credit terms of 12 months to the manufacturers.[2] The greater part of the Quaker merchants in Cork consigned to Norwich on their own account, and in the early 'seventies the Gurneys bought directly only Leinster yarns which their Cork correspondents could not provide. A very large share of the imports of yarn was also in the hands of the merchant John Pim. He was a member of a prominent Irish Quaker family, and had at one time acted as an agent for the Gurneys in their Irish business. But he moved to London at the end of the 1760s and in the 1770s was importing Irish yarn on his own account, both from Munster and from Leinster, where several members of the Pim family were themselves combers. This trade contrasts with the wool trade which preceded it, in which the wool had been bought by factors acting for English merchants.[3] It also contrasts with the trade in linen yarn, in which though imports on Irish account and long terms of credit were not unknown,[4] the bulk of imports was on English account, and even where the manufacturer was the importer the Irish merchant was reimbursed immediately.

[1] Cf. P.R.O., C. 107/161, Lloyd v. Nicholson. Papers of Clement Nicholson, merchant, Whitehaven, 1697-8. In two years the tobacco merchant Nicholson handled over £25,000 in tobacco as the agent of other merchants.

[2] The long terms of credit may perhaps also be a reflection of the acute competition in the yarn trade to Norwich in the second half of the century.

[3] Cf. B.M., Add. MSS. 21133, f. 56; *Calendar of Treasury Books*, vol. 10, pt. 3, p. 1,327; A.P. Wadsworth and J. de L. Mann, *The cotton trade and industrial Lancashire, 1600-1780*, p. 46.

[4] A.P. Wadsworth and J. de L. Mann, op. cit., pp. 47, 236.

In any event the fact that English manufacturers also had Irish agents purchase worsted yarn for them must not be overlooked.

The only important exception to the general trends in the financing of the import trade was sugar, which was generally imported on the account of the Irish refiners, who appear almost invariably to have been among the more substantial general merchants in the Irish ports.[1] On the other hand, if the Irish refiner decided to purchase his raw sugars in Ireland, he bought from a factor.[2] In addition, Irish merchants sometimes had small consignments of sugar or rum on their account on vessels sailing from the West Indies to Bristol, Liverpool or London, and in particular whole shiploads of rum on Irish account were entered in, and then cleared out for Ireland, from the ports of Scotland and the west of England. Small consignments of sugar or rum represented modest speculations by Irish merchants, who regarded the possibility of disposing of the goods in the English port of import as an insurance if conditions on their home market deteriorated. The shiploads of rum imported via England or Scotland arose from the exploitation of an anomaly in the Irish customs tariff, and much of the trade, while it lasted, was associated with the business of smuggling goods into Britain conducted on the north-east coast of Ireland.

Access to adequate capital or long-term credit facilities was a vital factor in trade. Irish merchants were particularly affected, as on account of buying their export commodities for cash it was difficult for them to grant credit to foreign customers. A bill at three months would, of course, have answered the Irish merchant's purpose, but the bill trade in Ireland, reflecting the limited capital resources of the Irish merchant community, was centred around the foreign bill at 21 days' and the inland bill at 31 days' sight. The smaller English merchants, also, had some reluctance in committing themselves in long-term outlay of capital in Irish ventures. The difficulty was at times got over by joint concerns, though such were not typical of Anglo-Irish trade in general. However, the difficulties involved in carrying on trade on a merchant's own account were lessened by advances made by the merchants or factors in the other country.

Such advances were generally associated with the guaranteeing or 'insuring' of debts on a *del credere* basis by merchants or factors. In

---

[1]The Houstons of Glasgow had dealings with several of the more prominent Irish refiners. National Library of Scotland, Houston MSS. Home Letter Book H.
[2]Cf. *Irish Parliamentary Register*, vol. 1, 2nd edition, p. 90, November 1781.

England, the stronger community, the merchants frequently made advances on the basis of such insurance, as, in particular, in the linen trade. In Ireland, on the other hand, advances were uncommon, although insurance of the proceeds of sales without advancing any money was itself far from being unknown and some merchants appear to have been prepared to assume the risks on these conditions more or less as a matter of course. Thus, the Dublin silk merchants Percival and John Hunt quoted their terms to a London silk merchant in 1754 as $2\frac{1}{2}$ per cent commission and 2 per cent *del credere*, but added—rather significantly—that 'if you please to stand the risque of debts yourselves it will be more agreeable to us.'[1] The relatively small resources of the Irish merchants and the lack of a bankruptcy law (prior to 1772) which made the recovery of debt a slow, tedious and uncertain task, all made it difficult for an Irish merchant to insure debts, and such dealings were probably untypical of the Irish importing merchant of the period. Francis Thomé who had been the Radcliffes' Dublin correspondent for ten years and who had recommended P. & J. Hunt to them as his successor does not at all times appear to have assumed the risk of debt on goods they dispatched to him. Operations of this nature may have widened in the last few decades of the century, when conditions improved so much in Ireland. The inland flour merchant, Robert Shaw, advanced the money to his correspondents on receipt of goods in his extensive inland[2] trade, and by analogy one may perhaps imagine a similar type of large merchant in the import trade.[3] In the case of imports of bark, certainly, the factor frequently 'insured' the money for the English merchant,[4] though this trade was somewhat exceptional as the demand was lively, and terms of credit very short. But even in this branch of trade the insuring of debt with or without the advance of the proceeds was far from universal.[5] The insuring of debt was also known to the cotton trade in the early nineteenth century, though in a modified form in which the Irish agent assumed a quarter of the

[1]Guildhall Library, Radcliffe Papers, MS. 6645/5, Percival & John Hunt, Dublin, 19 November, 17 December 1754.

[2]National Library, Dublin, Shaw MSS. 1785-97.

[3]Exceptionally, Robert Shaw junior, himself advanced £7,100 on a consignment of sugars from England in January 1797. National Library, Dublin, Shaw MSS. 5680, Letter Book, 1796-7, p. 185.

[4]Cf. *Minutes of Evidence before the Committee of the House of Lords*, 1785, p. 398.

[5]National Library, Dublin, Shaw MSS. 5678, Letter Book 1793-4, p. 492.

risk.[1] The *del credere* terms on English re-exports sent to Ireland did not necessarily have to be granted by the Irish merchant; in 1697 the Whitehaven tobacco merchant Clement Nicholson consigned tobacco on an apparently *del credere* basis to an English merchant who disposed of the tobacco on the Dublin market through the medium of his Irish correspondents.[2]

The advancing of the proceeds of sales, rather exceptional in English imports into Ireland even when the debt was 'insured' by the Irish importers, was on the other hand quite common in Irish exports to England on account of the Irish community's acute demand for cash and the English merchants' ability to satisfy it. The terms of credit Dublin linen drapers exporting on their own account in the first half of the eighteenth century granted through their London factors were six months, though in practice returns were often quicker.[3] As the Irish draper's disbursements only occurred by way of purchases of linens at fairly well-defined times during the exporting season, he was in a position to trade on his own account without an advance of money by the London merchant. In the case of the bleachers who became so prominent in the export trade from the middle of the century onwards, the need for reimbursement was much more imperative, and all the more so because of the almost complete lack of banking facilities in the North of Ireland.[4] The Dublin draper only purchased linens from May onwards, and with terms of credit of six months would already have received the net proceeds of his previous season's exports. The bleacher's commitments, on the other hand, commenced much earlier with the purchase of the first un-bleached linens from the peasant weavers by the end of the winter; and he was then involved in a continuous cash outlay during a bleaching season which lasted till Autumn. Without the proceeds of sale being advanced by the London factor, it would have been impossible for the bleacher of the 'seventies to conduct an extensive export business on his own account. His London factors, authorised to grant a credit of seven months, were drawn on by the bleacher

[1]Manchester University, McConnel & Kennedy MSS., Belfast Sales.

[2]P.R.O., C. 107/161, Lloyd v. Nicholson.

[3]Cf. 'I know no Irish factor but are pleased to be drawn on 5 or 6 months after linnen are sold but many are drawn on in half that time or sum people here would make a poor hand of it'. P.R.O., Chancery Masters' Exhibits, C. 105/15, Herne v. Barber, Elijah Chamberlain, Dublin, 10 January 1733–4.

[4]See *Journals of the Irish House of Commons*, vol. 11, app. clix., John Nevill, *Seasonable remarks on the linen trade of Ireland* (Dublin, 1783) p. 71.

once sales were effected in return for a commission of 6 per cent plus
½ per cent warehouse rent and insurance. The bleacher's Dublin
factors were authorized to grant a credit of two or three months to
buyers, and were drawn on for the proceeds of sale in return for a
global commission of 5 per cent.[1]

The exact length of time the bleacher was out of money on linens
shipped is not easy to estimate, though it is clear that the bleacher
during periods of quick sale was able to draw for the final proceeds
of individual consignments in three, six or nine months, whereas
when sales were slower the final pieces of linen included in a consignment might be disposed of only in 12, 18 or 24 months. Of course,
the bulk of the pieces in a consignment would be sold much more
quickly and the last pieces to be sold might be of inferior or unwanted
quality. In times of slow sales whole consignments might however
remain a long time unsold in the hands of the London factors. In
February 1787 for instance a consignment from a bleacher had lain
about nine months in the hands of a London factor, and another
quantity was unsold in London in February 1789, two years after
the unbleached linens had first been purchased by the same firm.[2] As
a result, returns were at times so slow that even despite drawing immediately on sale the Irish bleacher was forced to reduce his purchases
of brown linens for bleaching, whereas on the other hand in a boom
year the quicker returns enabled the bleacher to expand his business
by a significant proportion. The purchases of the Belfast bleacher
James Ferguson fell sharply in reaction to bad sales in 1777. Purchases which had been 1,425[3] pieces in 1775 and 974 in 1776 fell to
469 pieces in 1777 and 539 in 1778. The return of boom conditions in
the linen trade enabled him, however, to expand his purchases of
unbleached linens to 852 pieces in 1779, 1,611 in 1780 and 1,960 in
1781.

Had the whole of the trade been financed in this manner, the plight
of the bleachers would have been extreme during periods of slow
sales. Bleachers aimed at a turnover of their capital twice in the year,
and a single turnover in the year was regarded as minimal. In
July 1782 for instance John Andrews of Comber wrote to Isaac
Woodville a factor in Newcastle 'the trade in Newcastle must be come

---

[1]Public Record Office of Northern Ireland, Belfast, D.468, Ledger & invoices
of James Ferguson, 1771–84; Young, op. cit., part I, p. 107.

[2]Andrews Papers, Messrs. Isaac Andrews & Sons Ltd.

[3]Purchases to February 1776.

to a very low ebb when I cannot get a turn of my money once a year'.[1]
It took the bleacher roughly three months to bleach the green cloth,
and about the same length of time to have the finished commodity
disposed of on the London market. When sales were satisfactory, the
bleacher was enabled, through the merchant's advancing the proceeds
once sales had been effected, to lay down a second bleach and dispose
of it all in the same year. If sales proved slower, it was necessary for
the linen bleacher, if he wished to maintain his bleaching business at
a maximum output, to seek an advance from the factor on unsold
goods. Not all factors were of course prepared to be drawn on before
sales were effected. Even those who were felt some reluctance at
having their capital tied up in accumulating stocks of unsold goods
and in times of acute depression might refuse to make any further
advances before sales. The bleachers for their part were loath to draw
before the factors succeeded in selling goods, as interest on long
advances reduced their profits. However, the fact that sales very
frequently tended to be slower than would enable them to maintain
a satisfactory level of activity compelled them to draw on their
English or Dublin factors in advance of sales. A County Down factor
for instance wrote in 1781 to a London firm: 'You mention your not
being willing to advance money until you render the act. of sales of
the linens—under which restrictions I would not wish to consigne
linens to any house'.[2]

As a result much of the money was advanced in practice at the
time of receipt of goods, and not merely at the time when the factor
succeeded in selling them. Even as early as 1744 a witness stated
before a Parliamentary committee that it was 'customary for the
factors in London to advance money to the manufacturers on their
sending their goods to London for which the manufacturer paid
interest to the factors during all the time their goods lay unsold'.[3] By
the 1780s such advance had become very common,[4] and in 1785 it
was stated that 'there is not less than a million of money generally
advanced upon the Irish linens'.[5]

[1]Messrs. Isaac Andrews & Sons Ltd., Belfast. Letter Books, John Andrews,
13 July 1782.
[2]Messrs. Isaac Andrews & Sons Ltd., Belfast. Letter Book of Michael Andrews,
1780–82, 14 April 1781. The London firm was Bate & Henckell.
[3]*Report of the Committee on the Linen Trade*, 1744, in *Reports of the House
of Commons*, vol. II, p. 69.
[4]See *Irish Parliamentary Register*, vol. 8, pp. 320, 325.
[5]*Minutes of Evidence before the Committee of the House of Lords*, 1785, p. 243.

8

Although the function of the linen merchant was disappearing rapidly at the end of the eighteenth century, this was to some extent counterbalanced by a growing volume of direct investment by English merchants in the fixed capital of the Irish linen industry. English merchants were beginning to commission Irish bleachers to 'manufacture' on their own account or where this did not prove suitable to undertake capital investment in the Irish industry themselves. One London merchant for instance unable to obtain well bleached $\frac{7}{8}$ and yard wide linens wrote in 1765 of his intention to build 50 houses in Ballymote, Co. Sligo, with four looms each.[1] As early as 1773 a London importer of Irish linens had been 'concerned in manufacturing considerable quantities of linen in Ireland, one of which in particular consisted of from 3 to 400 looms in the article of dowlass and sheeting'.[2] This form of investment appears to have become fairly common at this time for Young in 1780 referred to 'English capitals, and English factors, and partners [who] have gone to the North of Ireland to advance that fabric . . .'[3] Most of this capital was probably provided by the English wholesalers now increasingly uncerned in imports from Ireland. In the early nineteenth century the firm of Sadler, Fenton and Company, linen manufacturers at Leeds and wholesalers of Irish linen, conducted their business both there and in Belfast.[4] The financial problems of the industry were also solved by the rise of large firms. In the early nineteenth century the numerous small bleaching concerns withered away. By the second quarter of the century the industry was conducted by a small number of firms with relatively large resources who granted short-term credit to their wholesale customers in England.

II. THE CHANGING STRUCTURE OF TRADE

The organization of Anglo-Irish trade, as of the other branches of English overseas trade, was subject to changes during the seventeenth and eighteenth centuries. As Ireland was primarily an agricultural community, these changes with their emphasis on large capitals

[1]Public Record Office of Northern Ireland, Belfast. Greer Papers, D. 1044/62, Edward Wakefield, London, 16 February, 1765.

[2]*Reports from Committee of the House of Commons,* vol. III, p. 110, 1773.

[3]Young, op. cit., pt. II, p. 1 57. See also Gill, *Rise of the Irish linen industry,* p. 196.

[4]H.R. Fox Bourne, *English merchants* (London, 1866) vol. ii, pp. 229–30.

enhanced Irish dependence in England. One of the characteristics of the changing structure of Anglo-Irish trade was a greater degree of specialization. Commodity specialization was becoming apparent on both sides of the Irish sea, although in Ireland especially its progress was necessarily limited by the relatively small size of the market. There were however many signs of its development, first and foremost in Dublin but also in the linen trade generally. Concurrently there also developed a tendency towards functional specialization. The merchant's specialization had hitherto been in his capacity as a general intermediary in foreign trade. In an age when communications were slow and imperfect, he had stood as the link between the manufacturers and wholesalers selling finished goods or purchasing raw materials on the one hand and on the other hand the foreign producers and distributors of raw materials or finished products. International trade was a business of small and unspecialized markets; the merchant's specialist knowledge of foreign markets enabled him to make some assessment of the risks which he was able to spread over several commodities. He imported and exported goods, conveyed them to and from the wharves, himself chartered or owned the vessels that carried them and through his intimate concern in foreign trade, performed a variety of banking and insurance services. Even his social life tended to be centred on the scene of his mercantile activities: the opulence of eighteenth-century merchant communities was sometimes reflected in the magnificence of the buildings on and near the waterfront. As communications improved, however, the role of the merchant began to decline and wholesalers and manufacturers in different markets were increasingly able to develop direct contact with one another. It thus became possible to dispense with the merchant's services, a development which was of course effected more quickly in trade with nearby countries than with distant regions. The decline in the rôle of the merchant is associated with commodity specialization, which brought many new intermediaries into commodity exchange, and his final supersession was made possible by functional specialization which overtook commodity specialization and gave rise to several new specialisms in the various services rendered by shipowners, bankers, and numerous classes of brokers who severally took over the function which the merchant had once performed in drawing markets together.

The most striking example in Anglo-Irish trade of the developments that led to the by-passing of the merchant comes from the linen trade.

This trade also emphasizes the fact that developments did not proceed at a uniform rate, and that generalization hides some wide variations in business organization. Commodity specialization was already fairly well developed on both sides in the linen trade early in the eighteenth century, although it is not difficult to uncover a number of exceptions to this tendency. In the early 1730s one Dublin linen draper for instance was able to combine his linen business with an interest in the corn trade, and throughout the second half of the century a County Down firm of bleachers conducted a flour-milling business. Functional specialization was somewhat slower in developing, and the rise of the bleacher in the export trade and of the wholesaler in the import trade was not yet complete at the end of the eighteenth century.

In the early eighteenth century the bulk of linen exports was effected through the hands of the Dublin linen merchants and wholesale drapers who bought on their own account or acted on commission for English importers. The linens were supplied to the Dublin drapers and merchants by the 'north country men' or inland drapers, who had purchased the unbleached linens from the peasant weavers in the north. Bleachers bleaching goods on commission for drapers gradually expanded their business, however, to include bleaching on their own account, and the more powerful inland drapers were likewise able to undertake their own bleaching. As the volume of business grew, such bleachers and drapers found it to their advantage to ship much of their linens directly to English customers instead of selling them to, or through, the Dublin drapers and merchants who hitherto had been the link between the Northern producers of linen and the English importers. The result was that whereas 88 per cent of the linens for Britain had been shipped through Dublin in 1710, the percentage had fallen to 65 per cent in 1750 and to 43 per cent in 1780. This change is in part indicative of the extent to which bleachers had assumed the responsibility of dealing with the English importers of linens.

Towards the end of the century, there was also a change in the nature of the English customer with whom the linen exporter dealt. The prominent merchants in London in the early days of the Irish linen industry were large merchants who specialized in the import of Irish linens, though in the second half of the century Irish linens were also imported to some extent by London firms concerned in linen imports from Europe, such as Boetefeur Dorrien Lewis and Company.

These importers generally held the linens on the account of Irish drapers or bleachers, and made advances to the Irish bleachers. When the linen merchant failed to sell all the goods consigned to him by the Irish bleacher, the bleacher might instruct him to place them in other hands. Thus in 1768 William Clarke one of the principal importers of Irish linens was instructed by a County Down bleacher to ship unsold linens to a merchant in Hull.[1] The stocks the importers held were considerable. In 1744, for instance, Patrick Adair, reputed the largest of the importers of Irish linens at that time, had £40,000 worth of Irish linens in his warehouse.[2] In 1773, Samuel Dyson held £43,000 to £44,000 worth of Irish linens, and another importer, Thomas Fletcher, £50,000 worth.[3] These figures admittedly relate to periods when the linen trade was depressed and stocks as a result inflated, but the extent of the business of the more prominent importers of Irish linens is made very obvious by their great importance in the bill trade between Ireland and London.

Yet however prominent they were, they never wholly dominated the trade. Even in the early decades of the century the wholesale linen drapers in London were regularly importing linens directly from Ireland, as is evident from the fact that Dublin linen drapers were receiving a good many commissions from London. The importance of wholesaling in the import trade is also evidenced from the fact that the merchant importers themselves sold linens direct to retailers in addition to their sales to wholesalers. Moreover, the bleachers themselves also came into direct contact with English wholesalers probably in the course of the 1760s but certainly by the early 1770s. The Andrews of Comber for instance at that time had substantial dealings amounting to at least 600 or 700 pieces of cloth per annum with drapers in Cumberland, Northumberland, Sunderland, Newcastle and Dumfries, and found it worth their while to send one of the family to the North of England each year to canvas orders from the drapers. Business with the wholesalers in linen in England continued to increase and in the early nineteenth century this trend

[1]Public Record Office of Northern Ireland, T. 1073/21, Black Papers, Robert Black, Belfast, 3 December 1768.

[2]Report from the Committee on the petition of the dealers in and manufacturers of Linen, 11 March 1744, in Reports from Committees of the House of Commons, vol. II, p. 69.

[3]Report from the Committee appointed to enquire into the present state of the Linen industry; ibid., vol. III, p. 110.

appears to have been associated with short-term credit granted to the wholesalers by the bleachers. The merchant importer, whether he dealt with only wholesale drapers or directly with the retailers as well, had lost his central position in the trade by the end of the first quarter of the new century. By then his function appears to have virtually disappeared from the pattern of the linen trade between the two countries and the Northern bleachers, now holding a place of pre-eminence in the linen industry, had developed direct contact with the wholesalers of bleached linens in London, in the west and north of England.[1] Shipments to a London merchant importer or factor on the bleacher's own account had become exceptional. Even as early as 1804 it was stated by the Irish Inspector General of Imports and Exports that over three-quarters of Irish linen exports were on English account.[2] Thus, by the early nineteenth century the pattern of the linen export trade had changed completely. The old mode of export by the Dublin drapers and linen merchants, and import through a specialized linen importer had lost its predominant place, and the Ulster bleacher by-passing at first the Dublin merchant or draper and at a later stage the specialist importer was in direct contact with the English wholesalers.

A rather similar development can be traced on the import side in the provision trade, and later in the early nineteenth century on the export side also. At the end of the eighteenth century the Irish exporter, who had once dealt only with merchants in the seaports on the other side, was frequently exporting direct to English inland merchants. The Waterford butter and pork merchants, Courtenay and Ridgway, had dealings, some of them on a fairly large scale, in 1792 with merchants as far inland as Bath, Devizes, Salisbury, West-bury, Winchester, Basingstoke, Crasdall near Farnham (Surrey),

[1] The first signs of the change in the nature of the bleacher's customers date from the 1770s, and by 1796-7, the Belfast bleacher, William McCance, appears to have done substantial business to the order of English customers (see P.R.O. of Northern Ireland. Invoices and covering letters of William McCance (copies)). The business of the Richardsons of Lisburn in the years 1815-22 was almost ex-clusively to the order of English houses and affords little evidence of dealings with English factors (See Gill's account of the firm in *The rise of the Irish linen industry*, pp. 247-63). Even in the business of the Andrews of Comber, much of whose business was still transacted through London factors in the early nineteenth century, a 'very material change' took place from 1824, and by 1838 exports on their own account had ended (See S. Andrews, *A history of the Andrews family . . .* op. cit., p. 115).

[2] *Report of the Committee on the circulating paper, the specie and the current coin of Ireland . . .,* 1804, reprinted 1826, p. 108.

Lewes and even Finsley near Sheffield.[1] The change in the nature of
the English importer meant that the Irish merchant's correspondence
was now much wider than it had been formerly. Over much of the
century the draper's or bleacher's exports were consigned to not more
than two or perhaps three English houses, but the bleacher at the
end of the century and in the early nineteenth century was shipping
to as many as 12 or even more customers. In the butter trade there
was also a great rise in the number of English importers.

Although not so strikingly as in the linen trade, the displacement
of the seaport merchant can be traced in other branches of Anglo-
Irish trade as well. To take one example: whereas the import and
disposal of raw materials for the old-established textile industries had
been in the hands of wholesale importers, many of the manufacturers
in the cotton industry, newly-established in the north of Ireland towards the end of the eighteenth century, were able to buy their cotton
yarns direct from the Manchester yarn manufacturers rather than
from the Irish wholesalers, or even employed or sent agents to Lancashire to buy on their account.[2] In a similar manner, an English
manufacturer of hats imported some of his raw materials—rabbit furs
and wool—from Ireland, only taking these goods from English
wholesalers when their prices were more attractive than such goods
would cost the manufacturer when imported on his own account.[3]
Tanners, whether in the seaports or in inland towns, likewise imported hides from Ireland.

Weaving firms in Lancashire either imported their requirements of
linen yarn from Ireland, or bought the yarn from English linen yarn
merchants. The Manchester weaving firm of J. & N. Philips & Company for instance sometimes bought their yarn in Ireland but sometimes from the Irish yarn merchants in Manchester, their conduct
being determined as in their imports from Germany by the fact that
'our manufactory obliges us to be particularly exact in our weights'.[4]
The scale of operations of a manufacturer or the continuity of his
requirements played the decisive role in determining whether he might
ship his finished product or import the raw material on his own
account. Where the quantities involved were small or infrequent, it

[1]Ledger of Courtenay and Ridgway, 1791-2, in the possession of Mrs. Olive
Ridgway, Rossmore, Mallow, Co. Cork.
[2]McConnel & Kennedy: Letters from Irish correspondents, 1793-1803,
University of Manchester.
[3]P.R.O., C. 107/104, French v. Davies, Foreign Letter-Book, 1771-92.
[4]A.P. Wadsworth and J. de L. Mann, op. cit., p. 292 and n. 2.

was scarcely worth his while to be directly concerned in the foreign trade, but when the position was otherwise the growth of communications and facilities made it feasible. In the early years of their business, when the scale of operations was relatively small and their financial difficulties acute, the bulk of McConnel and Kennedy's Irish trade was effected on the account of Irish cotton wholesalers or manufacturers, but once their initial difficulties were overcome, they shipped the yarns on their own account and employed a Belfast agent to dispose of them.[1] As an example of the extent to which the individual manufacturer might be concerned in foreign trade, Thomas Davies, the hat manufacturer of Stockport and London, who has already been referred to above, may be instanced: he imported some of his raw materials from Ireland, exported other raw materials such as 'vigonia' wools there, and in later years some hats.[2]

In the worsted yarn trade the Irish master-combers were too numerous and in many cases were too far inland to make direct contact between them and the Norwich yarn wholesalers practicable.[3] The Grubbs of Clonmel, however, who had the advantage of being near the port of Waterford, sometimes shipped their yarns direct to England, on other occasions sold them to Waterford or Cork merchants. The only combers who found it consistently possible to ship on their own account were the very large Cork houses like that of George Newenham or Abraham and Richard Lane. The bulk of the yarn from Cork was consigned to Norwich wholesale yarn merchants but by the early 1770s the Cork houses of Crowley & Sadlier and Joyce (the latter alleged to be supported by 'the Rich Roman Catholicks'), shipped direct to the Norwich manufacturers on commissions received from them. They thus competed with the more powerful and longer established Quaker firms in Cork, who shipped on their own account to the Norwich wholesale house of their coreligionists, Richard and John Gurney.[4] In contrast to the Norwich trade, supplies for Manchester were to a large extent drawn from Leinster. None of the Leinster combers (whose scale of operations was much smaller than that of their counterparts in Cork) engaged in exports on their own account, and in the early 1770s the export

[1]McConnel & Kennedy Records; University of Manchester; Letters from Irish Correspondents, 1795–1803; Belfast sales (1812–28, 1850–7).
[2]P.R.O., C. 107/104, French v. Davies.
[3]Library of the Society of Friends, London. Gurney Papers, sections I and II.
[4]Ibid.

trade appears to have been in the hands of the two Dublin houses of Pim and Abraham Wilkinson, and the Waterford firm of Jacob, Strangman and Watson. The Waterford firm also acted as factors for the Gurneys in the purchase of their comparatively small requirements of Leinster yarn. The Gurneys favoured the Waterford house's concern in the Manchester trade, and requested them 'to push at the Manchester business all in their powers for we agreed in one point that it would have a supply let the scarcity of yarn be ever so great in Ireland and therefore as under these circumstances its being in various hands would be attended with more prejudicial consequences than its being principally in their's'.[1]

In the nineteenth century the tendencies which had already manifested themselves in the previous century assumed greater importance. Some of the shipment trade in butter, formerly handled exclusively by a limited number of merchants in the larger seaports, passed into the hands of inland merchants who, instead of acting as hitherto as intermediaries between the exporter and the farmer, shipped directly to England. Exporting concerns also emerged in smaller ports which earlier had no share in butter exports. In some instances Irish country people crossed by boat from Dublin to the north of England to dispose of their produce, thus by-passing the Dublin merchants. English corn importers were also dispensing with the services of Irish merchants and sending their own agents to Ireland to buy for them.

These developments in the field of agriculture produce were parallelled in the industrial field. Even in the eighteenth century English manufacturers had developed extensive direct contact with Ireland. Significantly, many of the witnesses who gave evidence concerning Pitt's Commercial Propositions of 1785 were textile manufacturers, iron manufacturers, potters, brewers, tanners and factors or brokers; and not merchants from the port towns.[2] Wholesalers and manufacturers on both sides of the Irish sea were entering into direct contact. The dominant role of the foreign trade merchant in the economic life of the Irish seaport towns and of the English ports trading with Ireland declined and was replaced by links binding

---

[1]Ibid., part II/383. Richard Gurney to John Gurney, Norwich, 15 August 1772.
[2]P.R.O., B.T. 6/106, 109. Evidence printed in *Report of the Lords of the Committee of Council, 1785*. See also *Minutes of Evidence before the Committee of the House of Lords, 1785*; and *Minutes of Evidence taken before a Committee of the House of Commons . . ., 1785*.

14

manufacturers, wholesalers and distributive agents in the two countries. The decline was not merely that of the wholesale overseas merchants who traded on their own account, but also of the factor in the seventeenth- or eighteenth-century sense of the term.

Hitherto, the factor entrusted with goods to sell in return for a commission had enjoyed a widespread freedom as to how he disposed of them, but by the early nineteenth century they were often required to return monthly accounts of sales and remit at regular monthly intervals.[1] The declining importance of the factor was already apparent in the second half of the eighteenth century. As early as 1754 B. Molineux of Wolverhampton had a wholesale warehouse of ironmongers' goods and hardware in Dublin.[2] The larger English manufacturers as they entered into the Irish trade quickly dispensed with the services of factors. The London brewers employed agents in Dublin for disposing of their product,[3] and Josiah Wedgwood, the famous potter, had an agency in Dublin in the 1770s and again in the early nineteenth century.[4]

The growth and changing structure of Anglo-Irish trade in turn called for new intermediaries. In particular, dealings between manufacturers and wholesalers who had no direct concern in shipping led to the enhanced importance of the shipping agent or broker, and of the warehouseman. These individuals were of little importance in the trade of Irish ports in the early eighteenth century when so many merchants were directly concerned in foreign trade. However, the broker's importance was greatly enhanced by the rise of the Irish linen bleachers who, resident inland, could not without inconvenience attend to the formalities of shipping their linens. By the end of the century the bulk of linens shipped by bleachers passed through the hands of brokers in the ports of Newry and Belfast; and the growth in volume and variety of trade in general, and the increasing degree

[1]University of Manchester, McConnel & Kennedy Records. Letters from Irish correspondents 1795-1803: Hill Hamilton, Belfast, 28 August 1802; Belfast Sales, 1812-28, 1850-7.
[2]*Faulkner's Dublin Journal*, 30 July 1754.
[3]*A view of the present state of Ireland* (London, 1780) p. 66; *Report from the Committee* (of the Irish Commons) *appointed to take into consideration the petition of the Master Wardens and Brothers of the Corporation of Brewers*, 10 November 1773, p. 7, in (*Appendix to*) *Observations on the Brewing Trade of Ireland*, 1777.
[4]Wedgwood Papers, Wedgwood Museum, Barlaston, Stoke-on-Trent; *Report of the Lords of the Committee of Council*, 1785, p. 62. See for another example, *Minutes of Evidence before the Committee of the House of Lords*, 1785, p. 152.

of direct contact between wholesalers and manufacturers, led to the rise of a similar class of broker in Dublin and in some of the other ports. Indeed, the brokers themselves specialized in the type of trade they effected, some of them specializing in the linen trade and one, for example, even finding it possible to concentrate on the coastal trade.

Brokers were not necessarily exclusively dependent on brokerage for their income: they were frequently engaged on their own account as well. The Belfast brokers were prominent merchants and ship-owners and two of the brokers in Newry appear to have been themselves linen drapers. This does not, however, alter the fact that *vis-à-vis* the manufacturer or draper they were exercising a specialized function. A similar rise of the broker is discernible in England, as much of the goods passing through Liverpool, Chester and Bristol, to or from Ireland, related to transactions with inland wholesalers, textile or yarn manufacturers, and manufacturers in the already in-dustrialized Midlands. Brokers and warehousemen were, for example, prominent in the growing exports of woollen goods to Ireland. In one instance a London factor and warehouseman was handling exports to Ireland of the value of £30,000 per annum.[1] Brokers were also prominent in imports from Ireland to London, and there is some evidence of linen and butter being handled by them. By the end of the century some even of London's peace-time trade with Ireland was effected overland by Liverpool. As a result both of the improvement of inland communications and the increasing specialization of econ-omic functions, it was, for example, possible by 1790 to have woollen goods for a merchant in Stewartstown in Ireland sent overland from London, where they were handled by a warehouseman acting for a London factor, to Liverpool, where they were shipped by a broker.[2]

In war time especially Liverpool and Chester brokers and mer-chants reaped an advantage from their Irish connection. Direct trade between London and Ireland declined sharply at such times and a great deal of the goods was consigned through brokers in Chester in the early eighteenth century and through Liverpool by the end of the century. During the War of American Independence, the balance between the two ports was fairly even and competition for the custom of 'the gentlemen of the linen trade' existed between Newry brokers

[1]P.R.O., B.T. 6/109, 5 February 1785. Evidence printed in *Report of the Lords of the Committee of Council,* 1785, p. 18.

[2]Custom House Library, London, Letters Dublin and Newry, Bd. to Collr., 1790, 10 September 1790.

shipping through Chester and the Belfast brokers consigning their goods through Liverpool.

The rivalry between the various brokers in Belfast appears to have led to the formation of a committee of the shipowners and merchants concerned who appointed one of their number as agent. Later in or around 1790 a rival committee representing other Belfast shipowners and merchants was formed. The competition between the two committees led to regular sailings to an increased number of English ports. At the beginning of each of the three big linen fairs in Belfast, nine or ten vessels attended to take on board linens for Greenock, Glasgow, Whitehaven, and especially for Liverpool, Chester, Bristol and London. The growth of linen exports through Newry led to two merchants setting up in trade as regular brokers in that port at the end of the 'seventies and their success during the war period and the prospects of the Newry linen market encouraged another broker to set up in 1784. The competition between the various constant traders and their respective brokers must have been acute, and in 1790 the three brokers combined to act as agents under a committee of linen drapers and bleachers appointed by the owners to regulate the sailings.[1] The system worked efficiently and at a reasonable charge at any rate in its earlier and more competitive days. The degree of organization obtained must, however, have been sufficient to amount to a monopoly of regular sailings and appears to have been strong enough to exclude 'interlopers'.[2] This may have provided a means of raising commissions and freights, the Bangor cotton manufacturers of the late 1790s for instance preferring to have their yarns sent overland to Portpatrick and thence by ship to Donaghadee, rather than shipped to them via Liverpool and Belfast.[3] The brokers arose principally to provide a service for the growing class of merchants and manufacturers not actively concerned in foreign trade, but once their business was established firmly the facilities they provided and the regular sailings between Irish and English ports by an increasing

[1]*Belfast News Letter,* 9 November 1790. Cf. advertisement by John Neville, Newry, 19 October 1784. *Belfast News Letter,* 26 October 1784.

[2]Newspaper advertisements sometimes betray the opposition of the constant traders to 'interlopers' e.g. see advertisements by 'the Belfast constant traders' in the *Belfast News Letter,* 30 July 1782, and by the owners of three 'regular' vessels in Dublin in *Faulkner's Dublin Journal,* 26 November 1754.

[3]University of Manchester: McConnel & Kennedy Records. Letters from Irish correspondents, 1795–1803. The Belfast merchants had already acquired a reputation for excessive charges at an earlier date. See Public Record Office of Northern Ireland, D. 607/150, Downshire Papers, 12 March 1778.

number of constant traders encouraged a still further sub-division of trade along the same lines.

Changes in the structure of trade were further reflected in the emergence of specialist shipowners. Many of the earlier merchants concerned directly in overseas trade owned vessels or shares of vessels engaged in their trades. Thus, the Irish wool and yarn merchants owned vessels plying between Ireland and the west of England, frequently in joint ownership with merchants in the English ports.[1] On the other hand, although the wholesalers and manufacturers, who increasingly were dominating the trade in the latter half of the century, frequently owned shares in ships, it was as a rule more an investment of surplus funds than a case of working ownership directly linked with their own trade. There was some tradition of Irish ship-owning and sea-faring especially in trade with Southern Europe, but the financial limitations of Irish shipowning are especially evident from the extremely small number of privateering vessels fitted out in Irish ports in war time.[2] The small amount of Irish-owned shipping engaged in the trade between the two countries is a striking indication of the extent to which the control of Anglo-Irish trade had passed into English hands. In the coal trade poor profitability justified the absence of large scale participation in the shipping, but this consideration would not apply, as far as one can judge, to other branches of trade.

Irish ownership of shipping increased at a markedly slower rate than the volume of trade; this, combined with the growing variety and changing organization of trade, enhanced greatly the importance of the ship broker, as the intermediary between the merchant and the shipowners. Brokers not merely arranged the chartering of vessels, but in many cases, particularly in the ports with an economically active hinterland, received or dispatched goods for merchants; in the linen trade they also arranged for the regular attendance of vessels at the time of the fairs. However, the characteristic function of the broker was the chartering of vessels, and the earliest reference to a broker in Ireland in this connection is in 1720.[3] Opportunities for the broker's work in chartering vessels or handling goods were limited, however, in the

[1]Custom House, Liverpool, Register of wool vessels, 1739–92.

[2]See L.M. Cullen, 'Privateers fitted out in Irish Ports in the Eighteenth Century', *The Irish Sword*, vol. iii, no. 12 (1958).

[3]Public Record Office of Northern Ireland, Mussenden Papers, D.354/32, charter party, 3 March 1720.

first half of the century, and even in Dublin there were only two
brokers in 1751, one of whom was described as a 'French broker'.[1]
But during the rest of the century development was rapid. By 1780
there were six firms of brokers in Dublin, and in 1790 eleven.[2] In
1787 there were five shipbrokers in Cork; in 1795 six.[3] In Waterford
there were two firms in 1788, though on the other hand there was no
broker in Limerick.[4]

[1] *Dublin Directory* for 1751.
[2] *Dublin Directory*, 1780, 1790.
[3] *Cork Directory* 1787, *New Cork Directory* 1795.
[4] *A General Directory of the Kingdom of Ireland* (Dublin, 1788), vol. II.

CHAPTER VI

THE CORN AND COAL TRADES

THE same essential features of a changing organization and of a growing dependence on English credit were common to most branches of Anglo-Irish trade, though, of course, with varying degrees of emphasis. Two trades are, however, worthy of separate description; first, the *corn trade* on account of its flexible organization and highly fluctuating markets, and secondly, the *coal trade,* which was radically different in organization from the other branches of Anglo-Irish trade, and was the one least influenced by the new trends in economic organization. In particular the coal trade stood aside completely from the changes which were beginning to divorce shipowning from commerce, and commerce from the responsibility for the physical handling of goods in transit. Its static organization contrasted with an eight-fold rise in coal imports in the course of the century, and was increasingly unable to cope with the growth in sheer physical volume of the trade. Rudimentary organization must be associated with congestion in the ports on both sides caused by the expansion of the collier fleets in accounting for the unsatisfactory conditions of the trade. These conditions made for poor profits, a factor which in turn deterred new capital from entering the trade. Want of capital was, however, more evident in the sale or storing of coal than in the shipping itself which in a large port like Whitehaven represented a heavy investment in specialized vessels. Low profits, however, in conjunction with physical difficulties encountered in handling large quantities of coal and the fact that shares in colliers were highly fragmented rather than held in the hands of an active merchant class, prevented any developments that might have led to large scale or rational marketing. Business decisions in the coal trade were taken by numerous masters, whose psychology and reactions to fluctuations and price movements were more akin to those of the peasant producers in agriculture than to those of the businessman. When profits failed with particular severity the only recourse open to the masters was to lessen the number of sailings in the hope that a diminished supply of coal would raise the prices. However, successful combination proved as impossible in the coal trade as it has since proved among agricultural producers and the actions of the masters of coal vessels were a single element in rather than a cause of the abuses in the Dublin coal trade.

THE CORN TRADE

The organization of the corn trade with its uncertain and variable flow of commodities was, as one might expect, of a loose and flexible nature. A merchant might take advantage of a local surplus to buy grain and sell it on his own account on the English or Scottish market, and a local shortage might lead him to import on his own account. Similarly, as conditions in the Irish and their home markets warranted, English and Scottish merchants consigned corn or meal on their own account to Ireland, or gave buying commissions to Irish merchants. The Belfast merchant, Daniel Mussenden, accepted grain or meal on the account of British merchants, also imported on his own account, and in the course of dealings in the years 1756-8 with a Yarmouth merchant, Thomas Dawson, had offers of a joint concern in shipments both to and from Ireland. In years when shortages were likely to lead to a movement of grain or meal in either direction between the two islands, Mussenden had correspondence with merchants in the Irish ports of Limerick, Cork, Waterford, Dublin, Drogheda and Dundalk and with English or Scottish merchants in Wick, Peterhead, Edinburgh, Berwick, Yarmouth, London, Carmarthen and Liverpool.[1]

The corn trade was associated with much risk, especially in meal described as 'an uncertain and precarious article.'[2] Ships might therefore be dispatched to a correspondent in one of the Irish outports who had been previously instructed to advise the master as to the best or most likely Irish market, and a Dublin correspondent might at the same time be instructed to write to the provincial merchant with an account of the Dublin market. On the other hand, oatmeal bought in Ireland for the account of a British merchant might not be worth shipping, as prices in Scotland might fall perhaps to so low a level as to have the Scottish ports closed to imports. In April 1756, for example, Coutts Brothers of Edinburgh were unable to ship 400 tons of oatmeal in Drogheda, 50 tons in Dublin and some in Belfast for this reason.[3] In circumstances such as this, the Irish correspondent might be instructed to ship it to the most profitable Irish market.

[1]Public Record Office of Northern Ireland, Belfast, Uncatalogued Mussenden Papers, 1754-9.
[2]Scottish Record Office, General Register House, Edinburgh. Letter book of Alexander Oliphant, 1766-71, Ayr, 19 June 1767.
[3]Public Record Office of Northern Ireland, Belfast, Uncatalogued Mussenden Papers, Coutts Brothers & Company, Edinburgh, 3 April 1756.

When oatmeal or wheat arrived on a declining Irish market English and Scottish merchants sometimes had it shipped back to a more stable or rising home market. Market risks and fluctuations were most acute in the case of oatmeal which was a staple commodity both in the north of Ireland and in Scotland. The difficulties of the trade were heightened by the mob violence to which the attempted shipping of oatmeal at times gave occasion in both countries, even when prices were still below the limits that would warrant a closing of the ports. The difficulty, because of the sudden fluctuations in prices, in predicting the opening or closing of ports to exports or imports was an additional handicap for the merchants. Some evasion of the corn laws was, however, possible. The closing of the Irish ports to exports was not sufficient to prevent the shipping off of corn,[1] and on the other hand when individual English or Scottish ports were closed to imports of meal, it was possible to import Irish meal to ports which still remained open and then illegally ship it coastways to the other ports.[2]

In the wheat and flour trade, where there was an import trend into Ireland for most of the first eighty years of the century, and an overall export trend in the last two decades, a large degree of specialization appears to have existed, at any rate in the major consuming or producing areas. The haphazard oatmeal trade, however, was frequently transacted through the hands of general merchants except perhaps in the small ports of Drogheda, Dundalk, Newry and Wexford, which were in the main Irish producing areas. A great deal of the exports was on commission, and it would certainly have been disastrous for the Irish merchants to have relied heavily on dealings on their own account in so fluctuating an article. The growing volume of corn exports, both wheat and oats, led to the rise of Irish corn merchants of extensive business in the second half of the century. Much of their buying was on commission, though there was also an extensive amount of buying effected on their own account. Actual shipments, however, were probably for the most part on English account, as the extent of the exports was very considerable and the risks Irish merchants exporting on their own account would have to bear very large.

[1]Public Record Office of Northern Ireland, Belfast, Uncatalogued Mussenden Papers, Isaac Reed, Dundalk, 22 December 1756.

[2]Public Record Office of Northern Ireland, Belfast. ibid., Coutts Brothers & Company, Edinburgh, 3 April 1756. Custom House, Greenock, letter books, Collr. to Board, 1785–6, 25–29 May, 18–20 July 1786.

THE COAL TRADE

The coal trade was similar to the other branches of Anglo-Irish trade in that it was mainly on English account. Its organization was, however, otherwise unique. Whereas transactions in other commodities were regulated by contacts between merchants in the two countries, no such correspondence existed—or only exceptionally—in the coal trade. The control of the trade was in fact in the hands of the masters of vessels from the colliery ports.[1] The masters themselves held only small shares in the vessels, but as the ownership of colliers was fragmented and shares widely held among merchants and non-merchants in the hinterland of the coal-exporting ports, they were by virtue of their position in effective control of the colliers. The masters therefore shipped their coals without knowledge of conditions at the Irish ports other than what they had been on their previous visit, or were dependent for information on what they picked up from the masters of colliers returning in ballast. This absence of any regulation of the trade encouraged the periodic glutting of the Dublin market and resulted in the coal trade being throughout the whole of the eighteenth century distinctly an unprofitable business. In the earlier decades of the eighteenth century at any rate the lack of organization also led the masters to depend upon the over-stocked Dublin market, the only market with which they were acquainted, rather than develop trade with the smaller and more distant Irish ports. At best the low prices in summer, when the Dublin market was glutted, were barely sufficient to cover running costs, the masters depending upon the relatively high winter earnings to provide the year's profit. The low returns of the summer coal trade and the higher profits earned in foreign voyages to Norway encouraged some of the masters to leave the trade in summer and return to it in winter, when other freights were no longer available and the higher prices made the coal trade profitable. Shipping in Whitehaven was also attracted into the tobacco trade to Virginia, although in this business it was possible to take advantage of the seasonal rise in coal prices in Dublin by carrying a cargo of coal on the outward voyage to Virginia in winter or early spring. Vessels seasonally employed in the Virginia trade

---

[1]The organization and conditions of the coal trade are best illustrated in the Letters of Sir James Lowther to his Whitehaven agent, 1706–54. Record Office, The Castle, Carlisle, Cumberland. See also Customs Letter books, Custom Houses, Whitehaven and Ayr.

inflicted a hardship on the masters regularly employed in the coal trade, dependent as they were on the winter prices for a profit on the year's working, as the Virginia masters, inexperienced in the coal trade or anxious to get dispatched quickly, disposed of their coals at a low price, thus spoiling the market for the other masters.

The owners of the collieries were not themselves normally concerned in the shipping trade. But in Cumberland the two most prominent owners, the Lowthers and Curwens, did own some shipping, Sir James Lowther's purpose being to break any combination that the masters might form. The Lowthers were in a unique position. By judicious buying of property and large scale investment they developed a virtual monopoly of the West Cumberland coal trade, while the other Cumberland colliery owners and the other areas exporting to Ireland were unable in the first half of the eighteenth century to gain more than a relatively modest share of the Irish coal trade because of technical difficulties and a want of capital.[1] The Lowthers were in a position to take advantage of some of the economies of scale, and Sir James Lowther who controlled the collieries for the first half of the eighteenth century was determined to expand output and shipments over the summer months especially as working costs were then at their lowest. The coals were sold at fixed prices to the masters, and the result was that any losses consequent on the glutting of the Dublin market were borne exclusively by the masters.

No part of the benefit of greater production was passed on to the masters in the form of a reduction in shipping prices, and as the volume of shipping at Whitehaven had in the meantime been growing, profits dwindled all the more; some vessels were laid up for a want of sufficient capital to operate them, and masters either for want of opportunity to dispose of coals profitably or in the hope that fewer sailing might keep up the prices at Dublin, were making as few sailings as three a year. Talks of combining in the hopes of raising the prices in Dublin became rife and eventually at the beginning of the last quarter of 1728 the masters combined against shipping coals. The combination was successful in temporarily raising the Dublin prices from 15/- to 30/- a ton. Lowther, however, had some of the masters on his side, and also attracted 'foreign' shipping to Whitehaven. The resources of the masters were meagre, and they were not

[1] See W.H. Makey, 'The place of Whitehaven in the Irish coal trade, 1600–1750' unpublished M.A. thesis, London, 1952.

prepared for a long resistance. In January, 1729, the combination fell through.[1]

Seasonal variation in the output of the collieries and the inefficient organization of the shipping trade were themselves sufficient to account for fluctuations in the prices. But the inadequate organization of the trade was especially important in this respect. The masters controlled the actual shipping of the coals, and in Dublin sold their coals directly, or through factors, to the distributors and large consumers. By the opening of the eighteenth century at times of slow sale, the masters in the interests of economic working of their vessels had begun to unload their coals into gabards in the port of Dublin for disposal on their account in their absence. The Irish Parliament in 1705, viewing this as an attempt to influence prices to the prejudice of the consumer, forbade the owners of gabards to hold coals on board for longer than eight days, and empowered the Lord Mayor to have the gabards brought up to the public quay and the coals sold 'for the fairest price that can be had for such coals'.[2] This for the first time led to yarding in the coal import trade, leading many of the masters of colliers to 'sell or consign' their coals to the keepers of yards,[3] who in turn disposed of them to the retailers and larger consumers. Attempts at monopoly followed, however, especially by the ambitious Dublin merchant, John Mercer, and the Irish parliament limited the yarding of coals by any dealer to 1,000 tons, a figure subsequently raised to 1,500 tons.[4] This legislation, despite its alleged laudable intentions, obviated rational organization either on the part of Dublin merchants or on the part of the masters themselves. The Whitehaven masters appear to have continued to make some effort to control the disposal of coal, and employed at least one man in Dublin to keep a bank of coal on their behalf.[5] But more important

[1]For details of a combination among the masters against Lowther in January 1749, see Hughes, *North country life in the eighteenth century,* vol. ii, *Cumberland and Westmorland, 1700–1830* (London, 1965) pp. 62, 188.

[2]4 Anne, c. 8 (Ir.), section 7.

[3]P.R.O., C.O. 388/86, P. 15, *Petition of the masters and owners of ships of Whitehaven, Parton and Workington to the Lords Commissioners for Trade and Plantations,* (received 5 July 1710) (contains the signatures of prominent Whitehaven masters and owners).

[4]11 Anne, c. 4; 6 Geo. I, c. 2. See also entries nos. 1334, 1335, 1336 in L.W. Hanson, *Contemporary printed sources for British and Irish economic history* (Cambridge, 1963).

[5]Thomas Bacon of Whitehaven, brother of Anthony Bacon, the London merchant. W. Hutchinson, *History of the county of Cumberland* (Carlisle, 1794) vol. II, p. 41, note. Cf. L.B. Namier, 'Anthony Bacon, M.P., an eighteenth

than parliamentary measures in limiting the amount of coal yarded was a want of capital on the part of merchants and masters. The fact that the statutory limitation lapsed in 1728 and was not renewed until 1748[1] did not induce any striking increase in coal yarding.

Abuses, attributed mainly to the factors, continued in the coal trade.[2] As a consequence, in 1762 the factors were licensed, limited in number to forty, and required to take an oath to exercise their office 'faithfully, diligently and impartially between the sellers and buyers of coal'.[3] The factor's function was to take a vessel's cargo and sell it from the vessel, standing on the vessel himself or employing a purser to take his place. In return for his services he received from the master a commission of 2½ per cent. In practice, however, the factors bought cargoes in the bay, bringing them to market as they chose, and despite the fact that they were supposed to be acting on commission for the master, frequently charged the customer a price which might be as much as 10/- per ton higher than the price given to the master. Masters required a quick dispatch, and were therefore prepared to sell low to an immediate taker of their coals. Such was the factor's influence or power that, taking advantage of the custom whereby the master nailed a notice on the mast indicating the price at which the coals would be sold to the public,[4] he was able to require the master on his arrival to declare a high price that would discourage other customers with a view to taking the cargo himself at a lower rate.

The factor's monopoly position was enhanced by the want of coal yards as a result of which stocks were small in the winter months and factors therefore had not to withhold coals for long to raise the price. The consumers with the exception of the gentry, sugar-houses and breweries, who laid in their stocks at low prices in the summer months, were because of their small resources unable to lay in stocks in advance, and in winter time, therefore, were frequently forced to pay prices which could be on occasion six times as high as the shipping price or even higher. In an effort to supply 'the journeymen,

century merchant', *Journal of Economic and Business History,* vol. 2, no. 1, November 1929, pp. 20–70. Sir James Lowther stated in 1726 that 'I am very glad some of the masters are fallen into a way of yarding coals when the price is low in Dublin'. (Record Office, The Castle, Carlisle. Sir James Lowther's letters, London, 3 May 1726 (no. 13)).

[1] 21 Geo. II, c. 7.
[2] e.g. see *Journals of the Irish House of Commons,* vol. 7, pp. 99–100.
[3] 1 Geo. III, c. 10.
[4] In the last decade of the century this was a statutory requirement.

tradesmen, and manufacturers and the poor', public coal yards were
instituted in Dublin in 1762,[1] and in Cork in 1766.[2] The buying of
coals for the yards was not extensive,[3] however, and their role was
marginal.

There were, of course, other circumstances which also contributed
to the rise of prices. Unfavourable winds might for weeks prevent the
colliers from sailing with the result that Dublin prices might in winter
soar to famine level and then be plunged downwards when at last
the winds changed and a coal fleet bore down on the city. The great
increase in the coal trade in the second half of the century meant long
delays in loading vessels in Whitehaven and in finding a berth in
Dublin, thus adding to the delay and confusion in the trade. The high
prices were attributed however by contemporaries, who were much
concerned with the problem, not only to the physical difficulties of
the trade but to combinations among the Dublin coal factors, and to
collusive action between the factors and the masters.

The coal trade became a constant subject for parliamentary in-
vestigation and legislation.[4] Combination was proved, at any rate to
the satisfaction of the Irish Parliament, though it is not clear to what
degree the abuses were due solely to factors or masters acting by
themselves or to joint action by the two interests. The Dublin factors
did hold shares in some colliers, but only to an insignificant extent.
In the years 1786–1800 only eleven Dublin factors had shares in
thirteen Whitehaven vessels,[5] and in 1796 there were only seven
Dublin-registered coal vessels.[6] The likelihood that monopoly practices did exist is borne out in the fact that the coal owners exerted
pressures in this direction on the masters. There is evidence of this
from mid-century in Whitehaven.[7] The Scottish proprietors of the

[1] 1 Geo. III, c. 10.
[2] 5 Geo. III, c. 15.
[3] See Public Record Office of Ireland, Dublin, 1A–46–46. Committee of enquiry
into the management of the Public Coal Yards, 1778.
[4] For evidence, occasionally conflicting, of the organization of the coal trade
on the Irish side, see P.R.O.I, 1A–46–46. Committee Books of the Committees
on the Irish Coal Trade, 1790, 1791, 1793, 1796, Public Coal Yards Committee,
1778.
[5] Custom House, Whitehaven, Shipping Registers. 1786–1800.
[6] P.R.O., T. 64/182, an account of the number of vessels belonging to the several
ports of Ireland with their names and tonnage . . . Custom House, Dublin, 20
December 1796.
[7] See proclamation by the Lord Mayor of Dublin in *Faulkner's Dublin Journal*,
3 January 1756. As early as 1754 Lowther noted that 'it may be a proper time to
make the masters of ships pay their deposits to secure their owners from having

1790s made a much more extreme use of their powers. Masters were required to enter bonds to consign their coals to any of four Dublin factors, and when the prices at which they sold at Dublin exceeded 25/- prices to the shipping were raised by 1/- a ton to 9/- British and to 10/- a ton, once the Dublin prices reached 30/-.[1]

Legislation totally failed to solve the problem of high winter prices. The Irish Parliament in 1782 admitted failure by repealing most of its previous legislation relating to the coal trade.[2] Yet little improvement followed, and legislative action was again necessary in the early 1790s.[3] The capital involved in yarding large quantities of coals over the summer months was too considerable for the Irish factors and for the masters. Moreover yarding on a large scale was itself a highly speculative venture. There is only one known instance of yarding in substantial quantities. This significantly was effected by a broker in Liverpool, and was said to have resulted in a loss.[4] In 1793 the Irish Parliament was reduced in an effort to alleviate the shortage of coals to offer a bounty of 1/- per ton on quantities in excess of 4,000 tons yarded on or before 1 January 1794. To encourage large-scale yarding in the future, Parliament also made provision for an amount not exceeding £800 per annum for paying the annual rent of stores selling not less than 8,000 tons retail a year.[5] But the

their ships run out by their selling the coals at Dublin to loss' (Record Office, The Castle, Carlisle, Sir James Lowther's letters to his agent, no. 42, London, 6 April 1754). Lowther at the time actually foresaw the possibility that action to this end would be interpreted as an effort on his part to raise the price of coal in Dublin. The chances of the scheme being implemented were limited by the fact that the shipowners themselves were reluctant to accept it (Ibid., no. 54, 26 October 1754). The combination alleged by the Lord Mayor among the White-haven coal owners to direct certain factors to fix a selling price for coal in conjunction with the masters at a level not under 16/- for good coal or 15/- for bad, may refer to this scheme. The parliamentary committee of enquiry in 1761 discovered collusion between the masters and factors (*Journals of the Irish House of Commons,* vol. 7, p. 99), but does not suggest any connection by the Whitehaven coal owners with the scheme. This does not however exclude the possibility that Lowther may have been directly implicated in the scheme, as he was very discreet in his dealings with interests in the Irish coal trade.

[1]Public Record Office of Ireland, Committee books of the Committees on the Dublin coal trade, 1793, 1796.
[2]21 and 22 Geo. III, c. 17. Section XI reads, '. . . that every person or persons . . . shall be at full liberty to buy and sell coals at such prices and times, in such manner and quantities and from and to such persons as he, she or they shall choose.'
[3]31 Geo. III, c. 33; 33 Geo. III, c. 40.
[4]P.R.O. of Ireland, 1A–46–46. Committee Books of the Parliamentary Committee on the Coal Trade, 1796.
[5]33 Geo. III, c. 40.

organization of the trade remained as confused, if not more confused, than ever. High prices in winter were more a result of the organizational and physical difficulties of the trade than of combination. Combination itself was neither for master nor factor a guarantee against falling prices, if large coal fleets arrived or if with the return of milder weather demand slackened. The real problem was the shortage of capital, which prevented both merchant and consumer from buying in stocks when prices were low. As a result, the trade was at the mercy of recurrent changes in supply or demand: imbalance was reflected alternately in excessively high or unduly low prices.

No credit was granted by the masters in selling their coals; they accepted payment in specie, and waited till they had collected their payments before sailing. The drain on the country's supply of specie arising from the coal trade was a constant grievance to the Irish commentators of the period, and though the importance of the coal trade in drawing away specie was characteristically exaggerated there is no doubt that this remained the usual manner of payment in the coal trade throughout the century.

On the other hand some credit had to be granted by the colliery owners to the masters who purchased their coals.[1] This is not surprising: the masters of colliers had little resources of their own and could scarcely have met the costs of an outset were cash payment required for the coals they took. But the terms of credit were, as one would expect in a trade in which goods were sold for cash, extremely short, and payment appears to have been expected on the completion of a voyage. Certainly the Lowthers were very apprehensive about granting a load of coals to vessels already owing for one or two voyages. In the case of vessels loading coals for Ireland while outward bound to Virginia, the master was required to give security to pay within two or three months, though the fact that this was referred to on several occasions over the years by Sir James Lowther, suggests that the rule proved difficult to enforce. A suspected reason for the slowness of some of the owners to pay coal debts was that 'they may not want money for their tobacco ships.'[2] Masters therefore sought to leave their debt outstanding as long as the colliery owner would

[1]By way of contrast, no credit was granted by the Newcastle and Sunderland colliery owners. Record Office, Carlisle, Sir James Lowther's letters to his agent, London, 22 April 1727 (no. 12).

[2]Record Office, Carlisle, Sir John Lowther's letters to his agent, 25 July 1696 (no. 22).

tolerate it, and in 1706 Sir James Lowther was thinking of prosecuting those in debt for longer than six months.[1] The acknowledgment of debt for a loading of coals consisted of a note from the master to the colliery agent. This had the inconvenient consequence that where the master defaulted, the debt was difficult to recover. Sir James Lowther in 1719 considered means of finding a way to 'make the owners of ships easily to be come at where a master that takes coals dyes or fails',[2] and enclosed to the agent of the collieries a draft of a note to be signed by the part owners of ships going on long voyages, instructing him that if the owners refused to sign, he was free to insist on ready money from the master.[3]

The amount of outstanding debt was always fairly considerable. In 1696 it was £500, representing at the then current prices a total of about 3,000 or 3,500 tons. Over the first half of the eighteenth century it rose from about 8,000 tons to 25,000 tons on a quarterly average, a figure which represented about 25 per cent of annual output. In an attempt to reduce the amount, interest appears to have been charged on some of the arrears, and in 1725 Lowther remarked that 'I find the masters in general better since the notes to pay interest but my friends still set the worst example'.[4] However, it proved extremely difficult to reduce the volume of debt, and the amount expressed as a percentage of annual output always remained fairly stable. In 1754 Lowther ordered ready money to be demanded from masters owing for twelve months or more from the previous summer, adding that 'then I shan't lose by selling coals to those that are not fit to be trusted, which is what I have been a looser by'[5]. Nevertheless, the overall situation was never very unsatisfactory. Many of the coal boats were continuously engaged in the coal trade and their debts were, in a sense, self-liquidating. Again, almost all the Whitehaven shipping was seasonally dependent on the coal trade and, therefore, was not prepared altogether to forfeit Lowther's good will. Bad debts were few, and the majority of masters paid their debts promptly. An examination of the entries in an account book[6] for one quarter is

[1] Record Office, Carlisle, Sir James Lowther's Letters to his agent, 1 October 1706 (no. 16).
[2] Ibid., 17 October 1719 (no. 56).
[3] Ibid., 3 November 1719 (no. 60).
[4] Ibid., 14 October 1725 (no. 70).
[5] Ibid., 19 October 1754 (no. 51).
[6] Mining Department, Somerset House, Whitehaven. Book for Seaton colliery, 1770–82.

sufficient to illustrate the general pattern of payment. In the quarter 1 April–29 June 1771, 60 shipments were made from the Lowthers' Seaton colliery, 29 of them being paid for within the same period. Of these 29, 2 had been purchased for cash, 11 were paid for in less than one month, 13 in less than 2 months, and 3 in less than 3 months. As the bulk of the shipments had been effected after the 25 May, it is probable that the remaining shipments were paid for on lines similar to those already accounted for within the quarter. Coal debts of long standing were few. At the end of the quarter, the only debts still outstanding were, apart from the 31 shipments still unpaid, one from March 1771, three from the year 1770, and one from 1763. The position did not alter greatly in the following years and in fact improved after the mid-1770s, as coal debts outstanding at the end of each year from the previous year remained few and declined in number.

Table 24: Shipments from previous year's account owing on 26 December

1772 ⎫ 1773 ⎭	5*	1778	1
1774	11	1779	2
1775	12	1780	1
1776	5	1781	1
1777	2	1782	3

*Shipments for which payment was still due on 24 December 1774.

CHAPTER VII

SHIPPING, FREIGHTS AND INSURANCE

THE most frequented sea routes, apart from those in the coal trade, were those to Bristol, Liverpool and London. At the opening of the eighteenth century, however, there had been little direct trade with London. Sailings on this route only began to increase after 1713. Demands for cargo space grew with the expansion in Anglo-Irish trade, but despite the growth of the trade with London, sailings were still relatively infrequent even as late as the 1730s. By the middle of the century, however, the London route was well developed. Demands for freight continued to grow apace in the second half of the century. In London likewise there was a heavy demand for freights to Ireland. Discussing with Richard Gurney the possibility of a freight from London to Ireland for one of their vessels, Thomas Bland remarked in February 1772 that 'this is a season when ships are often wanted in London for Ireland'.[1] Difficulties were, however, still experienced on less frequented routes, and shipping yarns from Cork to Yarmouth sometimes presented problems. This was apparently why the Gurneys of Norwich employed vessels of their own in this trade, carrying cargoes of coal to Ireland in the intervals between shipments of yarn.

The large volume of trade led to the establishment of 'constant traders' on all the busier routes, and London, Bristol and Liverpool were linked to all the principal Irish ports by such vessels. As one might expect, such vessels were more profitable to their owners than vessels dependent on charters or occasional business[2], and an average of about five round trips per year was maintained. In 1790 the single firm of Dunn and Hincks in Dublin was handling 9 'regular' ships to London, 6 to Liverpool, 4 to Bristol, and 3 to Chester.[3] Cork in 1787 had 6 constant traders plying to Bristol alone[4], and all the other large Irish ports were served by numerous constant traders on the principal routes to Britain. The earliest constant traders were the linen ships, and to the end of the century they were the best and most

[1]Library of the Society of Friends, London. Gurney Papers, I/90B, 3 February 1772.
[2]The ships' accounts in ledger of Courtenay and Ridgway, 1791–92, appear to suggest this.
[3]*Wilson's Dublin Directory*, 1790, p. 11.
[4]*Cork Directory*, 1787, p. 7.

reliable. Sailing regularly and commanded by competent masters, they were in great demand among the merchants on both sides, who would not willingly entrust their goods (often uninsured) to other masters[1].

The most specialized type of vessel in Anglo-Irish trade was the Whitehaven collier, which in time became a large vessel of up to 200 tons, broad and 'floaty', and rather similar to the colliers engaged in the Newcastle-London trade. Carrying a larger cargo and more economically manned than the ordinary merchant vessel, it had better prospects of operating in the generally unfavourable conditions in the coal trade. To be fully economic the collier had to be intensively worked, making as many as 7 or 8 trips to Dublin in the year, though in the first two decades of the eighteenth century the low profits and reluctance of the masters had reduced the number to as little as three.[2] In later years the working became more intensive again, but by the end of the century congestion in the harbours reduced the number of trips again. A witness before the Irish Coal Committee of 1793 stated, for instance, that his ship which ought to have completed 7 trips was able to make only 5 in 1792.[3] The total number of colliers visiting Dublin in 1792 was 1,600—not necessarily different vessels—of an average of 150 tons and as they tended to arrive irregularly in fleets the extent of the congestion is easily imagined.

The low profits in the coal trade encouraged the vessels to seek other freights. Some of the early Whitehaven vessels were frequently engaged seasonally in the tobacco trade or the Norway trade, or on arrival at Dublin obtained freights back to Britain, to Europe or to America. Something of this pattern lasted up to the end of the century though by that time most of the Whitehaven fleet consisted of large vessels wholly specialized in the coal trade. In Scotland, on the other hand, none of the vessels were colliers by construction, and were of small tonnage by comparison with the Cumberland colliers. Some were even seasonally occupied in fishing[4]. Only a small proportion of the shipping was owned by the colliery owners themselves. In 1707

[1]Cf. 'You may send [the goods] by any other good ship that is in the Dublin trade. Strangers have so often met with accidents in their voyages hither that I would not choose to have any goods sent me per such'. Guildhall Library, London, Radcliffe Papers. Francis Thomé, Dublin, 25 August 1750. See also an advertisement by Belfast constant traders in *Belfast Newsletter*, 30 July 1782.

[2]W.H. Mackey, 'The place of Whitehaven . . .' op. cit., p. 127.

[3]Public Record Office of Ireland, 1A-46-46, Committee Books of the Irish Parliamentary Committee on the coal trade, January 1793.

[4]Custom House, Ayr, Letter book 1788-90.

Sir James Lowther wished to sell his share in a particular vessel for 'there is nothing to be gott by parts of ships but by seamen and merchants'[1], and one of his objects in continuing to hold shares was to oblige the more subservient masters.[2] The combination of 1728, however, determined Lowther to increase his holdings to enable him to break any further combination that might be formed against him; and as an example to the rest of the shipping, he also adopted a policy of selling his shares in the vessels of more obsolete construction and buying shares in more 'floaty' ships. Lowther's intention had only been to hold small shares, but in time he became major or sole owner of vessels. This enabled him to ensure their constant employment, especially in the summer months when the costs of working the pits were lowest. Sir James Lowther did not regard his vessels as a source of profit, but in the second half of the century the Lowther family took care to load their vessels with Howgill coals which though not fetching a higher price than other Whitehaven coals had a quicker rate of sale on the Dublin market.[3]

The vessels carrying Welsh coals to Ireland were less specialized than any other vessels engaged in the coal trade. In the other colliery areas the vessels were almost all seasonally dependent on the coal trade and were controlled by the masters. But in the small coal trade from Wales vessels carried coal in the absence of other freights and the masters acted on the orders of the merchant owners. The reasons for this are that though the ports on the south side of the Bristol Channel had an extensive import trade from Ireland, there was little to ship to Ireland (except in the case of Bristol), and the merchants were therefore forced to send their vessels to Wales for coal on the outward voyages to Ireland. The result was that there was a triangular pattern in much of the trade between ports on or near the Bristol Channel and ports in the south of Ireland.[4]

Generalization about trends in freight rates in Anglo-Irish trade is

[1]Record Office, The Castle, Carlisle. Sir James Lowther's letters to his agent at Whitehaven. London, 25 March 1707 (no. 1).

[2]See ibid., 8 April 1724 (no. 10).

[3]Public Record Office of Ireland, 1A–46–46. Committee books of the Parliamentary Committee on the Dublin coal trade, February 1796.

[4]See P.R.O., C. 104/11, 12, Cleek v. Calpine, where the roundabout pattern is illustrated in the records of an early Bridgwater firm with, as one would expect, special emphasis on the coal trade. For the years 1696–8 four shipments of coal to Ireland are recorded and two or three other voyages to Dublin, also commencing in South Wales, probably relate to the coal trade as well. On completion of the trips to Dublin the masters either sought a freight there or sailed

difficult, partly because the data are inadequate, partly because the rates charged for different commodities are not strictly comparable, and partly because some of the data relate to war years when rates were inflated. In particular, freight charges in some cases related to the weight or volume of the commodities, in other cases to ton of shipping capacity. Sugar exporters, however, preferred rates to be quoted by the ton rather than by the hogshead.[1] There is no evidence that rates rose with any marked emphasis in the course of the century, although it is worth noting that in the early 1790s coal freights appear to have risen.[2] Some evidence suggests that rings may have existed. For instance, the English master, William Vollum, in Dublin in 1799 thought he could advance the freight somewhat, but failed, '35/- being fixed by the merchants here, and I could not get any more'.[3] Where return freights were available, charges were likely to be lower, and it was said that for this reason the export freight from Dublin to Liverpool was not more than one half the import freight.[4]

Freight rates reflected in some degree the principle of charging what the traffic would bear. Charges on coal and other bulk commodities were for instance much lower than on more high-grade commodities. Of course despite the lower freight charges the incidence of transport costs bore more heavily on low-grade goods. Freight on coal was in the region of 50 per cent of the selling price on the Dublin quays. This greatly limited the ability of masters to raise their charges, and was an important factor in the low freight rates and poor prospects of profit in the coal trade throughout the century. On the other hand on goods such as linen cloth or linen or worsted yarn freight charges were only about one to two per cent of the prime cost and in some cases even less. In the early 1770s freight charges on linens shipped direct from Belfast to London were only a fraction of one

---

for Liverpool to load salt for south-west England or sometimes for Ireland. Some of the voyages assumed elaborate proportions. In 1698 the *Hope* sailed from Wales to Dublin where in June she secured a freight to Dunkirk. From Dunkirk the vessel went to Le Croisic to load salt back to Dublin, and in October carried a loading of wool from Dublin to Bridgwater and Minehead. The *Fly,* after landing a cargo of coal in Cork in September 1697, sailed to Liverpool for salt for Waterford, which was left in the hands of the firm's correspondent, who loaded the ship with provisions for the Canary Islands.

[1]National Library, Edinburgh, Houston, MSS., Home Letter book H, p. 87, Glasgow, 4 November, 1777.

[2]Public Record Office of Ireland, 1A-46-46. Coal Committee Books, 1793-6.

[3]P.R.O., C. 114/52, Wm. Vollum to John Reay, Dublin, 9 November 1799.

[4]Public Record Office of Ireland, 1A-46-46. Committee Books, 1796 (Committee to inquire into the Dublin coal trade).

per cent.[1] The addition of the other charges incidental to the transport of linens between the two ports did not increase costs very substantially. Even twenty years earlier in 1751 it had been stated that the cost of importing Irish linen to London did not amount to more than 2½ per cent, unless the premium of insurance was included.[2]

Freight rates were also affected to some extent by the existence of alternative routes. Many linen drapers and bleachers in the north of Ireland had for instance the choice of shipping through Belfast or Newry. On the other side of the Irish Sea, Chester and Liverpool were both rivals for the Irish trade. Over the greater part of the century, even in finer goods, overland routes were not competitive with the sea routes. Although in war time the risks of privateers and high insurance premiums resulted in much or most of London's trade with Ireland being effected overland through Chester or Liverpool, the return of peace always redirected trade to its wonted path around Lands End. Another example of the disadvantages of land carriage is seen in the worsted yarn trade with Norwich, which up to 1752 was conducted through Bristol because of anti-smuggling legislation which banned Irish worsted yarn from the English Channel for fear of its being carried to France. On the repeal of this outmoded legislation in 1752–3 the direct sea route between Great Yarmouth and the Irish ports of Dublin and Cork replaced the slower and more expensive overland route through Bristol.

On Irish linen sent to London from Bristol, Chester or Liverpool, costs were said to be near ½d. per yard.[3] The carriage of linen from Manchester to London was dearer than by sea from Dublin to London.[4] The advent of inland navigation must of course have had some effect in lowering inland costs, although a witness before a parliamentary committee in 1751 stated that 'the water carriage from Liverpool to Manchester was expensive as it comes through a private navigation'.[5] The development of canal navigation in the second half of the century, however, had a decided effect in lowering costs. A rough comparison with freight charges on the Irish Sea suggests that canal costs bore a rather low ratio to the already relatively competitive freight charges on the Irish Sea. Freight to Liverpool on a consignment of linen yarn in 1785 was £4 16s. 0d., on the canal thence

[1] Public Record Office of Northern Ireland, D. 468. Copy invoices of James Ferguson, linen bleacher.
[2] *Reports from Committees of the House of Commons*, vol. ii, p. 291.
[3] Ibid., p. 71 (1744).
[4] Ibid., p. 291.   [5] Loc. cit.

to Manchester 18/-. On another consignment the respective freights were 12/- and 2/3.[1] A merchant in estimating the costs of importing Irish worsted yarn computed freight to Liverpool at £0 15s. 0d. per cent, and thence to Manchester at £0 5s. 0d. per cent.[2] Even in the case of pottery, a relatively expensive commodity to transport, costs from Staffordshire to Liverpool were no higher than on the second stage of the journey, the Irish Sea crossing to Dublin.

The advent of the canals therefore had a pronounced effect in re-ducing transport costs for inland centres such as the Potteries or Manchester, which were connected by canal with Liverpool, a grow-ing centre of the Irish trade. Apart from transport on the canals, no sharp reduction was however effected in inland carriage, and overland routes were not competitive with the direct sea routes to any of the British ports. In particular, the overland movement of goods between London and the ports on the west coast trading to Ireland remained very limited except in war years. Moreover the real cost of overland transport was higher still than the nominal cost on account of the greater damage alleged by merchants to be suffered by goods con-signed overland.

A measure of the relative advantages of sea transport is afforded by evidence from the linen trade in the 1770s.[3] Freight on linens shipped direct from Belfast to London at that time averaged £1 to £1 5s. 0d. per consignment of two boxes containing about 100 pieces of cloth at a prime cost of about £150. This was considerably less than the charges incurred once the outbreak of war with France in the summer of 1778 necessitated shipment by wagon on the overland route from the ports of Chester and Liverpool to London. Freight to Liverpool and charges there amounted to around 15/- per con-signment and carriage to London to a further £2 18s. 0d. to £3 0s. 0d. The cost of carriage from Liverpool to London was therefore more than twice the cost of the freight in peace time direct from Belfast to London, and the overall costs via Liverpool more than three times higher. Moreover, the wide disparity in costs between land carriage and sea transport persisted despite the acute competition that existed while the war lasted between the wagon owners operating from the rival ports of Liverpool and Chester. In September and October 1780

---

[1]P.R.O., B.T. 6/106. See two invoices at the end of the volume. One of them is printed in *Minutes of Evidence before the Committee of the House of Lords*, 1785, p. 224.   [2]Ibid., p. 226.

[3]Public Record Office of Northern Ireland, D. 468. Copy invoices of the linen bleacher, James Ferguson.

advertisements in the *Belfast Newsletter* announced to the linen trade
that the costs of carriage by wagon from Chester to London had
been reduced to 6/– per cwt.[1] It is probable that land carriage was
now considerably cheaper than it had been years earlier when land
carriage for coarse linen from Chester, Liverpool or Bristol to London
was near ½d. per yard.[2] On such a basis costs for a consignment of
two boxes would have amounted to about £5. But land carriage was
still very far from competitive with the direct sea route. Once peace
returned in 1783 the constant traders sailing direct from Belfast to
London again bore the Irish linen trade. Only towards the very end
of the century is there some suggestion of rigid freight rates and port
charges creating a closer balance between the alternative routes in
Anglo-Irish trade.

Insurance was not usual. In peace time a great deal of the goods
shipped on the constant traders was not insured at all. This was
especially true of small consignments, of goods shipped on the short
Chester or Liverpool routes and of shipments outside the months of
winter. Insurance was most common in the case of bulk commodities
like provisions or corn, large consignments of which were sometimes
shipped on the account of a single merchant. Insuring was normal in
the continental trade even among the smugglers who probably alone
among Irish merchants effected insurance in France.[3] In war time
insurance became much more common in Anglo-Irish trade. Risks
were so considerable on the long and exposed route to London that
much of the London trade was effected overland via Chester or
Liverpool in war time, though under normal conditions costs on this
route were regarded as prohibitive in the case of goods like coarse
linen and higher than costs by sea on fine goods.[4] By shipping on the
short Chester or Liverpool route, it was frequently possible to avoid
the necessity for insuring. Insurance might not be effected when
privateers appeared to be absent from the Irish Sea or goods might
sometimes be placed on several bottoms to lessen the risks. Merchants were prepared to go to rather elaborate lengths to avoid

[1]*Belfast Newsletter,* 12, 15 September, 6 October 1780.
[2]See p. 135. note 3.
[3]See O'Connell Papers, Library, University College, Dublin. But some insuring
of Irish vessels had been done in the 1660s and 1670s by the Irish merchants of
St. Malo, and in the eighteenth century several Irishmen in France were underwriters or brokers.
[4]Relative costs were to alter in the early nineteenth century and much even of
the peace time trade with London was effected through Liverpool.

10

insuring: the London merchant, Thomas Davies, for example, delayed shipping a consignment of wool across the Irish Sea to Dublin,
'being afraid of running it and to pay insurance would eat up much
of the profit'.[1]

The opportunities for effecting marine insurance in Ireland were
limited. The main business of Irish companies was life or fire insurance. At least three Dublin insurance companies were however
prepared to transact marine business. In Cork there was already an
insurance office in 1747 'under the same regulations that are practised
in England for securing of interests in ships goods and merchandize
to all parts',[2] and in 1791 a 'Cork Insurance Company for ships and
merchandize' advertised its capital as being £50,000.[3] At the end of
the century a Belfast company also transacted marine business.[4]
Some underwriting of cross-channel shipping certainly existed,[5] but
it was of very small proportions, and occasional. The only Irish
marine insurance of any extent was in the coastal trade.[6] Insurance
on other ventures was normally effected through London correspondents or left in the hands of the British merchant dispatching
goods to Ireland. In the case of their Irish business Alexander
Houston & Company of Glasgow appear in some cases to have been
required to effect insurance through the London correspondents of
Irish merchants to whom they shipped sugar, whereas in other cases
they had apparently a free hand. In these latter cases insurance was
made locally in Greenock or Glasgow, and in Edinburgh. The extent
of local underwriting was, however, small, as in the insuring of the
same vessel application appears to have been made both to the local
and Edinburgh brokers. It was just possible that after application had
been made to the Scottish brokers the Glasgow firm might receive
news from Ireland that the Irish merchant had succeeded in having
the shipment underwritten in Dublin. In such a case the practice was
that the underwriters on both sides returned half the premium and
stood responsible for a correspondingly reduced risk.[7]

[1]P.R.O., C. 107/104, Foreign letter book, 10 September 1778.
[2]*Faulkner's Dublin Journal*, 24 October 1747.
[3]*Cork Hibernian Chronicle*, 30 June 1791.
[4]*Northern Star*, 4 January 1792.
[5]Public Record Office of Northern Ireland, D. 354/110, Mussenden Papers,
26 May 1744.
[6]*Report of the committee on the circulating paper, the specie and the current
coin of Ireland*, 1804, reprinted 1826, p. 108.
[7]National Library, Edinburgh. Houston MSS., Letter book H, pp. 128-31,
Glasgow, 27, 28 November 1777.

CHAPTER VIII

THE SMUGGLING TRADE

THE smuggling trade between the two islands in the eighteenth century was, in relation to the total volume of Anglo-Irish trade, of relatively little importance. Abuses were of course widespread, and a variety of frauds was at one time or another attempted. Merchants too in their correspondence at times referred quite casually to the bribing of revenue officers. But the volume of this business remained fairly limited in relation to the total volume of trade. Smuggling from Great Britain into Ireland on a large scale was restricted to a single commodity, tobacco. There was also some smuggling from Ireland to Britain, but this latter activity served to reduce the impact of smuggling on the balance of payments because the net outflow of cash must have been less than the value of gross smuggled imports. The goods smuggled to Britain were varied and some were novel, although in volume and hence in their economic significance many of the activities were limited. English copyright did not extend to Ireland in this period, and pirated editions, printed in Ireland, were smuggled into England. A still more unusual form of smuggling was the running of counterfeit coin and in 1765 the Collector of the port of Irvine in Scotland complained that 'this part of the country abounds with bad halfpence imported from Ireland'[1]. Also important in offsetting the quantities of tobacco smuggled into Ireland were the apparently thriving entrepot trade in smuggled goods developed on the north-east coast of Ireland on the suppression of the smuggling business in the Isle of Man in 1765, and the earnings of a number of Irish vessels concerned in smuggling goods directly from the continent into England or Scotland.

The pattern and methods of the smuggling trade between Great Britain and Ireland were in large measure determined by the close liaison between the authorities in the two islands. The Irish Revenue Commissioners were, in theory, entirely free from English direction, but from the end of the seventeenth century certain obligations were laid upon them and their officers by English statutes. These obligations were in fact unconstitutional, but were observed by the Irish

[1]Custom House, Troon. Letter Books, Irvine, Collr. to Bd., 1765-7, 27 December 1765. This may also help to explain why the Irish took a leading part in coinage forgeries in England (T.S. Ashton, *An economic history of England: the eighteenth century* (London, 1955) p. 175).

Commissioners.[1] In no trade is the liaison between the authorities in the two islands brought out more clearly than in the wool trade. Wool was not smuggled, of course, from Ireland to England, but because of the great importance attached to retaining the whole supply for the home industry in England and preventing any from reaching France, all possible efforts were made to prevent abuses under cover of export to England. Abuses were quite common in Irish wool exports in the second half of the seventeenth century, and cargoes entered for English ports at the Irish custom houses were frequently shipped to France.[2] Merchants shipping wool from Ireland to England were required to enter into bonds with one or more independent sureties that the wool would be landed in England, the bonds being cancelled only on presenting a certificate from the English port for which the wool had been entered as proof that the cargo had actually been landed there. This system of control itself gave rise to many abuses. The Irish officers were careless in accepting sureties, and false certificates were returned from the English revenue officers, or certificates were forged. To provide some degree of supervision, the English Treasury in 1674 ordered that a duplicate of each entry of a shipment of wool should be sent to the Treasury Office and another to the Commissioners of the Customs in London to be registered by them in their office and transmitted to the port of consignment.[3] The officers in the English ports, for their part, were to forward an account of whether these shipments had been landed in England to the Commissioners, who in turn were to represent to the Lord Treasurer all cases of failure.[4] These instructions appear to have been observed. In 1678 for instance the Treasury referred to the Commissioners of the Customs a petition from Euclid Speidel for a salary for registering the duplicates of the Irish wool cocquets, sending copies to the ports of discharge and for 'corresponding' with Ireland.[5]

---

[1]According to Kiernan (op. cit., pp. 100–01) these obligations were rejected by the Commissioners at a later date. He does not mention a date, but it must certainly have been late in the eighteenth century, probably during the more acute phases of the constitutional issue.

[2]L.M. Cullen, 'Tráchtáil idir Iarthar na h-Éireann is an Fhrainc, 1660–1800' (Trade between the West of Ireland and France, 1600–1800), *Galvia*, vol. 4 (1957) pp. 36–8.

[3]*Calendar of Treasury Books*, vol. iv, p. 632.

[4]Ibid., p. 635.

[5]Ibid., vol. v, pt. 2, p. 1140. Euclid Speidel, according to a work written in 1680 'informs that in the year 1678 there were 40 ships' lading of wool shipp'd off from Ireland, that according to the cockets ought to be unladen in England,

But this supervision was not in itself sufficient to eliminate abuses, for inadequate or insolvent sureties continued to be accepted, and false or forged certificates were still returned from England. Efforts were made on both sides of the Irish Sea to combat these abuses. There was also some collaboration between the authorities in the two islands in this work. In 1687 the deputy comptroller of the port of Exeter was sent to Ireland to give evidence concerning 'the discovery of certain counterfeated (sic) certificates or returns, wch had been produced . . . of the landing of great quantities of wool here which were really carryed . . . to France'.[1]

The system was, however, far from being a complete failure. It appears to have enabled many or most of the fraudulent shipments to be detected. The real reason for the continued smuggling of wool under guise of shipment to England lay in the easy and light composition for the penalties incurred. Compounding for these penalties was already a common practice in the early years of the Restoration, and when an office was established in 1662 for registering bonds and collecting forfeitures, the patentees, Sir Nicholas Armorer and Gabriel Silvius, were empowered to accept compositions from the holders of forfeited bonds and their sureties.[2] These compositions were considered to be a direct cause of the continued smuggling.[3] Despite the fact that the patent had been granted for a period of 21 years, it was finally determined in 1677 to buy the patentees out.[4] However, a new patent was issued in 1684 to Capt. Richard Coote[5] who, like his predecessors, followed a course 'not warrantable' and 'detrimental to the King', and in 1688 it was determined to cancel this patent also.[6] The main weakness of the patentees' administration had been their readiness to accept easy compositions. As these appear

---

but none of it arrived here'. John Collins, *A plea for the bringing in of Irish cattel and keeping out of fish caught by foreigners* (London, 1680) p. 5. On the correspondence between the authorities in the two islands, see also *Calendar of State Papers, Domestic, March–December, 1678,* p. 162.

[1]E.A.G. Clark, 'The estuarine ports of the Exe and the Teign', original of Ph.D. thesis (Geography), University of London, 1957, p. 693. See also *Calendar of Treasury Books,* vol. viii, pt. 3, p. 1786; pt. 4, p. 2049.

[2]*Calendar of State Papers, Ireland, 1660–2,* p. 590.

[3]E.g. see *Calendar of Treasury Books,* vol. iv, p. 73.

[4]Ibid., vol. v, pt. I, p. 708. See also *Calendar of State Papers Domestic, 1677–8,* pp. 402–3.

[5]*Calendar of State Papers, Domestic, 1683–4,* pp. 173–4, for the King's instruction to the Lord Lieutenant to grant the office.

[6]*Calendar of Treasury Books,* vol. viii, pt. 3, p. 1799.

to have amounted to as little as 12d. per stone of wool,[1] they served
to encourage the trade more than to prevent it. However, from the
time of the vacation of Coote's patent, the registering and collection
of bonds, if forfeited, was carried out by the Irish Revenue Commissioners, and the practice of compounding for the penalties was
abandoned.

The Irish Revenue Commissioners were also now required by
English statute to transmit to the English Customs Commissioners
every six months an account of wool exported, and to give the names
of the persons signing the certificates of the landing of the wool in
England and the dates of the certificates so that the same might be
compared with the accounts kept by the Customs Commissioners in
London.[2] The keeping by the Commissioners in London of a register
of wool imported from Ireland, which they had been first instructed
to keep in 1674, was itself made a statutory requirement in 1689, and
the certificates of the landing of wool from Ireland were required to
be signed by three of the principal officers of the port of discharge.[3]
Finally, the Irish ports entitled to export wool were in 1689 limited
to six, some of the smaller ports, like Galway, where customs administration had been considered very lax, being omitted.[4] In
England, the number of importing ports was also restricted. As it was
thought that freedom to ship wool to London and to the ports on
the south-east coast gave the wool smugglers greater opportunity of
plying their trade under cover of shipment to England, Exeter was
the only port beyond Lands End to which the import of Irish wool
was now permitted.[5] Subsequently in 1693 even Exeter itself was

[1]Ibid., vol. x, pt. 3, p. 1328.
[2]7 & 8 William III, c. 28 (Eng.), section 6.
[3]I William & Mary, c. 32 (Eng.), sections 4, 11.
[4]Ibid., section 6. The ports were Dublin, Waterford, Youghal, Kinsale, Cork
and Drogheda. The same ports were named in 10 and 11 William III, c. 10 (Eng.);
and New Ross was added by 4 & 5 Anne c. 7 (Eng.). Subsequently, in 1739 other
Irish ports were added (12 Geo. II, c. 21 (Eng.)) and in 1753 the export of wool
from any port in Ireland to England was permitted (26 Geo. II, c. 11 (Eng.)).
It may also be noted that some attempts at limiting the number of ports on both
sides of the Irish Sea concerned in the wool trade appear to have been made
prior to 1689 (*Calendar of State Papers, Ireland, 1660-2*, pp. 386, 398; *Calendar
of State Papers, Domestic, 1673*, p. 337; P.J. Bowden, *The wool trade in Tudor
and Stuart England*, pp. 189, 207).
[5]I William & Mary, c. 32 (Eng.), section 6. The named ports were Liverpool,
Chester, Minehead, Barnstaple, Bideford, Exeter. Whitehaven and Bridgwater
were added by 7 & 8 William III, c. 28 (Eng.), Whitehaven was omitted and
Milford Haven added by 10 & 11 William III, c. 10 (Eng.), and these ports were
confirmed in 12 Geo II, c. 21 (Eng.). In 1752 Lancaster and Great Yarmouth were

excluded from the Irish wool trade.[1] The practice of taking bonds in
the Irish ports was made a statutory requirement in 1699 by 10 and
11 William III, c. 10, which required that for every shipment bond
should be given by 'two sufficient persons, known inhabitants of and
residing in or near the place where the bond is or shall be given' in
double the value of the wool shipped.[2] The same statute also required
that, before wool from Ireland might be imported into England,
notice be given to the Collector of the port to which the cargo was
intended to be brought, and bond entered into there with one or more
sufficient sureties in treble the value of the shipment that the wool be
landed accordingly.[3] These measures, effecting a much closer liaison
between the authorities in the two countries, and the abandonment
of the practice of accepting compositions for the penalties, appear to
have eliminated abuses in the shipment of wool to England from the
early eighteenth century. Irish statistics for exports of wool to
England and the corresponding English figures for imports, available
in both cases from the end of the seventeenth century, tally almost
exactly, suggesting that the practice of carrying wool to France on
pretence of shipment to England was now at an end. Smuggling of
wool continued into the middle of the century, but it was now a
practice effected without entry at the Custom House. This means
that statistics of Irish wool and yarn exports, though not a complete
measure of total exports of wool and yarn from Ireland in the eighteenth century, are in fact a very reliable indication of the wool trade
with England in this period.

Difficulties were also encountered in eliminating abuses in the export trade from Great Britain to Ireland, either through the re-
landing in Britain of goods that had part of the duties drawn back or
through smuggling into Ireland. But in contrast to the wool trade no
system of detecting these abuses was built up in the early Restoration
period, and even when the first steps were taken the arrangements
were much less elaborate than in the wool trade. The authorities in
England were in fact much more concerned at first about the lax
observance in Ireland of the Navigation Acts in so far as related

---

added (25 Geo. II, c. 14 (Eng.); c. 19 (Eng.)), in 1753 Exeter (26 Geo. II, c. 8
(Eng.)), and subsequently in the same session the wool trade was thrown open
to all the ports in England (26 Geo. II, c. 11 (Eng.)).

[1] 4 & 5 William & Mary, c. 24 (Eng.), section 10.

[2] Section 5.

[3] Section 14.

to direct importation to Ireland from the colonies.[1] But in 1682 at the same time as the Treasury appointed Charles Horne to inspect the plantation trade in Ireland they also appointed Silvanus Stirrup to examine the quantities of coal, lead and tin landed in Ireland because of 'the great frauds frequently committed in the shipping of coals, lead and tin from England to Ireland'.[2] The appointment of Stirrup was the first attempt at detecting abuses in Anglo-Irish trade apart from the wool trade. The two officers were to have the 'sight and perusal' of the customs books of the Irish ports, and the assistance of the Irish revenue officers; and Stirrup appears to have had a part in the compilation of an elaborate and full survey of the quantities of Irish overseas trade in the early 1680s.[3] Two further officers were appointed successively to Horne's position,[4] though the office of keeping an account of imports of coal, lead and tin appears to have been allowed to lapse at a later date.[5] But in 1704 a new officer, Maurice Birchfield, was appointed by the Customs Commissioners in London to the post of surveying the plantation trade, and was also allotted the task of keeping an account of imports of coal, lead and tin, and, additionally, of salt.[6] The Irish Revenue Commissioners were asked to have their officers correspond with Birchfield, who was to reside in London, and for their part were requested to appoint a

---

[1]*Calendars of Treasury Books,* passim. See also instructions of the Lords of the Council to the Earl of Aran, Public Record Office of Ireland, Dublin. Wyche Papers, 1st series, 1/13. 12 December, 1683.

[2]*Calendar of Treasury Books,* vol. vii, p. 551; H.M.C. *Ormonde MSS.,* new series, vol. 6, pp. 404–5.

[3]A statistical summary of this activity is available in B.M., Add. MSS. 4759, Exports and Imports of Ireland, 1683–6, endorsed 'this abstract drawn out of the Books and examined by: Silvanus Stirrup, Martin Tucker'. (For a later reference to Tucker, see *Calendar of Treasury Books,* vol. xxiv, pt. 2, p. 516.) Apparently, a run of statistics of Irish overseas trade over a period of 6 years was compiled, for a later pamphleteer referred to an 'exact account of the exports and imports of Ireland for 6 years in the time of Ireland's greatest prosperity' (*An answer to a letter from a gentleman in the country to a member of the house of commons* (London, 1698), p. 24). Figures in B.M., Add. MSS. 4759 cover, apparently, the last four years of the run; and a few figures survive for the two earlier years. A pamphleteer in 1698 quotes a figure of £541,419 for Irish exports in 1682 (op. cit., p. 24), and Dobbs in 1729 gives Irish exports in 1681 as £582,814 and imports as £433,040 (*Essay on the trade of Ireland,* 1729, in *Tracts and Treatises illustrative of . . . Ireland* (Dublin, 1861), vol. ii, p. 334).

[4]See *Calendar of Treasury Books,* vol. xix, p. 387.

[5]Ibid., vol. xix, p. 339, 342. But not before 1695, as in that year Nicholas Culliford was appointed to the office. Ibid., vol. x, pt. 2, p. 945.

[6]Ibid., vol. xix, pp. 342, 387.

man who would transmit to them from England an account of goods shipped to Ireland.[1] The Irish Revenue Commissioners appointed Kendrick Vanbrugh to this position and the English Customs Commissioners were instructed to order their officers to correspond with him in London.[2]

This system of control was, however, too general to enable abuses to be detected and in 1708 and 1709 the Scottish Customs Commissioners proposed that no drawbacks should be granted for tobacco exported to Ireland till a certificate of its landing was returned, feeling that this would eliminate the frauds that happened 'notwithstanding all we are able to do in opposition . . . by corresponding with the Revenue Commissioners of Ireland'.[3] Accordingly a law was passed permitting no debenture to be paid for tobacco exported from Britain to Ireland until a certificate was returned from the officers in the port of landing in Ireland.[4] The payment of the drawback on the export of salt or rock salt had already been made conditional on the return of a certificate from the Irish officers in 1701,[5] and the system was subsequently expanded with effect from May 1719 to include all 'certificate goods' (i.e. goods entitled to drawback on re-export).[6] From 1710 bonds were required for the proper landing of coals shipped to Ireland[7] and coal thus also became a certificate commodity with the bonds being discharged only on the return of a certificate from the customs officers in the Irish ports. These measures eliminated abuses in the case of goods entered at the custom house for Ireland. A striking proof of this lies in the close degree of correspondence between the statistics of certificate goods compiled on both sides of the Irish Sea. But the control of high-duty exports from England by certificates returned from Ireland did not end the smuggling trade into Ireland. No certificates were required of the landing

[1]Ibid.
[2]*Calendar of Treasury Books,* vol. xx, pt. 2, p. 253. Custom House, Whitehaven, letter books, Bd. to Collr., 1703-10, London, 22 May 1705. At a slightly later date the Scottish Commissioners of the Customs also appear to have made some efforts to detect frauds in the Irish trade by a comparison of evidence on both sides. See *Calendar of Treasury Books,* vol. xxiv, pt. 2, p. 223.
[3]*Calendar of Treasury Books,* vol. xxiii, pt. 2, p. 414. See also vol. xxiv, pt. 2, pp. 179-80.
[4]8 Anne, c. 13 (Eng.), section 18.
[5]1 Anne Stat. I, c. 21 (Eng.), section 11.
[6]5 Geo. I, c. 11 (Eng.), section 5. Subsequently renewed from time to time. The requirement of a certificate from Ireland on teas exported there for purposes of the drawback of the inland duty is expressly stated in 21 Geo. II, c. 14 (Eng.).
[7]9 Anne, c. 6 (Eng.), section 6.

of goods in foreign countries[1] and tobacco smuggled to Ireland was carried therefore in vessels that cleared for foreign countries with their shipments.[2] Debentures were frequently stopped on suspicion of such practices, but evidence was difficult to obtain.[3] The extent of tobacco smuggling from England should not be exaggerated, however, as much of the tobacco was smuggled into Ireland from France, Holland, Guernsey or the Isle of Man. But on the other hand some of this tobacco may itself have been shipped from England with fraudulent intentions in the first instance.

Goods were of course also smuggled from Ireland to England. They included beef, butter and even cattle, but these were not items of permanent importance in the trade. Duties on spirits and colonial goods were much higher in England than in Ireland, and there was also a high inland duty on soap, candles and salt. This encouraged smuggling from Ireland. Small quantities of spirits were suspected of being smuggled from the vessels trading from Ireland, and the Commissioners of the Customs constantly passed on to the collectors of the ports in the west of England details they had received from the officers of the Irish ports of the quantities of spirits, salt or soap on Irish vessels clearing out for England.[4] Frauds of this nature were

[1]Apart from a requirement from 1701 of a certificate for calicoes and East-India silks re-exported (11 & 12 William III, c. 10 (Eng.), section 2) and from 1712 for tea and coffee exported (10 Anne, c. 26 (Eng.), section 34), given under the common seal of the Chief Magistrate in the foreign port or under the hand and seal of two British merchants there, before securities could be discharged or drawback allowed.

[2]B.M., Add. MSS. 21134, f. 44. 'It is a common practice in several of the ports of Scotland and England to ship off great quantities of tobacco for Bilboa or some other Spanish port and get the drawback on exportation and instead of going to Spain to run all the said tobacco into Ireland to the great prejudice of the revenue of both kingdoms'. See also R.C. Jarvis, *Customs letter books of the port of Liverpool, 1711–1813*, pp. 36–7, 43–5, 94; Custom House, Ayr, Letter Books, 1764–6, Officers to Board, Ayr, 13, 20 Feb. 1766; Custom House, Greenock, Letter Books, Greenock and Port Glasgow, Bd. to Collr. 1728–34, 31 December 1733.

[3]*Report of the committee appointed to inquire into the frauds and abuses in the customs*, 7 June 1733, in *Reports from committees of the house of commons*, vol. 1, p. 609.

[4]E.g. Custom House, London, Letter Book, Lancaster, 1728–34. See also B.M., Lansdowne MSS. 1215, f. 169. An account received from Ireland in 1745 of brandy and rum, wine, soap and candles, salt, entered outwards at the several underwritten ports and supposed to be run on the coast of Wales. It should be noted however that vessels sailing outwards from Ireland with soap, brandy or high-duty goods were also said to clear out for English ports other than the one for which they were really bound. Custom House, Whitehaven. Letter Books, Collr. to Bd., 1730–34, 18 October 1731.

made all the easier by virtue of the fact that not until 1772 were
certificates of the proper landing of goods in England required before
the payment of bounties or drawbacks in Ireland.[1] Smuggling of
spirits on vessels plying a legitimate trade between the two countries
was, however, limited; though the colliers especially had the reputation of smuggling goods, spirits in particular, either direct from
Ireland or by calling at the Isle of Man on their homeward voyage
in ballast. Soap from Ireland was constantly smuggled all along the
west coast of England and Scotland. The extent of this activity was
however greatly exaggerated by the English soap-boilers and the
quantities both smuggled and seized appear to have generally been
small, though the number of individual ventures was admittedly
high. As there was a high excise on salt in England, it was profitable
to smuggle salt back to England after it had been landed in Ireland.
Some of this business was effected on vessels clearing out regularly
for Britain though much of the trade, especially in the north-east,
was effected by small Irish or Scottish boats sailing outwards from
Ireland without a clearance. This trade was clearly on a rather large
scale on the west coast of Scotland,[2] though the proprietors of the
Scottish salt works tended to exaggerate its extent in their representations to the Customs Commissioners in Edinburgh.

The total volume of smuggling from Ireland was, however, very
limited in the first half of the eighteenth century. To a large extent
it consisted of small, though numerous, frauds in landing soap, spirits
or salt from vessels engaged in legal trade between the two islands.
There was virtually no large-scale smuggling into Britain from
Ireland. Indeed as long as the smuggling trade could be carried on
through the Isle of Man, Ireland had little attraction as a base for
the traffic in high-duty commodities. The Isle of Man was independent of English customs administration in this period because of
its anomalous constitutional position, and levied its own customs

[1] 12 Geo. III, c. 55 (Eng.), section 4. Rum, or other plantation goods, however,
under a somewhat forced interpretation of the Navigation Acts, could not legally
be cleared out from Ireland to England. See A short abstract of the Act of the
12th of Charles the 2nd, commonly called the Navigation Law, with some
observations on its relative force between England and Ireland (written c. 1780),
B.M., Add. MSS. 33118, ff. 25–31. There was some laxity in Ireland in following
this rule, and in 1772 the export of rum, sugar or coffee from Ireland to England
was expressly forbidden (12 Geo. III, c. 55 (Eng.), section 1).

[2] Customs Letter Books, Ayr, Custom House, Ayr; –do– Irvine, Custom House,
Troon; –do– Greenock and Port Glasgow, Custom House, Greenock; Thoughts
on the manufacture . . . of salt, by the Earl of Dundonald (Edinburgh, 1784).

duties. These were low, and were designed to encourage an entrepôt trade. Cargoes of dutiable commodities, imported into the island from France or Holland, were re-shipped for the shores of England, Scotland and Ireland.[1] The extent of this trade was very large, and goods from the island were smuggled ashore even as far away as Galway.[2] Thus, even as early as 1732, a customs officer coming back from a visit to the island reported 30 'sail of vessels' loading brandy and other goods for Britain and Ireland.[3] But in 1765 the English Parliament bought the rights of the island from the Duke of Athol for £70,000,[4] and with the establishment of English law on the island the smuggling trade from the Isle of Man was brought to an end. The closing of the island led to direct smuggling links with the continent, and goods were now smuggled ashore in Britain or Ireland direct from Gothenburg, Ostend, Nantes, Lorient or Roscoff. The importance of Guernsey as a smuggling entrepot was also greatly enhanced.

Some Irish capital had been employed in the trade in the Isle of Man. One Dublin firm, the Connors, may have had a smuggling branch there,[5] and the name of another island merchant, Simon Lynch,[6] suggests an Irish origin. Robert Black, a son of the Belfast merchant John Black, settled in Bordeaux, was a partner in a concern on the island, and brandies were consigned to him from Bordeaux.[7] In August 1765, shortly after the closing of the smuggling trade in the island, he wrote:

the late revolution in this country has taken up so much of my time as has made me a very unpunctual correspondent for some time past—the

---

[1] See R.C. Jarvis, 'Illicit trade with the Isle of Man, 1671-1765', *Transactions of the Lancashire and Cheshire Antiquarian Society,* vol. 58 (1945-6), pp. 245-67. For a contemporary estimate of the size of the trade in 1735 and 1745, see B.M., Lansdowne MSS. 1215, f. 170.

[2] P.R.O., Customs I ('Customs Minutes, Ireland'), vol. 43, f. 95, 26 October 1747.

[3] Custom House, Greenock, Letter Books, Port Glasgow and Greenock, Bd. to Collr., 1728-34, 12 April 1732. See also Custom House Library, London, Letter Book, Lancaster, 1728-32, Bd. to Collr., 6 April 1732.

[4] 5 Geo. III, c. 26 (Eng.). The purchase was effected on 30 April 1765.

[5] M. Wall, 'The rise of a catholic middle class in 18th century Ireland', *Irish Historical Studies,* vol. XI (1958) pp. 109-10.

[6] R.C. Jarvis, *Customs letter books of the port of Liverpool, 1711-1813,* p. 67.

[7] Public Record Office of Northern Ireland, Belfast. Black Papers. Robert Black was apparently a member of the smuggling partnership of Ross, Black and Christian on the island. John Black senior himself invested money in his son's ventures, and in 1761 there was owing to him in Ireland a sum of £54 by 'Denton the smuggler'. T. 1073/12/11.

late act of Parliament having effectually shut up every avenue to trade in this place. Many of the merchts. here are resolv'd as you observe to seek it elsewhere; for my part I am resolv'd to fix myself at Belfast as soon as I can settle my affairs here which I hope will be the case next spring . . .[1]

In the following year (1766) John Black wrote to his sons Alexander and James Black in London, of two other sons, Tom and Sam, being busy at the bleach green 'or fitting up my Robert's country dwelling Castle Hill for his reception when he parts from Douglas Isleman'.[2] Robert Black himself became a linen bleacher, exporting linens to London.

But not all the Irish smugglers abandoned the running trade like Robert Black. Before the trade from the island had been blocked, many Irish vessels were concerned in the business and ran cargoes from the island not only into Ireland, but into England and Scotland. The smuggling trade on the coast between Beaumaris and Chester was said to be carried on mostly in Irish wherries and this was said also of the clandestine trade in Aberystwyth and Cardigan.[3] These smugglers now began to run their cargoes directly from the continent. In the years immediately following the closing of the island, they appeared in Nantes, which had been one of the centres from which the island had been supplied with contraband goods and which had itself a direct smuggling trade with Ireland. The port's geographical situation, however, proved unsuitable for this activity, which although it continued to be conducted on the French side by the merchants of Nantes with whom the Irish smugglers dealt, was transferred as far as the physical handling of the goods was concerned to the more convenient ports of Bellisle, Lorient and Roscoff. The smugglers also began to build up a new entrepot trade using the north-east coast of Ireland as the base for their operations. This trade was in fact already in existence before the closing of the island, and in August 1765 the Isle of Man smuggler, Robert Black, wrote to a Belfast merchant and fellow-partner in a Belfast smuggling concern, that he was 'suspicious that the Ministry in England are determined to put an end to the

[1]Public Record Office of Northern Ireland, Belfast. Uncatalogued Mussenden Papers. Robert Black to William Mussenden, Douglas, 9 August, 1765.
[2]Public Record Office of Northern Ireland, Belfast. Black Papers, T. 1073/19/1, November 1766. Alexander Black was subsequently a plate glass manufacturer in London (see various letters addressed to him, 1782–99; ibid., T. 1073/19/24–46).
[3]B.M., Add. MSS. 9293, pp. 113, 117, 121. A survey (of the Customs) made in 1764 for 5 years to Xmas 1763 and down to the time of the survey.

trade carried on in the spirits branch from your place to Scotland'.[1] The closing of the island had enhanced the importance of this trade. In November 1765 the collector and comptroller of the port of Ayr informed their officers that they had received information that 'great quantities of spirits at Belfast are now filling up into small casks with an intention to obtain coast dispatches for the same to another port in Ireland and then to run the spirits upon this and the neighbouring coast'.[2] In the same month the collector of the neighbouring port of Irvine informed the Board in Edinburgh 'respecting the sundrie quantities of spirits intended to be run from Belfast in Ireland into the districts of Air and Irvine'.[3]

As no bonds were required in the Irish coast-wise trade, small Irish and Scottish boats were therefore able to carry on the smuggling of spirits with a good deal of impunity, and this business was a constant preoccupation to the customs officers in the west of Scotland ports in the years following the closing of the Isle of Man.[4] The extent of this trade is of course difficult to estimate. A large tranship-ment trade in rum, in which vessels entered cargoes in ports in Scot-land or on the west coast of England and then cleared them for Ireland, was developing at this time, and as its growth coincided roughly with the closing of the Isle of Man, the customs officers in Britain were inclined to think that most or all of this rum was for Scotland. The collector at Ayr, for example, wrote in June 1765:

since the Government had the possession of the Isle of Man where vessels formerly from the West Indies used to stop and land prohibited and high duty goods, we observe no less a quantity than 45,792½ gallons rum im-ported here between the 2nd October last and the 18th instant, the whole dutys thereon allowed to be drawn (back), as all of it appears to have been shipped for Ireland, from whence there is reason to believe that the greatest part of these spirits are intended to be brought back in small vessels and boats and run upon this coast and that of Galloway.[5]

---

[1]Public Record Office of Northern Ireland, Belfast. Uncatalogued Mussenden Papers, Robert Black to William Mussenden, Douglas, 9 Aug. 1765. The English government had already taken some action against this trade in the previous session and a clause relating to this trade was accepted by Parliament (5 Geo. III, c. 43 (Eng.), section 30). Some further clauses directed against this traffic were included in an act of 1772 (12 Geo. III, c. 55 (Eng.)).

[2]Custom House, Ayr, Letter Books, Collr. to Bd., 1764–6, Ayr, 14 Nov. 1765. See also ibid., 24 Feb. 1766.

[3]Custom House, Troon. Letter Books, Irvine, Collr. to Bd., 1765–7, 26 Nov. 1765.

[4]Custom Houses, Greenock, Ayr, Troon: Letter Books.

[5]Custom House, Ayr, Letter Books, Collr. to Bd., 1764–6. Ayr, 29 June 1765.

It is true that transhipment through Scottish ports coincided approximately with the cessation of the Isle of Man trade, but it is not quite true of the English ports where the emergence of the rum shipments dates from 1762. There was in fact as much reason for legitimate traders to tranship their rum as for smugglers. A flaw having been discovered at about this time in the Irish Customs Act, which enabled rum to be imported from Great Britain at half the poundage charged on direct importation, it was now more profitable to tranship rum in Britain, and by qualifying for a drawback by the fiction of entering the cargo at the custom house and clearing it for Ireland a few days later, ship it for Ireland as rum re-exported from Great Britain.[1] But the removal of the anomaly in the Irish customs duties in 1772[2] greatly reduced the transhipment trade. Rum exports to Ireland from England fell from 1,172,465 gallons in 1771 to 363,170 gallons in 1772, and in Scotland from 759,621 gallons in 1771 to 68,808 gallons in 1772. Total imports of rum from all parts into Ireland fell from their high level at the end of the 'sixties and in the early 'seventies. Imports which were 1,973,732 gallons in the year ended 25 March 1772, fell to 1,704,558 gallons in 1773; 1,503,086 gallons in 1774 and 1,322,507 gallons in 1775. This may in part be attributed to a fall in imports consequent on a heavier incidence of duty, and to some decline in home consumption in the early 1770s because of unfavourable economic conditions, but it may also to some degree illustrate the former extent of the smuggling trade in rum.

The entrepôt trade did not cease, however. Spirits illicitly landed in Ireland continued to be smuggled into Scotland and the north-west of England in the remainder of the century. In addition the smugglers' business was widened to include tea. Duties on tea imported from England to Ireland were much lower than the British duties and after 1767, when the Irish duties were themselves lowered and a complete drawback of the duties granted on tea re-exported from England to Ireland and America,[3] a smuggling trade emerged in which tea legally imported from Britain was run back into Britain. The volume of this business was fairly large, and much or most of the tea legally

[1] See Public Record Office of Ireland, Dublin, 1A–41–134. Series of 104 letters to Townshend, 1767–72.

[2] 11 & 12 Geo. III, c. 6 (Ir.). With effect from 1 May 1772.

[3] 7 Geo. III, c. 56 (Eng.). In 1772 the drawback was reduced to $\frac{3}{5}$ of the duties (12 Geo. III, c. 60 (Eng.)), but the full drawback on exports of tea to Ireland was restored by 17 Geo. III, c. 27 (Eng.).

imported into Ireland was said to be intended for smuggling back to Britain.[1] This is very much an exaggeration, however. The importation of tea increased sharply in Ireland from 1767, and though this may be attributed in part to the demand created by the rise of an entrepot smuggling trade, it also represents the substitution of tea legally imported from England for teas formerly smuggled from the continent. Moreover, the contraband trade in tea from France was itself very active during the 'seventies, and the quantities shipped from the north-west coast of France, especially from Roscoff, where this branch of the running was now concentrated, were very considerable. It is likely that the entrepot trade in smuggled tea was mainly fed from supplies run in from France.

The entrepot trade continued unrepressed to the end of the century and is therefore one of the main reasons for the active smuggling trade all along the coasts of Down and Antrim in this period. Red Bay at the mouth of Cushendall Glen appears to have become the main centre of this illicit trade in which goods were imported from France, Holland or Guernsey and then reshipped for Scotland or the north-west coast of England in small vessels without a clearance. In 1784 the Committee on illicit practices used in defrauding the revenue commented on the activities of 'luggers and wherries, and of large rowboats (some of them of a new construction, 40 feet long and rowing with 12 or 16 oars) which are almost constantly employed in bringing over tea, spirits, tobacco, etc. from Redbay and the north-east part of Ireland'.[2] In 1786 the collector at Ayr represented to the Scottish Customs Commissioners that 'the smuggling on the coast of Carrick being now carried on by small boats from Red Bay in Ireland where the larger smuggling vessels are in the use to land their cargoes, and that such small boats though they come upon the coast in the day time and are seen by the officers . . . yet by proceeding along the coast when it becomes dark', they succeeded in running their cargoes.[3] Two years later, the collector at Ayr again made representations about the smuggling of cargoes at Red Bay 'from

[1]Report of Commissioners of Excise on smuggling, London, 15 Feb. 1783, in A.L. Cross, *Eighteenth century documents relating to the royal forests, the sheriffs and smuggling* (New York, 1928), pp. 315–17. See also *First Report from the Committee on illicit practices used in defrauding the revenue*, in *Reports from Committees of the House of Commons*, December, 1783, vol. XI, p. 230.

[2]*Second Report from the Committee on illicit practices used in defrauding the Revenue*, March 1784, in *Reports from Committees of the House of Commons*, vol. XI, p. 263.

[3]Custom House, Ayr. Letter Books, Collr. to Bd., 1785–6, 16 Sept. 1786.

whence the goods have been conveyed to this coast in small boats from 10 to 15 tons burthen'.[1] Later still in 1789 the collector of the port of Campbeltown commented on 'the alarming height to which smuggling is carried on to and from the island of Sanda within 12 miles of this harbour towards the Mull of Kintyre', adding that 'the Breckenridges of Red Bay in Ireland have, we are assured, taken this island as a central situation for the conveyances of their smuggled goods from Ireland to the coast of Air'.[2]

It must be remembered, however, that only part of the goods run into Scotland was supplied from Ireland, for much of the smuggling was since the decay of the Isle of Man trade effected directly from continental ports or from Guernsey. Many Irish vessels, almost all from the Irish smuggling port of Rush, engaged in this trade and landed their cargoes on the west and north-west coasts of England and in Scotland. Rush first came into prominence in the days of the running trade from the Isle of Man, enjoying the advantages of being near the largest Irish market for smuggled goods, Dublin, and adjacent to the Isle of Man. Wherries from the port not only built up a large trade with Irish centres, but were already in the 1750s supplying goods from the island to Scotland and the north of England. On the closing of the island the smugglers from Rush developed direct links with the French smuggling marts of Bellisle, Lorient and Roscoff. Using much larger vessels, their activities were now more widespread and their daring and violence greater. Most celebrated of the many Rush smugglers was John Connor, nick-named Jack the Batchelor, who had been outlawed in 1767 for attacking two revenue vessels in the Bay of Dundrum.[3] Three years later he attacked the *Pelham* revenue cruiser in Beaumaris Bay in Wales, and after 'drawing' the crew out of her, plundered her and ran her on rocks at St. David's.[4] After his outlawry Connor and his confederates settled in Roscoff, the resort of many Irish smugglers, and he continued his smuggling to Ireland and Britain from his new headquarters. In 1772, according to Sir Edward Newenham, 'most of the goods now smuggled into this county (Dublin) are sent over by John Conner, alias the Batchelor, from France, where by his personal residence, he has

[1]Ibid., Collr. to Bd., 1786–8, 5 Jan. 1788.
[2]Custom House Library, London. Selections from the records in the Scottish outports, 1921, p. 41 (Letter from Custom House, Campbeltown, 9 March 1789).
[3]P.R.O., Customs 1 (Customs Minutes, Ireland). vols. 98, 99, passim.
[4]Custom House Library, London. Selections from outport letter books, 1662–1829, p. 191.

11

so ingratiated himself into the confidence of the French merchants, that they venture large cargoes on his credit and knowledge of our coasts'.[1]

Yet, Connor was only one of many smugglers from Rush, who were busy plying on the smuggling routes from the continent to the shores of Ireland and the western coasts of Scotland and England. Somewhat later than 1776 the Collector of the port of Carlisle wrote that the west and north coasts of Britain were frequented by 'very large smuggling vessels belonging to Ireland and other parts' and that 'they have not less than 50 sail of such vessels belonging to Rush in Ireland'.[2] The numbers of smugglers from Rush are in fact borne out in the many Rush men who served in French privateers—some of them with distinction—when war made the business of smuggling too hazardous.[3] As far as can be judged from the available evidence, little of the contraband for Scotland and England was on the account of the Rush merchants themselves. Goods smuggled into Scotland were generally on Scottish account, and supercargoes sometimes sailed on the vessels. Much of the goods transhipped in Red Bay was also shipped on Scottish account, and the name of the smuggling merchants in Red Bay, the Breckenridges, appears to confirm the Scottish connection. The Rush smugglers tended to be specialist ship-owners in the contraband trade, and contrast with the smuggling merchants and gentry of a slightly earlier period on the south and west coasts of Ireland, whose business was a purely Irish and localised one.

[1]Public Record Office of Northern Ireland, Belfast. Macartney Papers, D. 572/2/37. Sir Edward Newenham, Dublin, 2 April 1772.
[2]Quoted in 'Proposed review of the smuggling laws from Mr. Pitt' (n.d. apparently after 1776), in A.L. Cross, *Eighteenth century documents relating to the royal forests, the sheriffs and smuggling* (New York, 1928) p. 239.
[3]See L.M. Cullen, 'An Ceangal Tráchtála ... (Trade Relations ...) op. cit., pp. 327, 542–3.

CHAPTER IX

EXCHANGES AND BALANCE OF PAYMENTS

I. THE PAR OF EXCHANGE

OF currency matters in Ireland in the seventeenth century, little is known. There was, however, in this century as in the following, no Irish mint,[1] the Irish currency consisting of English coins and such foreign coins as were declared current and valued by proclamation. It would appear that English coinage passed in Ireland at its face value, and that therefore the par of exchange between the two countries in the middle of the century was simply £100=£100.[2] Foreign coin on the other hand was overvalued, but as this affected both gold and silver,[3] it produced no shortage of silver as such.[4] But the overvaluing of the foreign coin together with the worsening of Irish foreign exchanges as a result of the English Cattle Acts and the consequent demand for specie, placed a substantial premium on English coin over the remainder of the century.

The disadvantages inherent in the absence of a proper regulation of the Irish monetary system became particularly apparent in 1689 and afterwards when, because of political and economic difficulties, the valuations of the specie current in Ireland were altered. The course of exchange had been sharply rising in the last four years of the 1680s because of uneasiness among the Protestant merchant and propertied classes. In an effort to reduce the export or hoarding of specie the coinage current in Ireland was revalued in March 1689.[5] The new

[1]Excepting brass or copper money coined in Ireland on a number of occasions.

[2]See J. Simon, *An essay towards an historical account of Irish coins* (Dublin, 1749) p. 58; *Letters written by His Excellency Hugh Boulter, D.D., Lord Primate of all Ireland, etc., to several Ministers of State in England and some others* (Oxford, 1770) vol. ii, p. 159.

[3]See Petty, *Political anatomy of Ireland* (1672) in Hull, *Economic writings of Sir William Petty,* vol. i, p. 184.

[4]E.g. see a theoretical computation of the different kinds of specie in Ireland, which suggests no relative shortage of silver, by Sir William Petty in B.M., Add. MSS. 18022, ff. 67–8, 'An estimate of the moneys now current in Ireland . . . offered rather as an instance of what we mean than as an assertion that the particulars thereof are truth' (copy, n.d.).

[5]For seventeenth and eighteenth century proclamations relating to coinage see especially Simon, op. cit., and M.S. Dudley Westropp, 'Notes on Irish money-weights and foreign coin current in Ireland', *Proceedings of Royal Irish Academy,* vol. 33 (1916–7), Section C.

value of the guinea was 24/– and of the shilling 1/1d. This meant a
new par of exchange, on the basis of the respective valuations of the
shilling in both countries, of 8⅓ per cent (the percentage signifying
the surplus of Irish pounds purchased by £100 sterling). In effecting
the new valuations of gold and silver a mint rate higher than that in
England was established. This probably led to a tendency to export
silver and to use gold for internal use; although the real difficulty in
Ireland in these years was a scarcity of coin in general more than a
shortage of any particular metal. In May 1695 the valuations of gold
and silver were again raised, but without adjusting the Irish mint
ratio to correspond to that in England. The new value of the guinea
was 26/– and the shilling was raised to 1/2d. In England the monetary
situation was out of hand at this time, and the revaluation of coinage
in Ireland was probably an attempt at preventing a further draining
away of coin to England. But the Irish Government's attempt was
immediately nullified by the continuing deterioration of the situation
in England. In June, the month following the revaluation of the
coinage in Ireland, the guinea soared to 30/– in England. The result
was that Irish exchange on London now took on a favourable appearance,[1] sustained no doubt by the export of guineas to England,
and only became unfavourable again when in April 1696 the guinea
was reduced to 22/– in England. The apparently high rates of exchange in the last four years of the century are not in the main a
result of an adverse balance of payments.[2] Instead they reflect the
establishment of a new par rate brought about by the failure to re-
adjust the value of coins in Ireland to correspond to their changing
valuations in England. On the basis of the increased valuation of the
shilling the actual par was £100 sterling=£116.6 Irish, and in terms
of guineas was even higher once order was restored in the monetary
field in England and the value of the guinea there was reduced. Had
money in Ireland been reduced in value, the exchange would have
fallen in proportion,[3] and this did in fact happen in 1701 when the
value of coinage current in Ireland was reduced by proclamation.
The proclamation was issued in June, and exchange which was 22½

[1]See Record Office, The Castle, Carlisle. Sir John Lowther's letters to Whitehaven, London, 30 May 1696 (no. 14); 1 Aug. 1696 (no. 23).
[2]There appears in fact to have been a substantial inflow of specie to Ireland
in at least some of these years. In 1697 Mary Ffingall wrote from Liege that 'my
son writes that money was never so plentifull in Ireland as now'. National Library,
Dublin. Fingall MSS., MS. 8020. 23 June 1697.
[3]See, e.g., P.R.O., C104/12, letter book, Edward Hoare, Dublin, 18 May 1696.

per cent in the previous month (May) had in the beginning of July fallen to 10½ per cent. The par of exchange was now back at the level determined in 1689, and was to remain at this level officially till the separate Irish currency, which was itself purely conceptual as it had no distinctive physical embodiment, was abolished in 1826.

As a result of the proclamation of 1701 the mint ratio in Ireland was lower than in England. But once the guinea was reduced from 21/6d. to 21/- in England in 1717 and the mint ratio thereby reduced to 15.21 the unaltered Irish mint ratio was higher than the English and encouraged the export of silver coin there. The situation was worsened by the fact that the valuations set on foreign gold coin by the proclamations of 1712 and 1715 were maintained, and that when the New Portuguese Gold was valued by proclamation in 1725 it was valued in the light of the previous proclamations relating to foreign gold, and not in the light of the altered mint ratio in England. The faulty mint ratio soon reduced the Irish currency to a state of chaos. Silver and the only slightly overvalued English guineas were both exported and replaced by the more heavily overvalued foreign gold. By 1737 the coinage in Ireland consisted substantially of moydores and New Portuguese Gold, the coins in which the margin of over-valuation had been greatest. Silver had become acutely scarce. Because of the great number of overvalued gold coins of large denominations, small cash transactions were both complicated and difficult, and silver could be obtained only at a premium. The high course of exchange in the 1720s and 1730s is only to some degree a result of adverse trading conditions and poor harvests. The permanently high rates over the period 1717–37 are a reflection of the deterioration of the coinage in Ireland in those years. As the bulk of the coinage came to consist of overvalued gold, the old par rate of 108⅓ did in fact cease to apply, and the real or effective par rose to 110 or 111, though it would be truer to say that there were now several par levels of exchange, depending on what coin the remitter had or was able to acquire.

After years of controversy over the state of the coinage in Ireland[1] the foreign gold was at last reduced to its real value by a proclamation of August 1737, and the guinea reduced from 23/- to 22/9d., thus establishing a mint ratio exactly the same as that in England. The

---

[1]The reduction of the gold coinage was strenuously opposed by the Irish bankers and remitters. See *Letters written by His Excellency Hugh Boulter . . .op. cit.*, 2 vols., passim.

proclamation was completely effective in bringing to an end the distortions of the course of exchange between Dublin and London, and the sudden fall in the rates of exchange at this time reflects the re-establishment of a par rate of $8\frac{1}{3}$ per cent. But the revaluing of the gold coin failed to restore the supply of silver, of which there remained a severe shortage to the very end of the century. As silver was itself undervalued in England and was being exported to regions where a more favourable mint ratio held, the mere maintenance in Ireland of a mint ratio corresponding exactly to that in England was not in itself sufficient to restore a supply of silver to Ireland. Had a slight premium been placed on foreign silver in Ireland at the same time as the gold was reduced,[1] the Irish mint ratio would have been more favourable than the English and would have encouraged the inflow of silver. But the proclamation left the valuations of silver unaltered, and one may detect in the inability of the Irish Government to take any action, however modest, to rectify the situation the influence of the English Treasury which feared that any such steps would reduce the already limited supply in England.

II. THE INSTITUTIONAL STRUCTURE OF THE
IRISH FOREIGN EXCHANGE MARKET

London was the chief overseas centre for Irish remittances, though London's own share of Anglo-Irish trade did not become significant till the second decade of the eighteenth century. The reasons for London's primacy in the Irish exchange business are clear. On the one hand, Irish absentee landlords tended to settle in London or at least to incur debts there, and as a result there was a regular demand for bills payable in London. On the other hand, London being the centre of English trade, finance and insurance, most merchants in the English outports had correspondents there. In these circumstances payment through London worked to the advantage of both Irish drawer and English debtor-merchant. The Irish merchant by drawing on a London correspondent found it easier to pass bills in Ireland; and at the same time the merchant in the English outports also found bills on London to his advantage because many of his other payments

---

[1]The Irish Government itself made the moderate demand that the bullion price of silver in Ireland, where all foreign silver passed by weight, should be raised to the middle price of silver bullion in England. See *Calendar of Treasury Books and Papers, 1735–8*, p. 201.

and receipts were already channelled through the English capital. As a result the great bulk of financial transactions between Ireland and the English outports was already being effected through London in the 1660s. Indeed, long before the union between England and Scotland, Irish exchanges with Edinburgh were transacted through London.

There was of course some direct remitting of funds between Ireland and a few of the outports. But the volume of this business was during most of the century negligible. There were some small direct dealings with Bristol, occasioned by that city's closeness to Bath, where many of the Irish gentry sojourned during the season. Some Irish merchants and bankers were prepared to provide facilities for Irish remitters by drawing on Bristol correspondents, and on the other hand merchants in Bristol as in Chester at the head of the main overland route from London to Ireland occasionally drew on Irish correspondents. The Dublin banking firm of La Touche and Kane, for instance, had some small balances in the hands of a correspondent in Chester and of another in Bristol over the years 1719–26.[1] Direct dealings with the outports were relatively few, and both the demand for, and the supply of, such bills was very small. In Chester, even at the time of the great linen fairs, bills on Dublin were not available. One Irish merchant who attended a Chester fair in 1734 sent the guineas he received in payment for linens to London, hidden in a bale of linens, in order to have his money remitted from there.[2] Towards the end of the century there were some direct exchange transactions with Liverpool and Glasgow, both from Dublin and Belfast, for which market rates were quoted. However, this business was limited both on the side of demand and of supply. Bills were not always available and on the other hand, because of the relatively small demand for them, merchants drawing on Liverpool or Glasgow were able to sell their bills only by charging a lower exchange than the current rates on London. Moreover, with the exception of some remitting from Glasgow to both Dublin and Belfast, these exchange dealings arose exclusively from the export business. Glasgow alone of British provincial ports was a centre of any importance in the exchange business with Ireland, and a fairly substantial portion of Irish trade with Scotland in the last decade of the eighteenth century appears to have been financed

[1]National Library, Dublin, MS. 2785. Abstract Ledger of La Touche and Kane.
[2]P.R.O., C 105/15, Elijah Chamberlain to Jas. Hudson, Chester, 1 July 1734.

by direct dealings from both Dublin and Belfast. There was little or no demand for bills on other centres in Scotland, and a Dublin bill merchant wrote that in Dublin 'drafts on the interior parts of Scotland unless payable in Glasgow can seldom be negotiated without great inconvenience'.[1] In a few cases merchants were able to finance transactions by dealings outside the regular foreign exchange market, but this was exceptional. Thus, Robert Gemmill, a Belfast cotton manufacturer and yarn wholesaler, also had a manufactory in Paisley, and was therefore able to establish a credit with the Paisley Bank. The yarns he purchased in Scotland for his Belfast business were paid for by the discounting at the Bank of bills drawn either by Gemmill himself or by the yarn spinning firm on Gemmill.[2] With these exceptions it can be said that the bulk of the outport trade was financed through London and that this pattern was maintained into the nineteenth century.

The nature of the personnel concerned in the exchange business with Ireland tended to change in the course of the century. Over most of the century a great part of the exchange business had been dominated by the Irish bankers acting through their London correspondents, and by a limited number of London merchant houses, who had commercial and financial dealings with Ireland. But the supersession of the specialist merchant by the manufacturers and wholesalers toward the end of the century brought many London financial and commercial houses into the bill trade in their capacity as London agents for the manufacturers in the English outports and industrial areas. And, on the other hand, because of the greatly increased volume of payments, the Irish manufacturer or wholesaler requiring to finance his imports was able to purchase a bill or bills on the Dublin exchange and establish a credit with a London house, instead of having to rely, as previously, on exchange facilities provided by Irish merchants or bankers through the medium of their London correspondents.

That payments between Ireland and England were effected through London was in itself a factor in developing the remission of funds between the English outports and London by multiplying inland transactions. On the other hand, in Whitehaven, where the receipts

---

[1]National Library, Dublin, MS. 5679. Letter book of Robert Shaw & Son, 1795-6, p. 533. 26 July 1796.
[2]University of Manchester, McConnel & Kennedy MSS., Letters from Irish correspondents, 1795-1803.

of coal exports to Ireland were remitted back in specie and not in
bills on London, exchange with the English capital was extremely
difficult. Bills were scarce, money might have to be sent into the
neighbouring counties to procure bills on London, or entrusted to
the carriers operating between Kendal, forty miles from Whitehaven,
and London.[1] Because of their strong position in these circumstances,
the carriers were able to exact high rates for their services and at one
stage Sir James Lowther, owner of the Whitehaven collieries, was so
dissatisfied with the expenses involved in having funds remitted to
him in London that he considered the possibility of having them remitted via Dublin.[2] The tobacco trade, extensive in Whitehaven up
to the middle of the century, was the only source which gave rise—
but only seasonally—to drawings on London by the Whitehaven
merchants. However, the merchants were heavily dependent on the
cash brought in by the coal trade to Ireland in having their bills discounted, and when the coal trade failed discounting was not easy.[3]
Much of the tobacco imported in Whitehaven was re-exported to
Ireland, and it is therefore not surprising that some of the drawings
by Whitehaven merchants were on London merchants having Irish
business.

An additional reason for the importance of London in the Irish
exchange business was that there was little direct exchange dealing
between Ireland and the continent.[4] The merchants in Cork at times
urged the merchants in French ports to avoid the loss on exchange
through London by seeking direct remittance from France,[5] but such
bills were comparatively few and the great bulk of payments between
the two countries was channelled through London.

Though remitting through London was normally unfavourable in
the provision exporting season to the foreign buyer, merchants still
had the benefit of smooth remitting and also at times of a gain in

[1]Custom House, Whitehaven, Letter Books. Sir James Lowther observed that
'the scarcity of bills of exchange shows the poverty of the town'. Record Office,
The Castle, Carlisle. Sir James Lowther, London, 21 March 1723-4 (no. 127).

[2]Record Office, The Castle, Carlisle. Sir James Lowther, London, 17 Feb.,
19 Feb., 5, 12, 15, 22 March 1737 (nos. 86, 87, 92, 95, 96, 99).

[3]Custom House, Whitehaven. Letter Book, no. 1, 5 Feb. 1729.

[4]See L.M. Cullen, 'An Ceangal Tráchtála . . .' (Trade relations . . .). op. cit.,
pp. 83-91.

[5]A merchant in Cork in 1734 advised a Bordeaux merchant 'tacher un (sic) autre
fois de trouver des remises en droiture. Vous les trouverez toujours en prenant
vos temps (sic)'. Archives Departementales de la Gironde (Bordeaux), 7B 1779,
Bradshaw, Cork, 25 August 1734.

similar exchange dealings transacted outside the period September to December. Remitting through London would at all times have been easier than direct exchange dealings. Direct dealings with the continent would have reflected the seasonal nature of Irish commodity trade, and remitting in one direction or in the other would at all times present difficulties. On the other hand, in remitting through London advantage was taken of the large and continuous flow of payments between the principal continental centres and London, and between London and Dublin. This easy remitting of money was of especial importance in the Irish provision trade, which was to a large extent carried on by factors with limited capital, who having to purchase on cash terms required to be put in funds before they could fulfil foreign orders. Direct remitting from France or Spain was uncertain and would have involved delay. Consequently, in the interests of economy of time and correspondence, the most convenient course for a foreign merchant was to have funds or a credit in London, and have his correspondent there remit or more commonly be drawn on by the Irish merchant. There continued to exist some direct exchange with the continent, but the amount was inconsiderable. On the one hand bankers and merchants in Ireland were prepared to draw small bills to the order of non-commercial remitters to the continent. On the other hand merchants in France were sometimes able to remit small bills on Dublin, and Irish merchants and bankers in France provided some foreign exchange facilities for Irish travellers on the continent as well as for residents there. Some of the smaller Irish merchants and smugglers of the seventeenth and early eighteenth century, however, financing their homeward cargoes with the proceeds of an outward one, scarcely had need of remittances of any nature.

French merchants sometimes purchased bills on London to remit funds to Ireland. Such bills were, however, difficult to negotiate both in Cork and Dublin,[1] and did not feature prominently in the financing of Franco-Irish trade. Business between Ireland and France and other foreign countries had therefore to be financed almost invariably through London correspondents. Thus the English agent for the Bordeaux house of Pelet was Thomas Thomas and Son, and in the

---

[1] See Archives Departementales de la Gironde, 7B1575, Blocks and Murray, Dublin, 28 August 1784; 7B 1800, Thomas Thomas, London, 8 August 1726; B.M., Egmont Papers, Add. MSS. 47004, p. 189, Richard Purcell, Canturk, 16 October 1739.

'twenties and 'thirties he remitted to Cork or was drawn on by Pelet's factors in Cork.[1] Thomas also acted as the London agent of another Bordeaux house, that of the Irish family of Black.[2] John Black had retired from business in 1750, and spent much of the remainder of his life in Ireland, leaving the Bordeaux business in the hands of his sons. At the time of his retirement he had £3,200 in British annuities 'under Messrs. Thomas of London's directions',[3] and in the course of the following years Messrs. Thomas and Son continued to carry out financial transactions relating to trade and exchanges between Ireland and France for him, partly by realising some of his English annuities.[4] Exchange through the hands of London correspondents was, of course, typical of the other sectors of Irish overseas trade as well, and trade with Spain, Portugal, Northern America, the West Indies, and with the Baltic was usually financed in this manner. The Belfast merchant, Daniel Mussenden, for example, effected his foreign exchange dealings in the 'fifties through a London firm, Allen and Marlar. He remitted bills to them and in turn Mussenden's Rotterdam agents, Rocquette and Van Zeylingen, on whom Mussenden's creditors, even as far away as Drontheim (Trondheim) in Norway and Dantzig, drew, had funds remitted from or drew on Allen and Marlar.[5] The Dublin bankers, La Touche and Kane, also normally held a small cash balance arising from their exchange dealings in the hands of a Rotterdam correspondent, Peter de la Motte, though as it is invariably included among their English balances, it would appear that these dealings were effected through London.[6] A striking example of Ireland's dependence on the London exchange market is afforded by the example of the Dublin house of Dillon, provision merchants, wine importers and bankers who, although concerned in trade with Holland, France and Spain effected little

[1]Archives Departementales de la Gironde, 7B 1779, 7B 1800.
[2]Public Record Office of Northern Ireland, Belfast, Black Papers, T.1073/7, 8, 16.
[3]Ibid., T.1073/7/1, 2. Account of John Black's Estate, 1 Jan. 1751. Again, in 1752 Black instructed Messrs. Thomas to employ his 'liquid balance of acco' in public funds.
[4]In July 1756 at a time when Messrs. Thomas had accepted his sons' draft, Black's public funds had fallen from 106 to 88⅝, and to avoid a loss in selling Messrs. Thomas proposed to advance the sum required to honour the draft of 5,000 livres, at 5 per cent on the security of £700 of the public funds. T.1073/8/9, 1 July 1756.
[5]Public Record Office of Northern Ireland, Belfast. Mussenden Papers, uncatalogued collection, 1754-7.
[6]National Library, Dublin. Abstract Ledger of La Touche and Kane, 1719-26.

exchange business direct with the continent. On the other hand they transacted a large volume of remitting with London, where a member of the family was their correspondent. Another member of the family was a merchant in Rotterdam. His bill drawings on Dublin were infrequent, and sometimes merely represented transfers to the account of the London house. Bill drawings on the Dublin branch of the firm by correspondents in Cadiz, Bordeaux or Dunkirk were very rare. Apart from the limited volume of bill drawings by Theobald Dillon of Rotterdam the only regular call on the resources of the Dublin house by continental correspondents lay in the bills, generally of a small value and to the order of non-merchant remitters drawn by the Irish houses of Waters and subsequently of Woulfe in Paris.

Dealings with Ireland must therefore have formed a considerable part of London's foreign exchange business, and many London agents acted financially for interests in Ireland. Already in the second half of the seventeenth century many London merchants and goldsmiths were much concerned in exchange dealings between the two countries. But once the Irish banks began to develop from the end of the century onwards, they gradually dominated the exchange business between the two countries, acting through their agents or correspondents in London. Burton's Bank already had a correspondent, Haistwell, in London in 1696, and soon employed a second one. Writing from Dublin in 1707 to a remitter in the Irish countryside, Burton's partner, Harrison suggested to him: 'When you have any such occasion again send to me and I will give you directions to Messrs. Mitchell and Finlay who are people yt I now imploy as well as Mr. Haistwell for he has disobliged several people, yt will not now goe near him.'[1] One of the most prominent of the London agents was Nathaniel Gould who in 1737 was described as 'the great remitter from Dublin and Cork both . . . his correspondents that draw on him from Dublin are Hugh Henry and Company and at Cork they are Harper, Mitchell and Armstrong, who draw bills upon him payable here at 21 days sight'.[2] The bankers and their agents were sometimes allied by religious ties. The Huguenot house of Puget acted as a London agent

[1]Public Record Office of Ireland, Dublin. Sarsfield Vesey Papers. Correspondence, no. 65. Fran. Harrison to Agmondisham Vesey, 6 Sept. 1707. Finlay may be the Robert Finley (sic) in London, who with another London banker Cairns, was described in 1720 as 'the two bankers for Ireland'. B.M., Egmont Papers, Add. MSS. 46985, p. 112, Percival, London, 29 Sept. 1720.

[2]Record Office, The Castle, Carlisle. Letters of Sir James Lowther, London, 17 Feb. 1736/7 (no. 86).

for the Dublin bank of La Touche through the century, besides acting from 1783 as London agent for the Bank of Ireland, of which a member of the La Touche family was first Governor. The London Quaker merchant Jonathan Gurnell was a correspondent and 'intimate old friend'[1] of Joseph Fade, the Quaker merchant and banker in Dublin, while a member of the Quaker merchant and banking family of Hoare in Cork moved to London and married into the house in 1744, the house now being styled Gurnell and Hoare.[2] Among other London houses acting for Irish banks were the house of Bartholomew Burton,[3] correspondent in the 1750s for the Dublin bank of Lennox and French, and the house of Nesbitt and Stewart, who, besides their other Irish business, were appointed correspondent in 1789 of the newly founded Bank of Limerick.[4] The business was controlled mainly by the Irish banks, the London correspondents being employed in the capacity of agents in return for a percentage commission on the volume of dealings. This did not, of course, exclude them from transacting business for other Irish bankers and merchants, or from engaging in exchange dealings on their own account. In 1764 the London merchant and banker, Sir George Colebrooke, opened a Dublin bank which stopped payment temporarily in 1770, and failed in 1773, a year before Colebrooke's London failure. But apart from this short-lived challenge the Irish houses were secure in their position in the exchange business throughout the century.

In addition to the banks and their London agents, exchange dealings, especially with the continent, were effected through merchant houses in London, such as Thomas Thomas & Son, and George Fitzgerald, the merchant from County Waterford, who had a wide correspondence both in Ireland and on the continent. The importers of Irish linen in London also developed an extensive bill trade at first mainly with Dublin, but later with Belfast also, where there was no

[1]National Library of Ireland, MS. 8020. Fingall MSS. Dillon and Cruise, London, 24 March 1742/3. Joseph Fade was founder of the Dublin bank later styled Willcocks and Dawson.

[2]Samuel Hoare of Cork, in April 1744, married Grizell Gurnell and became a partner in the mercantile house of Jonathan Gurnell. He died only in 1796, and a ledger covering his partnership and personal accounts over the years 1744-96 survives in the Public Museum, Cork.

[3]Burton was a London Dutchman. See Wilson, *Anglo-Dutch commerce and finance*, pp. 134, 161.

[4]E. O'Kelly, 'The old Limerick private bankers', *Journal of the Old Limerick Society*, vol. I, no. I (December 1946) p. 15.

banking system. The bleachers therefore discounted their bills on London with local or Dublin merchants, who thus established a credit with the London linen importers, which in turn they drew on or had their English creditors draw on as occasion required. In this manner the London linen merchants built up a large Irish bill business which far exceeded the requirements of the linen trade. In the 1770s, for instance, sugar refiners in Belfast effected insurance on sugar imports from Glasgow through the linen merchants in London, a fact that suggests that by taking the bills of bleachers they accumulated funds in the hands of the linen merchants in London. This pattern of business was established at an early date, and already in the 1750s the financial transactions of the trade between Belfast and North America were cleared through the linen merchants in London.[1]

The functions performed by the London houses for Irish merchants and bankers were primarily those of bill agents. But they also did other business. Thomas Thomas, for example, sometimes ordered commodities in Cork on the account of merchants in the French ports, and other London merchants might like Allen and Marlar act as brokers in receiving sugars from the West Indies for re-shipment to Ireland. Insurance of ventures on Irish account not only in Anglo-Irish trade but in Irish overseas trade generally, was commonly effected through the London houses, and in this connection it is significant that both Thomas Thomas and George Fitzgerald were members of the London Assurance Company.[2] Several of the London bankers engaged in exchange dealings with Ireland had at one stage been merchants, and the bill trade of both bankers and merchants reflected to some extent at least the nature of the commodity trade in which they were, or had been at one time, engaged. Some of the London houses also made advances to Irish merchants. The linen importers in particular served a vital function in the financing of the linen trade by advancing money to the bleachers either on arrival of the linens in London or later at the time of sale on long credit terms to buyers. They also appear to have been prepared to allow some temporary accommodation to merchants engaged in the trade between Belfast and North America. In some cases, London agents may have advanced sums to Irish manufacturers. In 1785, for instance, in

---

[1] New York Historical Society Library. Letter Book of Greg and Cunningham, 1756-7.

[2] A.H. John, 'The London Assurance Company and the marine assurance market of the eighteenth century', *Economica*, May 1958, p. 134.

a list of the debts of Robert Brooke, the founder of the famous cotton factory at Prosperous near Dublin, a sum of £1,300 was owing to 'Messrs. Nesbitts and Stewarts' of London.[1] But there is little evidence of such lending by London houses, apart from the special case of the linen industry. The fact that a house was committed to long-term loans would have caused great uneasiness among its exchange customers, even had the nature of the Irish bill trade, with its emphasis on the 21 day bill, permitted such. The house of Gurnell, Harman and Hoare were by the 1770s granting long-term accommodation, but by this time the house had become primarily a banking business in the London area, and appears to have virtually withdrawn from the Irish exchange business, apart from keeping the English balances of some of the Irish Quaker merchants.

On the Irish side, Dublin never quite dominated Anglo-Irish payments as did London at the other end. There was at all times a fairly substantial amount of business transacted from one or more provincial centres in Ireland. However, in the second half of the seventeenth century Cork was the only centre outside Dublin to effect dealings on a fairly large scale. Direct exchange dealings from Belfast, at this time a minor port, were very occasional. There was only one substantial merchant in the town, and as much of the port's staple commodity, butter, was shipped to Dublin, or exported directly on the account or by order of Dublin merchants, Belfast's exchange business with London was for the most part effected through merchant correspondents in the Irish capital. The primitive economy of the north-east in this period is evident from the fact that the landlords of the region, even as late as 1667, refused the merchants in Belfast any allowance for exchange on remittances to Dublin or London, and where exchange was charged it was by individual agreement between remitter and merchant.[2] Belfast was, however, a growing town. The rapid expansion of the linen industry in the surrounding areas from the early eighteenth century, led to a more widespread negotiation locally of bills drawn directly on London, although the bills themselves generally originated in shipments of linens through Dublin. As early as 1739 at least, there is evidence of a fairly regular course of exchange on London. But it was still primitively organized and even into the second half of the century much of the remitting

[1] *Journals of the Irish House of Commons,* vol. 12, p. ccxxi.
[2] Linen Hall Library, Belfast. Letter Book of George Macartney, merchant, 1660–7.

was effected through contact between landlord's agents and drapers or bleachers, though the latter were now in a position to charge an exchange for their dealings which tended to follow the rates on the much larger Dublin exchange.

The Belfast exchange market remained at all times heavily dependent upon the Dublin market. Most of Belfast's linens and butter were sold in or shipped through Dublin, and as a consequence direct exchange dealings with London remained subsidiary to business effected through Dublin. Nevertheless, despite the large and growing volume of commodity trade between Belfast and Dublin, remitting of money between the two centres remained difficult until well into the eighteenth century. As late as 1748 rents could be remitted only seasonally to the capital with any readiness through applying to linen drapers or corn merchants who had sent goods to the capital. But difficult as was remitting between the north and Dublin, it was no more difficult than in the other provinces. Exchange in Cork at this time enjoyed a certain degree of independence of the Dublin market. Exchange rates in Cork normally fell heavily in the last four months of the year, when Cork merchants were drawing on London for their exports, becoming as much as 2 per cent or more less unfavourable than the current rates in Dublin. Landlords in Dublin were anxious to remit through Cork to avoid the higher rates in Dublin, but despite the fact that Dublin and Cork were the only two large ports in the kingdom, this presented great difficulties. It was not possible to remit large sums at short notice and either by bill or exchequer acquittance it was necessary to start remitting in May, June, July or August to benefit by the falling exchange in September or October.[1] Difficulties in the inland exchange business were not, of course, peculiar to business between Dublin and Cork and Belfast. They were country-wide. In the more primitive parts the volume of the bill business was extremely small, and even opportunities of sending the specie by safe hand were few. Remitting by exchequer acquittance or Collector's receipt was frequently the only resort, and in remote areas the Collectors of the Revenue were the only bankers. This method was itself highly unsatisfactory. In the under-developed districts the revenue was exiguous and insufficient to cover even the costs of collection. The collectors themselves were dilatory and did not always give satisfaction. Even in the busy port of Cork the payment of exchequer

[1]See P.R.O., C. 110/46, bundle O, nos. 1, 3. Owen Gallagher to Oliver St. George, Dublin, 8 Jan., 19 Feb. 1729.

acquittances was 'tedious, because the Collector dales (*sic*) that way, and pays his own first'.[1] Exchequer acquittances were a last resort, and were never popular with remitters.

Conditions were, however, slowly improving. Banks and embryonic banks had become more numerous in the 1710s and 1720s, and though they generally originated in foreign exchange business the difficulties of inland exchange encouraged them to enter that field as well. Indeed, it was essential to their other business, because in consequence of the dominance of the Dublin exchange market much of their foreign business was on behalf of country clients. Landlords especially encountered great difficulties in having their rents remitted to Dublin or London. They, therefore, despite some initial distrust, favoured the new movement.[2] One short-lived bank was actually founded by two landlords, and even in the second half of the century there were several lesser banking establishments in Dublin run by land agents or rent receivers. Already in the 1720s the Dublin banks had widespread country commitments, though their services were inadequate as yet to satisfy fully the demand. But by the middle of the century the Dublin banks were doing a country-wide business,[3] and remitting large amounts of rent to England. Internal remitting was now fairly smooth. Lord Downshire's rents, for instance, which previously could be sent from the north to Dublin only with great difficulty, were from the beginning of the 1750s transmitted with ease;[4] and this development was repeated throughout the whole country.

As the volume of internal remitting grew, the rates on London in the several Irish centres became more interdependent. The Belfast rates were, of course, always dependent on the Dublin market, but for the second half of the century there is no evidence that exchange in Cork showed the same large seasonal deviations from the Dublin rates that it exhibited previously. Exchange rates in Belfast and Cork were always somewhat more favourable than those in Dublin, but apart from this slight permanent difference, itself a reflection of the

[1]Ibid., bundle O, no. 10. Owen Gallagher, Dublin, 4 Nov. 1729.
[2]'Before these blows, all gentlemen were becoming bankers or involved with them, now they begin to draw out'. H.M.C., *Report on MSS in various collections,* vol. VI, p. 61, 10 May 1734. Some of these gentlemen were, like Agmondisham Vesey, both merchants and members of the landed gentry.
[3]Cf. Primate Stone to Sackville, Dublin, March 11, 1753; 'The country gentlemen, old and young, are subject to the bankers and they are in the power of the Treasury'. H.M.C., *Stopford-Sackville MSS,* vol. I, p. 193.
[4]P.R.O. of Northern Ireland, D. 607. Downshire Papers.

12

favourable balance of payments arising to these ports by their large export commodity trade, there was in the second half of the century little variation, other than marginal, between the course of exchange in all three centres. This came about from the growing volume of internal trade and remitting. Importers in Dublin had now extended their business into all four provinces and, on the other hand, Dublin was a growing centre of consumption of Irish commodities. The growth of a large inland corn trade, both coastwise and by land-carriage, converging on the capital, especially contributed to the easing of internal remittance. It is, for example, significant that the large discounting business of the Dublin merchant Robert Shaw arose from his dealings as a commission agent in the inland flour trade.[1]

The growth of Irish internal trade, the use by merchants and bankers alike of correspondents in other towns, and the specialization in the bill trade developed by many merchants were all factors which, especially in the latter half of the century, made for a more closely integrated financial system. As Dublin was the greatest home market and the movement of goods tended in its direction, the capital was now coming for the first time to dominate the country's economic activity rather than to be just the most prominent regional centre. Purchases by a provincial merchant or shipper from a local merchant now tended to be paid for to a large extent by drawings on a Dublin bank or agent. Bills on Dublin were a common means of payment in the provinces, and because of their ready acceptance supplemented the rather sparse circulation of bank notes outside the two large banking centres of Dublin and Cork. The supply of Dublin bills in the provinces appears on the whole to have exceeded the demand and, as a result, there was generally a loss in passing bills on Dublin.

The loss on bills passed in the provinces is in contrast to the exchange regularly charged in Dublin for drawings on the country. In the 1720s for instance a not inconsiderable share of the income of the Dublin bank of La Touche and Kane originated in their Cork, Limerick and 'country' exchange business.[2] It was therefore more profitable to have a sum remitted to Dublin by taking bills in the provinces than to pay a 'great exchange' to someone in the capital prepared to pay cash for a balance in the country.[3] This tendency

[1]National Library, Dublin. Shaw MSS. 1785–97.
[2]National Library of Ireland, MS. 2785.
[3]Eusebius Low to Dr. Eaton Edwards, Dublin, 18 April, 1738, in the possession of Mr. Adrian E.O. Waters, Kilmacsimon, Bandon, Co. Cork.

appears to have been permanent, and in 1778 a creditor in Cork in a letter to Walter Butler at the Castle in Kilkenny, reminded him that 'there is always a loss on Dublin bills'.[1] Bills on Dublin were procurable in Cork at a less favourable rate than par only in the exceptional circumstance of Cork exchange rising above the Dublin exchange on London. Thus, in 1742 at a time when exchange on London was higher in Cork than in the Irish capital, his Cork agent informed Egmont that he had to pay twenty shillings exchange on a remittance of £150 to Dublin 'which is a very uncommon thing having never known before that a Dublin bill could not be had here at least at par'.[2] London bills on Dublin were also sometimes used to effect remittances from England to Cork, but this was a procedure which was little employed. Because of the relative weakness of the demand in Cork for means of payment on Dublin, there was a loss in passing these bills in Cork, which amounted for instance in the 1720s to ½ per cent and sometimes 1 per cent. In other words the loss on these bills reflected the course of inland exchange. In Cork serious remitting difficulties were again encountered during 1784. A northern bleacher informed a Dumfries correspondent on the subject of a sum of money due in Cork that 'as bills are extremely difficult to get there on Dublin, [I] am afraid it will be some time before I get the money, and attended with a great deal of expense'.[3] 1784 was a particularly bad year. Food prices were high; in contrast to the normally large surplus the balance of trade showed a deficit in the year ended 25 March 1783, and only a small surplus in the following year. In Cork a reluctance to accept bank notes developed, and there were rumours in the course of the summer that all was not well with Warren's Bank.[4] The change in the course of exchange between Cork and Dublin would thus appear to have foreshadowed the banking difficulties in Cork and the eventual failure of Warren's Bank in September 1784. In fact even as early as February a Dublin merchant had

[1]National Library, Dublin. Ormonde MSS., vol. 180, p. 295. Anastasia Foley, Cork, 24 June 1778.

[2]B.M., Egmont Papers, Add. MSS. 47007, p. 11. Richard Purcell, Cork, 13 Feb. 1741–2. Cf. B.M., Add. MSS. 46980. p. 107, Berkeley Taylor, Ballymacow, Co. Cork, 12 July 1715. See also National Library, Dublin, Microfilm N.3142, Thomas Bousfield to Theobald Dillon & Sons, Dublin, Cork, 9 July 1734; Macnemara & Whyte to do., Cork, 24 March 1727–8.

[3]Isaac Andrew & Sons Ltd., Belfast. John Andrews to Robert Donald, Dumfries. Comber, 3 June 1784.

[4]E. O'Kelly, *The old private banks and bankers of Munster* (Cork, 1959) pp. 48–9.

complained of a bill on Cork that 'there will be a greate loss on it at least 3 per cent. Tell Mr. Thom Burke not to receive bills on Cork—even Cork bank notes leaves a loss of 3 or 4d. a pound'.[1] Apart from temporary difficulties of the sort they encountered in 1784, the receipts of Cork merchants and bankers, augmented by their large scale discounting and negotiating in Dublin of bills on London which they took locally, were more than ample to meet the demand for remittances to Dublin.

Seasonal or temporary difficulties in remitting to Dublin were not infrequently encountered in some of the smaller centres in the first half of the century. In contrast to the position later in the 1770s it was for instance difficult to remit money from Kilkenny to Dublin in the 1730s and early 1740s.[2] In Galway in November 1734 it was stated that there were 'noe bills here now at parr'[3] and in March 1740 another Galway merchant complained that 'I cannot gett Dublin bills without paying 3d a pound exchange'.[4] However, it is clear that merchants were not always at this disadvantage in remitting. In November 1739 a Galway merchant promised to remit a sum to Dublin 'as soon as I gett a bill at parr of the money'.[5]

Because of the flow of payments to the provinces country bills payable in Dublin were in little demand, and the Bank of Ireland was not prepared to discount such. In August 1796 a Dublin discount house informed a bank in Waterford 'that country bills payable in Dublin are of no manner of use here as the Bank of Ireland will not discount such for any person nor have they ever been in the habit of doing so'.[6] The permanent loss on bills on Dublin, indicating as it does the great facility of drawing on the capital, is an indication of the extent to which the inland bill trade had developed. In the previous century, on the other hand, the scarcity of bills had been so acute that when Belfast exchange rates on Dublin and London first emerged in the 1670s, the merchants were seasonally able to exact an exchange of 2 to 2½ per cent for their drawings on Dublin.[7] But by the 1780s the

[1]National Library, Dublin. Blake MSS. John Blake, Dublin, 28 February 1784.
[2]National Library, Dublin. Microfilm N. 3142. Silvester Langton to Thomas Dillon & Co , Kilkenny, 4 April 1737, 11 February 1739-40.
[3]Ibid., Anthony Bodkin to Thomas Dillon & Co., Galway, 29 November 1734.
[4]Ibid., John Kirwan Patk. to Thomas Dillon & Co., 11 March 1739-40.
[5]Ibid., Anthony Bodkin to Thomas Dillon & Co., Galway, 20 November 1739.
[6]National Library, Dublin. Shaw MSS. 5680, Letter Book, 1796-7, p. 28, 30 August 1796.
[7]Linen Hall Library, Belfast. Letter Book of George Macartney, merchant, Belfast, 1678/9-1681.

bill trade between Belfast and Dublin had developed to such a degree that the Belfast merchants were forced to allow the full legal discount of 1½d. in the pound to the takers of their bills (at 31 days sight) with, at times, an additional allowance of ½d. Fluctuations in inland exchange would of course tend to be confined within the limits of the legal rate of interest and of the risks and costs of transferring specie[1] which declined as the eighteenth century progressed.

The bills employed in the inland trade were generally at 21 or 31 days sight, sometimes at shorter sight. Bills at longer usance became less uncommon in the last decades of the century. But the bulk of the trade was still effected by the 21 or 31 day sight bill, and the Dublin banks, including the Bank of Ireland, were generally not prepared to discount paper with more than two months to run. The importance of the Dublin discounting business was enhanced by the founding of the Bank of Ireland in 1783. The Bank was prepared to re-discount suitable paper and thus strengthened the discount houses and private banks operating in the Dublin market. Moreover, the Bank of Ireland was compelled by its charter to discount at 5 per cent, one per cent less than the legal maximum rate of interest in Ireland. The Dublin private banks and bill merchants followed suit and reduced their rate to 5 per cent. The country banks, on the other hand, continued to discount at 6 per cent, and the existence of the differential of one per cent between the rates of discount in the capital and in the country, added to the necessity of maintaining balances in the hands of their Dublin correspondents to finance their inland bill trade, encouraged provincial bill merchants and bankers to rediscount at Dublin houses the bills on England passed to them in the provinces.

Even in the early decades of the century provincial bills on London were readily negotiated in Dublin. In 1713, for example, an agent in Cork remitted a bill on London to his landlord then in Dublin, 'not readily meeting Dublin bills to my mind, and beleeving London bills to be always ready money in any trading town of the kingdom, spetially (sic) Dublin where at all times the bankers take bills'.[2] The bankers in Cork, Limerick and Waterford made a large use of this facility;[3] and this development, though itself a result of the growth and ease of remitting between the provinces and the capital, added

[1]See *Annual Register,* vol. 8, p. 326.
[2]B.M., Add. MSS. 46979, p. 266. Berkely Taylor to John Percival, Dublin, 31 May 1713.
[3]National Library, Dublin. Shaw MSS., 1785–97.

to the forces making the subsidiary centres of exchange closely dependent on the course of exchange between Dublin and London. A high Dublin exchange on London encouraged provincial merchants and bankers to rediscount or negotiate in Dublin, the English bills they took locally; and a fall in Dublin exchange led them to pass their bills locally, thus reducing the local exchange and bringing it into line with the market rates in Dublin.

As a consequence of these developments, Dublin in the last decades of the century dominated Irish foreign exchange dealings to a greater extent than ever previously. Dealings from Belfast and Cork were, of course, substantial, but the exchange market in these centres was by its nature subsidiary to the Dublin market. The dealings arose purely from the great export trade carried on in the two centres. Belfast merchants and Cork merchants and bankers quoted rates on London, but on the other hand, there was no London exchange on Cork or Belfast, and direct remittance from London to either centre was limited. In the last three decades of the century there were also some small direct exchange dealings on London from Waterford, which rivalled Cork in the butter trade to England, and probably, also from Newry, whose linen exports to England equalled, and at times exceeded, those of Belfast over much of the second half of the century.[1] Occasional business was also done from Londonderry and at the end of the century a small discount house in Galway also was prepared to draw on London. But Dublin alone, with its country bill trade and its large import trade, had a fully developed exchange market, and remittances to and from Ireland for that reason tended to centre on it.

Although at the end of the century over a half of the linen exports were being shipped direct from the North, even Northern bleachers exporting directly continued to carry out much of their exchange dealings through Dublin. This arose from the existence in Dublin of relatively abundant discounting facilities. Bleachers negotiated and, where necessary, discounted many of their bills on London with the linen factors in Dublin, and financed their purchases of unbleached cloth by the cash acquired from the sale of their inland bills on Dublin. In the North, the demand for gold by the landlords and, consequently by the peasant weavers, made the successful operation of a local banking or large discounting business impossible.

---

[1] A Newry rate on London certainly existed in 1803. See *Report of the Committee on the circulating paper, the special and the current coin of Ireland,* 1804, reprinted 1826, Appendix M.

III. SEASONAL AND SHORT-TERM FLUCTUATIONS
IN EXCHANGES

Exchanges between Ireland and London were, of course, subject to seasonal influences, especially as Irish exports were predominantly agricultural. The relatively heavy discounting of bills in the second half of the year, therefore, tended to bring exchange rates down, and on the other hand pressure to remit to London both by importing merchants and landlords' agents raised the rates in the early months of the year, when opportunity for Irish merchants to draw on London was smallest. Seasonal influences were most pronounced in the seventeenth century when the Irish foreign exchange market was relatively primitively organised. It was stated in this period that bills were only 'procurable at a moderate rate of exchange', in two months, May and October.[1] These two months corresponded roughly to the Irish exporting seasons. By May factors in the Irish ports were beginning to receive funds for purchasing butter and wool, and by October the beef-slaughtering season was in full swing. However, the effect of seasonal factors was less apparent in the eighteenth century, though in Cork exchange rates in the first half of the century continued to fall heavily in the last four months of the year, as a result of the great foreign demand for beef. But in the latter half of the century there were no violent fluctuations in the course of exchange in Cork, and the seasonal movements of exchange rates corresponded broadly to those in Dublin and Belfast.

Seasonal or short-term factors, besides occasioning movements in the course of exchange, also tended at times to distort the normal relation between the level of exchange on both sides of the Irish sea. Under ordinary circumstances London quotations on Dublin were one per cent higher than Dublin quotations on London. This difference represented interest for two months on a remittance from London by way of 21 day bills.[2] The fact that the charge for interest was

[1] Irish MSS Comm., *Calendar of Orrery Papers,* ed. E. MacLysaght, p 184.

[2] The position is explained clearly in a letter from a Dublin merchant to a merchant in London in 1731: '. . I think its' more to thy advantage to be drawn on for notwithstanding that exch. is generally 1 per cent higher with you than here yet consider when thou art drawn on I receive the money a month at least before thou pays it, and if thou remitt, (thou) must pay ye money a month before I can receive it here wch. makes 2 months add ye interest of which is above 1 per cent.' P.R.O., C. 105/15, Wm. Clarke to Jas. Hudson, Dublin, 1 Jan. 1731–2. See also Foster: *Essay on exchanges* (London, 1804) p. 64, and Appendix VII, p. 208; F.W. Fetter, *The Irish pound* (London, 1955) p. 19, note.

additional to London exchange on Dublin and not to Dublin exchange on London arose because the great bulk of bills originated
directly or indirectly in movements of goods and as the balance of
Irish overseas trade was highly favourable, the Irish merchants and
Irish bankers doing exchange business were normally in a far better
position to draw bills on London than were English merchants or
bankers to draw on Dublin. Dublin was in fact the activating centre
of the exchange business between the two countries. However, the
spread of one per cent between the charges in the two centres was not
a fixed one. When drawings in Dublin happened to be exceptionally
low by comparison with the demand for remittances, the pressure to
remit raised Dublin exchange as high as that in London or even above
it. This was, however, unusual, because of the generally favourable
trends of Irish overseas payments, but in the 1720s, when the balance
of payments tended on the whole to be unfavourable to Ireland,
Dublin exchange appears to have been frequently as high as the exchange in London. A more common phenomenon was that the
differential in favour of the Irish exchange on London become wider
than one per cent, as a result of the great seasonal drawings for Irish
exports. These drawings tended to depress the exchange, and their
influence is most noticeable in the rather limited Cork bill market,
where in the first half of the century rates became much more favourable than the course of exchange between Dublin and London during
the last four months of the year. But from the middle of the century
the spread between the rates appears to have been on the whole stable
except under the stress of exceptional market conditions. A financial
crisis in Dublin with the resulting decline in the discounting of bills
by merchants and bankers also made the Dublin exchange fall below
the course in London. The low state of credit and the inactive discount market in Ireland in 1770 explains why in December of that
year exchange on London was only $6\frac{3}{4}$ per cent, whereas the quotations in London held as high as $9\frac{1}{5}$ per cent.[1] In March 1797 exchange
had declined to as little as $4\frac{1}{2}$ per cent because of a dull discounting
market, whereas in London exchange was at the time as high as 9
per cent. Conversely, during the height of the South Sea Bubble panic,
the fall in rates in Dublin to a level well below London exchange is
accounted for by Irish doubts of the creditworthiness of the London

[1] News from Dublin, 22 December, in *Cork Hibernian Chronicle,* 24 December
1770.

correspondents and merchants on whom bills were drawn. Ireland was not directly implicated in the crisis, and London quotations on Ireland remained high, since bills on Ireland were for that reason much less distrusted. A local shortage of coin was also capable of producing a fall of exchange, and such a shortage occasioned by cash purchases of provisions was one reason contributing at times to the sharp seasonal decline in Cork rates in the early eighteenth century.[1]

Large variations in exchanges, either in the seasonal movement of the course of exchange or between the quotations on both sides of the Irish Sea, were exceptional in the second half of the century. An enlarged supply of specie and falling costs of transporting it were one factor in achieving this result. Whereas costs of remitting specie between the two countries amounted to 2 per cent or more in the first half of the century, they had fallen as low as one per cent to $1\frac{1}{2}$ per cent at the end of the century. Again the elaboration of the Dublin exchange market had a powerful effect in lessening the impact of seasonal heavy drawings on London or of temporary pressure to remit, which had made rates swing so markedly up to the early eighteenth century. As early as 1720 the Dublin banks appear to have been discounting on a much larger scale than they drew on London in the last half of the year, and with the balances they thereby accumulated were better enabled to meet the demand for remittances to London in the early months of the year. Variations between the level of rates charged in Dublin and London were moreover eliminated by the actions of speculators. If the spread between the rates in the two centres was wide enough it became profitable to ship gold from the centre with the higher exchange rates to finance bill drawings. The increased bill drawings in turn served to reduce the exchange. Where a gap persisted, speculators could also make a profit by purchasing bills at the centre with the lower rate of exchange and remitting the proceeds in bills purchased at the other end.[2]

---

[1]Archives Departementales de la Gironde, 7B 1779, Carré to Pelet, Cork, 28 Sept., 1731; B.M., Egmont Papers, Add. MSS. 46978, p. 305, W. Turner, Churchtown, 31 Jan. 1709-10; Add. MSS. 46998, p. 187, William Taylor, 16 Oct. 1733.

[2]A Dublin discounting house wrote in March 1797 that 'we are in the habit of remitting bills and perhaps drawing at a shorter sight or letting them become due and have returns made us'. (National Library, Dublin, Shaw MSS. 5680, p. 232, 14 March 1797.)

IV. LONG-TERM FLUCTUATIONS AND THE
CHARACTER OF THE BALANCE OF PAYMENTS

The course of exchange was on the whole against Ireland at the time
of the Restoration.[1] Remittances were effected at about 2 to 4 per
cent, though in the spring and again in August exchange might fall
to par.[2] The Cattle Acts and war conditions, however, raised the
exchange, and in April and May 1666 rates rose to 5 and 6 per cent.[3]
They worsened in the following years under the full impact of the
Great Cattle Act of 1666, and in 1672 when the export trade was
hampered by the outbreak of the Dutch War rates rose to as much
as 15 per cent with an overall average of about 10 per cent during the
year. However, such a rise was exceptional, and over most of the
'seventies and 'eighties the course of exchange appears to have
averaged 7 to 8 per cent.[4]

The actual rates fluctuated seasonally between 10 per cent and 5
per cent, and exceptionally declined to 3 per cent in September 1679
as a result of very brisk butter exports. In the last four years of the
'eighties the exchange rose sharply again on account of the political
uneasiness of the Protestant merchant community which was leading
them to transfer their effects to England. In February 1687 it actually
rose to 14 per cent. Exchange rates rose to a very high level in the
years 1696-1701 and again over the years 1717-37, but both periods
represent plateaux caused by an alteration in the effective par level
of exchange, arising from the deterioration of the Irish currency in
these periods. If allowance is made for this rise of the par of exchange,
the exchanges in these years were not as a rule quite so strikingly

[1]According to a document written after the Cattle Acts: 'as a result of an
unfavourable balance of Irish payments, 95£ in England was worth about 100£
of the like money in Ireland in the free time of trade'. Public Record Office of
Ireland, Dublin. Wyche Documents III/35. Considerations relating to the Improvement of Ireland, not only as to the encreasing of its domestick wealth, but
also of its money and bullion (By Sir William Petty?). Cf. H.M.C., *Ormonde
MSS.*, new series, vol. 3, p. 70, and *A Letter sent to Mr. Garway (a member of
the Rt. Hon. the House of Commons of England) by an English Gentleman*, 27 Dec.
1673.

[2]Irish Manuscripts Commission, *Analecta Hibernica*, vol. 1, pp. 111-12;
National Library, Dublin. Abdy MSS., MS. 325, nos. 24, 26, Feb. 1662, 18
March 1662.

[3]*Calendar of State Papers, Ireland, 1666-9*, pp. 94, 103.

[4]Around 1686 Petty remarked that 'exchange between London and Dublin [is]
about 7 per cent one time with another'. The state of the case between England
and Ireland, *The Petty Papers*, ed. Marquis of Lansdowne, vol. 1 (London, 1927)
p. 58.

against Ireland, and indeed frequently were at least seasonally favourable. Over the remainder of the century the course of exchange was on the whole favourable to Ireland. Long runs of markedly unfavourable rates were registered only in 1742, 1745, 1753–4,[1] 1759–60, 1767, 1770–1, 1772–3, 1777–8, 1782–4, 1793 and 1796.[2] These periods, all representing occasions when specie was short or the country affected by commercial crisis, correspond to the major crises in the banking or discounting business in Ireland.[3] In 1742, 1745, 1753–4, 1759–60, 1770–1, 1772–3, 1777–8 and 1782–4, the crisis was associated with a marked decline in the trade surplus. With the exception of 1759–60 and 1777–8 the deterioration in the balance of trade is attributable in particular to a rise in grain and flour imports. The relatively shortlived crisis in 1793 on the other hand was not precipitated by a reduction in the trade surplus. The fact that exchange rates rose above par for the four middle months of the year, despite the wish to convert paper claims into cash because of the increased liquidity preference of the merchant community, does however suggest that there was some temporary pressure on the exchange market for reasons not connected with the trade balance.

In the event of a widespread commercial crisis developing in the economy, however, the increased demand for liquidity, reflected for instance in the fall in the prices of government stocks and public funds, might eventually affect the paper offered on the exchange market as well. Because of the demand for cash, banks and discounting houses became reluctant to discount even short-term bills. The resultant decline in discounting activity reduced the liquidity of and hence the demand for bills more than the supply of bills offered for discount. But as the supply of bills if anything tended to increase at least in the short run during a general move to a cash basis, the decline in discounting resulted in a fall in the quotations on the exchange or in other words in the price of bills. A widening in the differential between the rates of exchange in Dublin and London is in fact under such circumstances a reflection of an increased demand

[1]Exchange rates were also above par in February 1755, the month preceding the banking crisis of March 1755.

[2]As might be expected evidence of a time-lag may sometimes be detected between the adverse movement in the balance of trade and the subsequent onset of an exchange crisis.

[3]Excepting the rise in exchange rates in the first half of 1742, occasioned by large corn imports, which, although sharp, does not appear to have led to a banking or commercial crisis. The period is however the aftermath of the very severe famine of 1741 when stagnation was probably general.

for cash in the centre where the exchange rate falls. The commercial crisis of 1796-7 affords some illustration both of the effects of adverse moves in the balance of payments and of an increase in liquidity preference. The trade balance declined sharply in 1796, and as a new loan to the Irish government was made only in December 1796[1] there was no compensating inflow of specie during the year such as was occasioned by the previous loan, payment of which had been completed in January 1796.[2] Some pressure on the exchange market is discernible, and exchange rates exceeding par were quoted on the Dublin market in five of the last seven months of the year. However, the pressure to remit to London appears to have been fairly limited, as the course of exchange at no time appears to have exceeded 9 per cent and a substantial inflow of specie which commenced at the end of the year[3] brought the exchange below par. The fall in exchange is also associated with a marked rise in liquidity preference. An internal drain of cash had already developed in Ireland, where political conditions were becoming more unsettled and invasion from France appeared imminent, in the course of 1796.[4] Banks were becoming reluctant to discount bills, and merchants, placing cash at a premium, ready to sell bills below the par of the exchange. The rates of exchange in Dublin in September and again in October had temporarily declined below par, and from January 1797 the decline in rates because of the very small volume of discounting activity was very marked.

In Britain likewise the demand for cash was pressing. Cash was becoming scarce in part because of an internal drain, in part because of an external drain, to which the flow of specie to Ireland from the end of 1796 was of course contributory. The merchant community was anxious to hold cash rather than paper claims, even short-term ones. Bills of exchange were therefore difficult to pass. One result was that it was necessary to offer a relatively large premium in Irish pounds to effect the sale of bills drawn on Dublin. This tended of course to widen the spread between the rates of exchange in London and those in Dublin where local conditions were producing the

---

[1] *Third Report of the Committee of Secrecy appointed to examine and state the total amount of outstanding demands on the Bank of England,* 21 April 1797, p. 16. British Parliamentary Papers, 1826 (iii) 26.

[2] Ibid., p. 30.

[3] See ibid., pp. 6, 16, 19, 24, 31, 75.

[4] Public Record Office of Northern Ireland, Downshire Papers, D. 607, nos. 728, 856, 909, 2 Sept., 9 Nov., 1 Dec. 1796. National Library, Dublin. Shaw MSS. 5680.

contrary result of depressing the exchange quotations. The spread
was made all the wider by the fact that the fall in exchange in Dublin
—or the price of bills on London—was accentuated and perpetuated
by the difficulty of discounting the bills on the London market. Under
normal conditions the widening of the spread between the rates in
the two centres would have encouraged activity on the exchanges.
But the prolonged period during which cash was in demand in both
countries reduced the volume of transaction on both sides; and
greatly slowed down the return to equilibrium on the exchange
market. The demand was for cash in both capitals, and because of
this, speculators were unable to take advantage by arbitrage of the
possibilities offered by a divergence in the degree by which the price
of bills fell in the two centres. As a result, although exchange fell
below par in Ireland in the course of December, it remained well
above par in London into January 1797. Although rates in both
capitals were below par by the end of January 1797, the abnormally
wide spread between the rates which first appeared in September 1796
persisted into the middle of the year. Equilibrium in the exchange
market was restored only in June 1797.

The favourable course of exchange over most of the century was
reflected in the increasing stock of specie, especially gold, in Ireland.
Even in the first three decades of the century, when pressure was most
severe, there appears to have been some increase in the supply of
specie. In the following decades the position eased considerably and
on the basis of contemporary estimates the supply increased three- to
four-fold between 1730 and 1776. As the supply had been heavily
reduced by severe drains abroad in the early 'fifties, in 1759–60 and
again in 1770, it seems clear that the major increase occurred after
1760, when the Irish economy began to undergo the benefit of sharply
rising prices for agricultural commodities. These favourable trends
were intensified in the last decades of the century and, if contemporary estimates can be relied on, the supply probably trebled between
1776 and 1797. This conclusion is, of course, in contradiction to
much contemporary opinion in Ireland. But contemporary assertions
of a chronically adverse balance of payments were formulated first
in the aftermath of the Cattle Acts and later during the short but
recurrent periods of crisis, and were generalized as arguments in the
constitutional campaign against English rule in Ireland.

The three main features of the Irish balance of payments were,
firstly, the large favourable balance of trade; secondly, offsetting this,

a great drain by way of remittances of rents, salaries and pensions to absentees, and through charges for freight, insurance and banking services in London; and, thirdly, a capital inflow. The balance of trade was almost invariably favourable, even in the decades immediately following the enactment of the Cattle Acts.[1] In the 103 years from 1698 to 1800 an unfavourable balance was recorded in the ledgers of Irish exports and imports only on seven occasions. The balance which had declined to a low level in the early years of the century had grown to above £200,000 p.a. in the 1710s and 1720s and to £400,000 in the 1740s. From the end of the 1750s the balance frequently amounted to £600,000 and in the last two decades sometimes exceeded £1,000,000. Admittedly, the statistics are a very inadequate measure of the balance, since the valuations employed in assessing the balance are, apart from their other limitations, unsatisfactory in that they relate only to the prices of Irish exports in the home ports and to the supposed prices at which the imports were purchased in ports abroad. In the case of Irish exports, the omissions are not so serious as much of Irish overseas trade was effected on commission, and the profits and earnings from freights and insurances were limited. In the case of imports, however, this method underestimates the expenditure, as it makes no allowance for freight and insurance which were more commonly a loss to Ireland, and for the profits, less commission to Irish correspondents, accruing to English merchants. Yet despite their inadequacy in this direction, the statistics probably still underestimate the extent of the favourable balance to Ireland: prices of Irish export commodities were rising more sharply than those of imports, and as a consequence the prices current on the wharves in Ireland in 1802 of imports were only 32 per cent above the official rates, whereas the prices current of exports were 69 per cent above the official rates.[2]

A separate balance of Anglo-Irish payments is impossible to assess even remotely, but it would in any case be of limited interest as the great bulk of Irish overseas payments was of course cleared through

---

[1]There was almost complete contemporary agreement on this point, and the view is reiterated in eighteenth-century opinions referring back to this period (Cf. *Irish Parliamentary Register*, vol. 3, p. 123). Figures for both exports and imports in the same year are available only for 1681, in which exports amounted to £582,814 and imports to £433,040 (Dobbs, *Essay on the trade of Ireland*, 1729, in *Tracts and treatises illustrative . . . of Ireland* (Dublin, 1861) vol. ii, p. 334).

[2]*Report of the Committee on the circulating paper, the specie and the current coin of Ireland*, 1804, reprinted 1826, p. 99.

London. The favourable balance of Anglo-Irish trade itself was only a small one in the early eighteenth century. As the relative importance of Anglo-Irish trade grew, however, it increased rapidly, and in the last two decades of the century was generally greater than that of Irish overseas trade as a whole. The statistics of the English Inspector General, however, show a large balance in favour of England in all but the opening two decades of the first eighty years of the century. In the last two decades of the century the extent of this balance is greatly reduced, and in some years is replaced by an adverse balance. The valuations in the English ledgers are much less useful for the purpose of measuring the balance of trade than those employed in the Irish accounts. As the English valuations remained stable, they do not register the fall in the price of colonial goods in the first half of the century, whereas the Irish ledgers record this fall. In part, as a result of this, the balance against Ireland in the English ledgers is purely an apparent one. It is also exaggerated, especially in the second half of the century, by the extent to which the values of Irish imports were underestimated in the English ledgers.[1] The import price of linen was only half the price of linen in the Irish statistics in the last decades of the century, and the price of butter, the second most important item in imports from Ireland, only 65 per cent of the Irish rate, although the rates both of linen and butter, even in the Irish ledgers, were below current prices in Ireland in the final decades of the century.[2]

Remittances to absentees, because of their enormous size, were an important factor in determining the trends and organization of the

[1]By the end of the century the undervaluation of imports generally was much more marked than that of British exports in the official valuations (See *Official and real or current value of the Imports and Exports of Great Britain to and from Ireland*, 30 July 1804, P.P. 1803–4, viii, 190). In 1799 the Inspector-General's statistics fell short of current values by 45 per cent for imports and 26 per cent for exports, and in 1800 by 44 per cent and 22 per cent respectively (G.D.H. Cole, *British trade and industry, past and future* (London, 1932) p. 39). Official prices of re-exports were actually above current values (in 1800 to the extent of 15 per cent). Import prices were less seriously underrated officially, when compared with prices of domestic exports. In 1800 the official prices of imports were only 55 per cent of current prices, while official prices of domestic exports were 61 per cent of current values (Professor Ashton's introduction to Schumpeter, op. cit., p. 8.).

[2]While the valuation of linen fell below its real value late in the century, it should be noted that earlier in the century the official valuations may on occasion have exceeded market prices. Stephenson in 1759 thought linen at 16d. a yard 'too highly estimated'. *A letter to the Right Hon. and Hon. the Trustees of the Linen Manufacture* (Dublin, 1759) p. 18.

exchange business; and the exchange dealings of the Irish banks arose in part from the fact that they held the Irish balances of a partly absentee class. Rents remitted to England were estimated at around £100,000 per annum in the second half of the seventeenth century, and a writer in 1698 estimated total extra-commercial remittances to England at £200,000.[1] By the 1720s these remittances to England were commonly estimated to be about £600,000 per annum, and in 1780 Arthur Young suggested a figure of £732,000 for absentee rents, and a total sum of £1,000,000 for non-commercial remittances. Large as these remittances were, the evidence of a favourable course of exchange and of an enlarged supply of specie suggests that the total inflow of payments more than exceeded the total outflow. Even in periods of acute distress, when the rent drain was most obvious, the low agricultural prices and the failure of tenants tended to reduce the amount of remittances far below the level they might otherwise attain. It is, however, still likely, having regard to the extent of rent and| other remittances which approximated to the trade balance, that the trade balance can have exceeded them only marginally under favourable conditions and that in many instances it must have fallen short of them. In these circumstances the fact that the course of exchange remained almost continually favourable throughout the century (apart from well-defined periods of economic difficulties) suggests that there must have been an offsetting capital inflow. This is the third feature of the Irish balance of payments, and the one whose existence and significance are least appreciated. But its existence is beyond doubt, and there is abundant evidence of transactions constituting a short-term or long-term capital inflow into Ireland.

Ireland being a poor and relatively undeveloped country, capital remained scarce, though the favourable balance of payments is clearly of significance in relation to the country's rapid rate of progress in the second half of the eighteenth century. The rate of interest was reduced from 7 per cent to 6 per cent only in 1731, and remained one per cent higher than in England right to the end of the century. The market rates of interest in Ireland were almost invariably at or near the legal maximum. As the interest on private borrowings was 1 per cent higher than the yield on the 4 per cent government debentures,[2]

---

[1]*Discourse concerning Ireland and the different interests thereof in answer to the Exeter and Barnstaple petitions* (London, 1698) p. 10.
[2]*Parliamentary Register,* vol. 8, p. 294.

this meant that private borrowings could only under exceptionally favourable conditions be effected under 5 per cent. In actual fact, excepting the particularly favourable periods of the early 1750s and late 1780s, it is probable that most private borrowings were effected at 6 per cent. The market rates declined in the years of prosperity from the end of the 1740s. In the early 1750s the price of the 4 per cent debentures had risen to 107 or 108,[1] and low interest rates appear to have had their effect in the numerically increased Irish merchant community and growing imports at that time. The decline in interest rates at this time was of course also a reflection of the ending of government deficit financing and the paying off of the National Debt, which had grown rapidly in the preceding decades. The sound financial position of the early 1750s was not, however, repeated in the following years. In particular, the commercial crisis of 1777–8 and the mounting deficit in the government accounts during the French war raised interest rates sharply. The price of the 4 per cent debentures, which was 101 to 103 in 1777, declined to as low as 80 in the early 1780s. Recovery however set in, and aided by sound financial policies the price of the debentures returned to par in 1786–7. The government were able to take advantage of the favourable market conditions to fund the debt in 1787–8 and reduce the rate of interest to $3\frac{1}{2}$ per cent. The price of the new debentures continued to rise from 90 to 95 in 1788 to 98 at the end of 1791. The outbreak of the Revolutionary war and a growing deficit disorganized Irish finances in the following years, new Government borrowings were at higher rates of interest, and in March 1797 even the price of the new 5 per cent debentures, which was 94 in August 1796, had sunk to 70.[2]

Better investment facilities in England clearly had some success in attracting Irish capital. But the amount was in the aggregate comparatively small. Much of the investment was in any event financed out of income remitted to absentees, and where it was not, interest on the investment entered usefully into the balance of payments on the credit side. On the other hand, apart altogether from the large volume of temporary or seasonal accommodation allowed to the Irish merchant community by the more powerful English merchants,

[1]Ibid., pp. 291, 295.
[2]National Library, Dublin. Shaw MSS. 5680, pp. 29, 209, 240. The prices of Irish funds in the period 1777–93 are quoted in *Faulkner's Dublin Journal,* and the *Freeman's Journal.* No regular quotations are available for earlier years, and an organized market for Irish funds can not go back, at the earliest further than the 1730s.

13

the higher rates of interest appear to have encouraged much long-term lending. The higher yield on Irish public funds than on English may also have attracted British investors. Further, the Irish lotteries and the tontines attracted an inflow of money. As the business correspondence of the period testifies, English merchants like their Irish counterparts frequently purchased Irish tickets. In one instance the London house of Nesbitt and Stewart were the purchasers of the whole lottery, thus producing an inflow of £97,500.[1] The Irish tontines were also an investment which attracted much foreign money to Ireland. A Geneva syndicate, placing their investment through the medium of the London banking house of Peter Thellusson and Co., invested £50,000 in the Irish Tontine of 1777. Independent investors in Geneva contributed a further £40,000. Genevese investors thus contributed £90,000 of the total tontine of £300,000, of which 41.83 per cent was held by English investors.[2] When the Irish debt was funded in 1788, there was some agitation for the reduction of the legal rate of interest. This was not effected, and the reason appears to have been—significantly—that the reduction would have lessened the amount of lending from England.[3]

The large favourable balance of trade, the interest on Irish money absorbed through the London money market, and apparently large-scale lending to Ireland were all factors contributing to a steady growth of wealth and investment in Ireland in the second half of the century. The physical embodiment of this investment is seen in the erection of country houses; in urban house building, planned and executed in an orderly manner; in the expanding port towns and some inland centres; and in industrial and commercial development, extensive although somewhat thinly spread and not always well directed.

[1]*Faulkner's Dublin Journal,* 6 March 1792.
[2]Charles Gautier, 'Un Investissement Genevois: La Tontine d'Irlande de 1777', *Bulletin de la société d'histoire et d'archéologie de Genève,* tome x, 1951.
[3]See debates on reducing the rate of interest in 1788, *Irish Parliamentary Register,* vol. 8, pp. 275–300, 307–30. The measure succeeded in passing the Commons, but was rejected in the House of Lords.

CHAPTER X

THE EXCHANGE BUSINESS
OF THE IRISH BANKS
IN THE EIGHTEENTH CENTURY[1]

IN the second half of the seventeenth century inland and foreign exchange business in Ireland was almost exclusively transacted by dealings between merchant and merchant or remitter. Merchants were, however, already showing some tendency to specialize in the bill business. Some Dublin merchants already had an exchange business that probably substantially exceeded the immediate requirements of their own commodity trade, and provincial merchants acted as agents for them in securing acceptance of bills or in remitting the proceeds to Dublin. These developments were embryonic, however, and there were no banks in Dublin apart from a few which specialized in mortgages on land. In the provinces there was only a bank of sorts, conducted by the Cork merchants Edward and Joseph Hoare, whose overseas trade at the end of the century enabled them to draw bills on merchants in Bristol and London and on the Commissioners for Victualling the Navy. Remitters generally had to have recourse to merchants who were only prepared to draw on London as the course of trade enabled them to do so. In Dublin, as the chief centre of Irish trade, there was, however, already a class of 'exchangers', loosely described as bankers, in the business between Ireland and London. It was around this foreign exchange activity that, in contrast to the position in England, Irish banking developed.

As a consequence, most of the early banks were mercantile in origin. Such, for example, was the famous Dublin private bank of La Touche. David Digues La Touche established a silk, poplin and cambric manufactory in Dublin at the end of the seventeenth century and also acted as a Dublin agent for many of the Huguenot manufacturers in the Irish provinces. It was thus but a small step forward to undertake the regular remission of funds between Dublin and various Irish provincial centres. Nor is it surprising that when the bank was established on a formal basis, the names of several of its correspondents were French: Vashon and Son in Waterford,

---

[1] A slightly re-cast version of a paper published in *Economica*, November 1958.

Alexander Crommelin in Lisburn, William Crommelin in Kilkenny, Solomon Le Blanc in Lurgan. Once engaged in the internal remission of funds, La Touche was led as a matter of course into the remission of money to London. As several of La Touche's correspondents belonged to the Crommelin family, who helped to promote the modern Irish linen industry, it may not be altogether fanciful to surmise that La Touche's foreign exchange business had its origins in discounting bills drawn by linen drapers and shippers. Certainly, his English correspondents were in London, Chester and Bristol, the three points of entry for the bulk of the Irish linen exports, and his sole continental correspondent was in Holland, from whence part of Ireland's supply of flax-seed came. Similar examples in the rise of Dublin banking are the bank of Dillon founded by a merchant family trading with Holland and France, and having members of the family established in Rotterdam and London; and the bankers James Swift, Thomas Gleadowe, John Macarell and Thomas Finlay.

The mercantile origins of the provincial banks are no less striking. With perhaps one or two exceptions, they were all established by merchants and remained subsidiary in many cases to the trading activities of their founders. Apart from merchants who opened banking houses, there were others who, like Edward and Richard Weeks, merchants in Waterford, issued promissory notes payable not as bankers' notes to bearer but to 'persons or their orders'. As these notes circulated,[1] it is obvious that a tenuous line divided merchant and banker. An act of Parliament passed in 1756, shortly after the failure of three Dublin banks closely identified with the merchant community, prohibited bankers from engaging in trade as merchants.[2] Loose in wording, it was at first ineffective in practice, because merchants could still issue notes without assuming the formal status of bankers. Merchants were therefore able to retain their note issue, as in the case of the great Cork merchant house of Lawton, Carleton and Feray, who continued to transact a banking business with only a slight change in the style of their notes. But the failure of many merchant houses in the crisis of 1759–60, along with the disappearance of six Dublin banks and two small banks in Galway over the years 1754–60, appears to have made Irish merchants decline future commitments in the way of a note issue. The house of Lawton, Carleton and Feray was itself involved in a grave scandal in 1760

[1] *Journals of the Irish House of Commons,* vol. 4, app. cxxii, 29 Feb. 1739/40.
[2] 29 Geo II, c. 16 (Ir.).

through the failure of its cashier, who had been supported in mercantile business on his own account by the credit of the firm. There seems to be no evidence whatever that in the decades intervening between 1760 and the eve of the suspension of gold payments in 1797 Irish merchants engaged in the issue of paper.[1]

The rapid growth of banking in the eighteenth century was a response partly to the development of trade, partly to the acute shortage of coin which made bankers more capable of forcing their notes on the community which, in turn, was ready to accept them in the place of the medley of worn or underweight English and foreign gold. From the start, exchange became their most important function. Dublin's first regular bank, that of Burton, embarked from its foundation on the discounting business and as early as 1696 Sir John Lowther, writing from London, informed the agent of his collieries in Whitehaven that, 'if any money could be returned out of Ireland there is one Burton at Dublin which makes ye most returns and his correspondent here is one Haistwell of my acquaintance'.[2] Many other Dublin banks were to follow. A few had a long life, but many were ephemeral. Their pattern of business was, however, alike in all cases, and as London was the centre through which the greater part of Irish commercial finance was transacted, all had agents in the English capital. Thus, in their first year, Messrs. Swift and Co. spent £100 in 'charges in sending a person to London and [to] sundry persons in Ireland to fix upon proper persons for correspondents for the company'.[3] The amount of commission paid by them in that year to their correspondents for bills of exchange negotiated was considerable, being £672 9s. 7½d. It was far and away their greatest

[1]The Limerick merchant, Philip Roche John, in January 1797 advertised that he was withdrawing his notes payable to bearer 'during the present situation of credit' (Eoin O'Kelly: *The old private banks and bankers of Munster* (Cork, 1959) pp. 85–6). This is the sole reference to bearer notes in the decades immediately prior to the suspension of cash payments in 1797, and it is probable that their use by Roche was an innovation introduced in his autumn purchases of commodities in 1796 to counter the growing shortage of coin in free circulation. This would also appear to be borne out in the wording of the notice, which appears to suggest that the notes had been only recently introduced.

[2]Record Office, The Castle, Carlisle. Sir John Lowther's Letters to his agent at Whitehaven, London, 14 July 1696 (no. 19).

[3]J. Busteed: 'Irish private banks', *Journal of the Cork Historical and Archaeological Society*, vol. 53 (1948), p. 33. The Sarsfield Vesey Papers in the Public Record Office of Ireland, Dublin, contain some items relating to the bank's business. The bank's London agents were probably Wogan and Aspinwall who in 1725 were described as acting 'for the new Bankers in Dublin' (B.M., Egmont Papers, Add. MSS. 46990, p. 109. Percival, Charlton, 24 July 1725).

charge, amounting to 40 per cent of their total expenses. La Touche and Kane's banking followed a similar pattern. They had correspondents not only in the principal towns of Ireland but also in Bristol, Chester and London; in whose hands were funds enabling La Touche and Kane to draw bills for their Irish customers.[1] These balances must have originated in bills discounted by the bank and paid for by their own note issue, and the bills when honoured increased the funds in the hands of their correspondents in London and elsewhere. By keeping their discounting and drawing of bills at a fairly even rate, they maintained their London balances at a steady level, and a pamphlet of 1729 suggests that the varying of the exchange with this object in view was already a normal procedure among Irish bankers.[2]

The prominence of exchange dealings in the business of the Irish bankers arose primarily from the pattern of Irish commodity trade. The balance appears to have been highly favourable under normal conditions, which meant that it was not always easy for a merchant to find a ready purchaser for a bill drawn on London. There was, of course, a large body of temporary or permanent Irish absentees, requiring the remission of their rents to London, but direct dealing between an absentee's agent and merchant was difficult. The merchant might not be in a position to draw at any time or for the amount the remitter might require. This provided the opportunity for the bankers. By taking bills from all merchants and at all times, it was possible for the banker to meet all demands on him for remitting funds to London. To an increasing extent throughout the first half of the century, merchants seem to have discounted their bills with the banks rather than among their fellow-merchants, and remitters to London increasingly relied on bankers' bills.

One surviving abstract of a ledger of La Touche and Kane throws some light on Irish banking of the early eighteenth century.[3] Their business relates practically exclusively to the internal or external exchange of money, and of the quarterly balances in the hands of their correspondents those in England invariably form between 40 and 70 per cent. Their principal business was with London where they had two well known correspondents, Jonathan Gurnell &

---

[1]An abstract ledger of the firm for the year 1719-26 survives, of which there is a photostat copy in the National Library, Dublin, MS. 2785.

[2]*Observations on coin in general* (Dublin, 1729) pp. 38-9.

[3]See n. 1 above.

Company and John Puget, and conducted intermittent dealings
with Edward Flower & Son and Ellijad Edward. The balances in
the hands of La Touche's agents there were far greater than those
either in Bristol and Chester or in their largest provincial centre in
Ireland. The size of the bank's English balances increased steadily
over the years 1719–26. Table 25 reproduces a summary of their
October-December balances, normally the largest of the year.

Table 25: Bank of La Touche and Kane

'Abstracts of accounts as they stand: places and correspondents'
names: cash in their hands'.

Oct. 1– Dec. 31	London English a/c	Dutch a/c	Bristol	Chester	Total
1719	3,868– 7–5¾	—	—	108–19– 5¾	3,977– 6–11½
1722	5,267– 1–7	27– 0–0	567–16–2	271– 8– 0	6,133– 5– 9
1723	5,047– 5–3¼	185–15–0	728– 5–7	247–10–11¼	6,208–16– 9½
1724	8,697–13–0	740– 0–0	954– 8–4½	204– 5–10	10,596– 7– 2½
1725	9,642– 0–0	870– 0–0	1,201–14–9	1,722– 0– 0	13,435–14– 9

These sums indicate a rather large business and assuming that all
bills were at 21 days' sight, as was the practice in Anglo-Irish payments, their turnover must have been substantially greater than the
actual balances in the hands of their correspondents at the end of the
quarter. The drawings on the bank's resources were most extensive
in the first half of the year, but as one would expect from the nature
of the Irish economy they were always able to increase their balances
in the second half, when their discounting was most active.

Table 26: Cash in the hands of La Touche's English correspondents

Year	1 Jan.–31 Mar.	1 Apr.–30 June	1 Jul.–30 Sept.	1 Oct.–31 Dec.
1719	—	—	—	3,977– 6–11½
1720	3,627–14– 2½	5,920–0–7	—	—
1721	4,171–10– 0¼	2,357–0–0	5,461–10–9¼	—
1722	—	—	5,433– 3–6½	6,133– 5– 9
1723	3,177– 0–11½	4,205–9–1	3,573–17–4	6,208–16– 9½
1724	5,715– 1– 3½	6,048–1–1	7,319– 5–4	10,596– 7– 2½
1725	5,211– 9– 0¾	7,166–7–7½	13,074–11–3	13,435–14– 9
1726	12,597– 6– 5	—	—	—

By the early 'thirties there were as many as six or seven banks in
Dublin, and the growth in their number and volume of business is to
be associated with the high exchange of the 'twenties. This high
exchange led to a disappearance of most of the exportable specie;

and thus the greater demand for, than supply of, bills was an important factor in forcing many remitters to have recourse to the bankers.

A sure sign of the progress of Dublin banking is that the bankers were now remitting government money to England. The sums involved in official transfers were too large for merchants to handle and for that reason recourse was had in the seventeenth century to London goldsmiths to effect these transactions. The growth of banking in Ireland, however, meant that there were now individuals in Dublin with sufficient resources to remit large sums. In 1730, for example, £40,000 was paid to the bankers Henry and Burton to remit to England.[1]

Another proof of the prominence which the bankers of the 'twenties were acquiring in exchange is that they were doing a large business in endorsing merchants' bills to remitters, and that they were able to charge a rate for their own bill-drawings which was about one per cent higher than that charged by merchants. This suggests that merchants' bills were becoming relatively few on the Dublin or Cork exchange market compared with demand, partly as a result of the increased tendency of merchants to pass their bills to the bankers, and that the bankers were therefore in a position normally to force a higher rate for their endorsements and drawings. In 1726, for instance, a land agent promised to remit a sum of money to an absentee 'at the easiest and surest terms I can and to be sure it will be at least $1\frac{1}{4}$ per cent less than from the bankers'.[2] The Dublin banker Henry was described as 'one of the dearest in town, always 1 per cent dearer than one could get good merchants' bills'.[3] On the bills they endorsed to remitters, the bankers charged a premium of $\frac{1}{2}$ per cent above merchants' exchange. The basis for this charge was reasonable, as in endorsing the bills they took the bankers 'insured' them for the remitter and had to make good any loss. The justification for a charge of a further half per cent for their own drawings lay in the fact that the bankers allowed a half per cent commission to the London correspondents on whom they drew. The proportion between

---

[1]Public Record Office of Northern Ireland, Belfast. Transcripts of the State Papers, Ireland, T. 693, p. 1. (Jan. 2 1729-30). See also F.G. Hall, *The Bank of Ireland, 1783-1946* (Dublin, 1949) pp, 7-8, and government accounts in *Journals of the Irish House of Commons,* passim.

[2]P.R.O., C. 110/46, bundle 1, no. 71. Owen Gallagher to Oliver St. George in London, Dublin, 4 January 1727.

[3]Ibid., bundle 1, no. 48, Owen Gallagher, 14 January 1726.

drawings and endorsements in a banker's business probably varied according to the flow of payments. When bills on London were seasonally scarce, or when the balance of payments was unfavourable, as for example over much of the 'twenties, a great part of the business would be effected by the banker's own bill-drawings. On the other hand, when bills on London were plentiful, endorsements probably formed a greatly increased proportion of the business, and surplus bills discounted would accumulate in London balances, which helped to finance the banker's own drawings, when the supply of merchants' bills was seasonally reduced.

Bankers were able to draw so freely only as a result of the large numbers of bills which they discounted and which, being at very short sight, meant that a perpetual stream of funds was becoming available to them in London. As merchants' exchange consisted largely of drawings to the order of remitters, the bankers were the sole persons to charge a regular discount; and in 1727 the agent, Owen Gallagher, informed his landlord that the reason why bankers took bills at 'a quarter or half per cent less [exchange] than others is that they take bills every post from such as have bills to pass, and others take bills but now and then, as their occasions require'.[1] The deduction of a charge for discount was not at this time common in Ireland among the smaller merchants and remitters, and the practice appears to have become general only from around 1760, when the usance especially in inland payments began to lengthen.

Bankers' rates being high, remitters who had the necessary acquaintance among merchants and who were not under immediate pressure to remit, often sought merchants who were in a position to draw. Where an absentee or agent was likely to have frequent sums remitted, and a merchant had funds regularly accruing to him in London, an agreement between the two parties was at times possible. The merchant then drew bills at a fixed and lower rate than the current course of exchange in return for cash regularly placed at his disposal.

Less important, but still very significant, was the inland exchange business. Swift's bank in its first year appointed country correspondents, and over the seven years 1719–26 La Touche and Kane had 19 correspondents in 15 provincial centres. Their dealings with Cork and Limerick were by far the most important, and there was apparently a separate course of exchange on each of these centres.

[1] Ibid., bundle 1, no. 74, Owen Gallagher, 30 January 1727.

Dealings with agents in other centres were much smaller and appear to have been effected under a single course of 'country exchange'. The more important towns comprising this country exchange were, in rough order, Clonmel, Galway, Waterford, Belfast, Kilkenny, Sligo, and there were smaller and more intermittent dealings with agents in Londonderry, Youghal, Lisburn, Lurgan, Carlow, Drogheda and Birr. These correspondents were, in most cases, and perhaps in all, merchants and manufacturers, some of whom were eventually to enter banking on their own account. Thus, John Bagwell was a merchant in Clonmel, and was the founder of a well-known local bank. Caleb Falkiner, merchant of Cork, was the father of Riggs Falkiner, merchant, who opened Falkiner's bank in Cork before 1760; and the Boyle, who as a partner with Lenox, was another of La Touche's Cork correspondents, is almost certainly of the firm of Boyle, Calwell and Barrett, merchants in the provision trade and embryonic bankers. Again, the names of La Touche's Waterford correspondents, Newport and Knuckle, suggest the origins of the Waterford bank of Newport. From the early decades of the century the existence of the Dublin and provincial agents contributed to the ease of internal exchange, as was the case in a rather similar manner in England. As the provincial banks became more numerous after the middle of the century, and generally selected a Dublin private bank as one of their correspondents, it is easy to understand how the passing of the century witnessed a growing ease of internal remitting.

Some contemporaries writing after the crash of the bank of Malone, Clements and Gore in 1758 were led to believe that the main business of Irish banking was lending on mortgages,[1] and later writers have been misled into following the same beliefs by applying to the bankers of the period in general the terms of two subsequent Acts of Parliament.[2] There is, however, not the slightest evidence to substantiate this view, and it is certainly one which was not held by most contemporaries. Early eighteenth-century pamphleteers accused the banks of having wilfully exported, because of their interest in exchange, the country's supply of silver and English gold. At a still later date a hostile critic claimed that the banks had wrested the

---

[1] *Considerations on the present calamities of this kingdom and the causes of the decay of public credit* (Dublin, 1760) p. 4. See also *Proposals humbly offered to Parliament for the restoration of cash and public credit to Ireland* (Dublin, 1760) p. 6.

[2] 33 Geo. III. c. 4; c. 14 (Ir.).

business of exchange from the merchants,[1] and a writer in 1780 stated that 'the principal object of the banking trade in Ireland is the business of discounting'.[2] Indeed, the Bank of Ireland itself was in the early years of its existence primarily a discounting bank.[3]

As all the Irish banks were committed to exchange dealings, intermittent shortages of specie made them extremely vulnerable during a period of high exchange rates. These shortages were most pronounced in the seventeenth century, and during the first six decades of the eighteenth. The supply, already scarce in 1660, had been reduced still further as a result of the unfavourable exchange in the decades following the Cattle Acts of the 1660s. At the opening of the eighteenth century it was even found necessary to enlarge by Act of Parliament the time for purchasers of forfeited estates in Ireland to make payment of the purchase price, because immediate payment had ceased to be possible on account of the want of money.[4] Though the coinage appears to have increased in the early years of the century, mainly as a result of a favourable balance of payments over the years 1706–15, the increase barely corresponded to the growth of domestic and external trade.[5] Cash remained acutely scarce, especially silver, and in some cases tenants were unable to pay their rents through sheer scarcity of coin. In the poor trading conditions of the 'twenties, worsened by bad harvests and at times famine conditions, exchange was frequently unfavourable to Ireland, even allowing for the fact that the bulk of the coinage now consisted of overvalued foreign gold. There was thus a strong demand for specie to remit abroad, which imposed a great strain on the banks. They were, therefore, ill-prepared to meet a run by holders of their notes. The fact

[1]*Observations on and a short history of Irish banks and bankers* (Dublin, 1760) pp. 8–9.
[2]*A view of the present state of Ireland* (London, 1780) p. 91.
[3]Hall, op. cit., pp. 50–53.
[4]2 & 3 Anne, c. 19 referred to in *Calendar of Treasury Books,* vol. xxvii, pt. ii, p. 46 n.
[5]The Irish currency in the second half of the seventeenth century seems to have amounted to between £300,000 and £400,000 (Sir William Petty, *Political anatomy of Ireland,* 1672, in Hull: *Economic writings of Sir William Petty,* vol. 1, p. 187; *Report from the Council of Trade 1676,* ibid., p. 214; W. Harris, *Remarks on the affairs and trade of Great Britain and Ireland,* 1691, p. 31; *Some thoughts on the bill depending before the . . . House of Lords for prohibiting the exportation of the woollen manufactures of Ireland to foreign parts,* London, 1698, p. 5; *An answer to a letter from a gentleman in the country to a member of the House of Commons,* London, 1698, p. 25). But Irish writers of the 'twenties and 'thirties estimated the coinage at various totals between £400,000 and £600,000. See also H.M.C., *Diary of the First Earl of Egmont,* vol. 3, p. 329.

that notes continued in circulation and that only two important banks succumbed to 'runs' in the 1720s or early 1730s[1] may perhaps be attributed to the replacing of guineas and silver by overvalued foreign gold. This now formed the mainstay of the Irish circulation and its cost of transfer would have equalled the high cost of bills.

Favourable conditions returned in the early 'thirties and the devaluing of the foreign gold in 1737 brought the exchange below par. This encouraged the inflow of guineas though, as silver continued underrated, the scarcity of the smaller coins remained. The course of exchange remained favourable over most of the next 15 years and during this period with a probable inflow of gold no difficulties were encountered by the bankers apart from a run due in part to political causes in 1745.[2] After the Peace of 1748, however, imports increased sharply and reached a climax in 1753 and 1754. Bad harvests were an aggravating factor. The balance of trade itself did not become unfavourable, but as the volume of remittances to absentees was a constant factor or in years of increased exports a rising one, exchange now became unfavourable. This led to a demand for guineas to remit, and the bankers were again in difficulties. A pamphleteer writing in 1760, six years after the failure of Dillons' bank, declared that 300,000 guineas, which they had imported in two years, had been exported as fast.[3] But Dillons' circumstances were exceptional as the holders of the bank's notes had become aware of the financial difficulties of the bank's foreign correspondents and partners in trade. However, all the Irish banks were affected by a general shortage of cash. This was due in part to the stop put, in 1751, to the currency of the Spanish pistoles which, as they had been slightly overvalued in the proclamation of 1737, now formed a not insignificant part of the Irish coinage. The shortage was further aggravated by the rise in the rates of exchange,[4] and by the fact that the Portuguese gold reduced in 1737

[1]The Bank of Meade and Curtis in 1727 and Burton and Falkiner in 1733. The only other failures recorded are those of an unnamed Limerick banker (*Reasons offered for erecting a bank in Ireland in a letter to Hercules Rowley, Esq.* (Dublin, 1721) p. 10) and of a Cork merchant and banker, Holland Goddard, in 1729 (B.M., Add. MSS. 46994, p. 143, 30 August 1729, Egmont Papers).

[2]The rise in the exchanges preceded the political crisis by several months. As early as 15 June 1745 *Faulkner's Dublin Journal* had noted that 'by the great drain of money from this kingdom for corn, exchange is now at $11\frac{1}{2}$ per cent, which is higher than hath been known since the reduction of the gold coin'.

[3]*Letter to the author of a pamphlet entitled Some Thoughts on the Nature of Paper Credit* (Dublin, 1760) p. 18.

[4]The 1804 Currency Committee, mistakenly, accepted that the rise of exchange in these years was occasioned by an over-issue of bank paper (*Report of the*

was much more readily exportable. The want of cash was acutely felt in the country, and as the balance of payments deteriorated pressure to remit forced exchange in the absence of a sufficient stock of specie to a high level; 'but even at that rate bills are very scarce and 10 per cent has this day been given; this proceeds from ye great scarcity of money among us'.[1] It is not surprising that the Dillons failed at this juncture. Their collapse made the task of the other banks more difficult. Another bad harvest in the autumn of 1754 added to the difficulties of the situation. In March 1755 the banks of Willcocks & Dawson and Lennox & French succumbed. The merchants agreed to accept the notes of the remaining banks and this succeeded in tiding them over their difficulties. But in 1759–60 exchange rose above par again amid a shortage of coin, and two further banks collapsed. Later in 1770 in somewhat similar conditions, there was a very severe run on the banks.

The bankers' interest in exchange was the factor which made them most vulnerable. Under unfavourable external payment conditions the bankers had to protect themselves by charging a higher exchange on their bills on London, but this increase itself encouraged the cashing of bankers' notes by private individuals now more anxious than ever to remit specie on their own account to avoid the loss on bankers' bills. Almost all the Irish banks which collapsed did so in periods of high exchange, when specie was short, the only clear exception being the bank of Malone, Clements & Gore. During the last thirty years of the century the balance of payments was definitely favourable and the ensuing low exchange led to the inflow of gold, often in large quantities. With a growing stock of gold in the country, the banks were free from danger and more able to survive by lessening their discounting of bills in time of commercial or political crisis. In 1773 the house of Colebrooke failed. In the 1778 crisis the house of Finlay had temporarily to stop payment, but no bank failed although three lesser establishments which had issued notes, those of Mitchell, Underwood and Birch, failed. In 1784 the house of Warren failed in Cork. There was a complete absence of difficulty in the following years until 1793. In that year the bank of Sir Thomas Roberts and

---

Committee of the House of Commons on the circulating paper, the specie, and the current coin of Ireland, 1804, reprinted 1826, p. 7). But its opinion was based solely on the evidence of William Colville, who gave a confused and inaccurate account of what he remembered of events fifty years previously (ibid., pp. 121–2).

[1]Guildhall Library, Radcliffe Papers, MS. 6645/5. Francis Thomé, Dublin, 28 Feb. 1754.

Company in Cork had to close temporarily, and in Dublin the house of Lawless and Coates withdrew from business, the first major withdrawal from business since the failure of Colebrooke twenty years previously.

The shortage of cash had already as early as the 'twenties[1] led to a great use of notes issued by the banks principally in return for the bills they discounted. La Touche & Kane, for instance, increased their note issue from £44,489 in the October-December quarter of 1719 to £63,482 in the same quarter of 1725. Table 27 reproduces their note issue for those quarters for which figures are available.

Table 27: Note issue of La Touche and Kane, 1719-25

	1719 £	1720 £	1721 £	1722 £	1723 £	1724 £	1725 £
Jan.–March	—	39,352	19,669	32,581*	47,860	51,649	53,634
Apr.–June	33,979	37,337	26,784	—	52,528	57,515	62,946
July–Sept.		—	23,712	37,545	56,085	48,690	55,365
Oct.–Dec.	44,489	—	—	—	—	45,795	63,482

*1 Oct. 1721–1 April 1722.

The security for their outstanding notes lay in cash, in other bankers' notes and in bills discounted. Cash in hand and other bankers' notes taken together formed a fairly stable ratio of about 30 per cent to their liabilities. However, though the total percentage of cash and bankers' notes remained steady, the proportion contributed individually by the two items followed a sharply contrasting trend. Their cash in reserve, which amounted to as much as £20,000 to £34,000 quarterly in the years 1719 and 1721, had in 1725 dwindled to £7,000, whereas on the other hand bankers' notes grew from £1,262 in the quarter 1 January 1721-31 March 1721, the first quarter in which this item is indicated, to £22,946 in the same quarter of 1725, and to £30,991 in the next quarter (1 April–last June 1725). This is a reflection of the acute scarcity of money in Ireland, and of the increasing circulation of bankers' notes in Dublin. By the first quarter of 1725 La Touche and Kane eliminated their liabilities other than that to their note issue. This had the effect of reducing the amount of their outstanding commitments, raising the proportion of cash

[1]'Were it not for bankers' notes which we have been passing in good plenty, it would be impossible to manage our domestick traffick half so well as we do.' (*Observations on coin in general*, Dublin, 1729, p. 45. Cf. Berkeley, *The Querist*, 1735 (Dublin, 1935, ed. J. Hone), Pt. I, no. 35).

and other bankers' notes to between 40 and 60 per cent of their assets. The items eliminated included acceptances and some commitments of a relatively long-term nature. The fact that banking profits were buoyant suggests that La Touche and Kane were concentrating on the more liquid and more profitable bill trade.

Table 28: Banking profits

Year ending 31 March	La Touche & Kane[1] £	James Swift & Co.[2] £
1720	1,215– 6–11	
1721	898–13–10¼	
1722	1,330– 3– 0¾	
1723	1,270–13– 7¼	947–16– 1
1724	1,533– 0– 2¼	1,980–11– 9
1725	1,922– 2– 3¼	1,412– 6–11
1726	1,711–19– 7½	

The growth in the number of issuing banks led to an expanded note issue, and the import 'boom' from 1749 onwards witnessed an increased use of paper pumped into circulation in the discounting of merchants' bills.[3] The failures in the 1750s produced a painful contraction of credit, which was a cause of concern in Parliament itself.[4]

[1]National Library, Dublin, MS. 2785. Abstract Ledger of La Touche & Kane.
[2]J. Busteed, 'Irish private banks', Journal of the Cork Historical and Archaeological Society, vol. 53, pp. 33–4.
[3]The total in circulation may have reached £1 million. This was not in itself excessive, considering that the bankers' circulation in Ireland had been estimated at the modest total of £400,000 in 1729 (Scheme of the money matters of Ireland (Dublin, 1729) p. 17), but it greatly exceeded the capital of the banks issuing it (Journals of the Irish House of Commons, vol. 5, p. 378).
    A pamphleteer in 1721 claimed that the paper credit of Ireland for the previous twenty years was never less than £600,000, 'and if I be rightly inform'd the sum was much greater' (Mr. Maxwell's second letter to Mr. Rowley, wherein the objections against the Bank are answered, 1721, p. 6). This would appear to be an exaggeration of the circulation of the Irish banks. The circulation of La Touche and Kane in the years 1719–25 varied between £20,000 and £60,000, and at the time of its failure in 1733 the longest established of the Irish banks, that of Burton & Falkiner, had outstanding notes valued only at £90,000 (Faulkner's Dublin Journal, 4 August 1733). Even as late as 1760 a Dublin bank, that of Richard and Thomas Dawson, had an outstanding issue of only £54,133 (Faulkner's Dublin Journal, 12 April 1760). On the other hand, when the note issue of the Dublin banks was at its largest Willcocks and Dawson were said to have an outstanding issue of £212,200 on 1 Jan. 1755 (Remarks on Willcocks and Dawson's estimates laid before the creditors the 5th of this instant at Guild-Hall and published in the newspapers the 8th of this instant (Dublin, 1755).
[4]A writer in 1762 stated that the circulation of the Irish banks prior to the many failures was above £1,000,000 and that it was now 'eclipsed' through the banks being in disrepute (Some hints on trade, money and credit, humbly addressed to the True Friends of Ireland, by Arthur Jones Nevill, Dublin, 1762, pp. 21–3). The note issue of the Dublin private banks in 1797 was estimated at £700,000 (Report of the Committee on the circulating paper, specie and the current coin of Ireland, 1804, reprinted 1826, pp. 9, 92).

Recovery in Irish banking in the subsequent decades was slow. The number of Dublin houses, which had been six at the beginning of the 1730s[1] and eight in 1754,[2] was reduced to four by the early 1760s.[3] One other house, that of Coates and Lawless, probably dates from the same decade, at least in its early stages as a quasi-banking business, and in the same year as the failure of Coates and Lawless, 1793, the house of Beresford opened, the first addition to the Dublin private banking business in over a quarter of a century. The progress of banking in provincial centres was likewise faltering in the decades following 1760. Only six banks were opened in four centres, and the extent of their operations was limited.[4] The circulation of the Belfast Bank, founded in 1784, never exceeded £30,000;[5] in Cork, next to Dublin, the largest banking centre in the island, the outstanding notes of Roberts' Bank amounted in 1793 only to £76,133. The provincial note issue, with banks in only three or four towns other than Cork, grew much more slowly than the volume of commercial transactions, and in the capital itself the private banks towards the end of the 1790s can at best have built up a circulation no more extensive than that of the Dublin banks of the 'fifties. The need for an increased supply of media of exchange was in part made good by the founding of the Bank of Ireland, which in 1797 had a paper issue equal to that of all the Dublin private banks combined; in part by the steady inflow of specie under a favourable course of exchange both on private account and for the account of the Bank of Ireland.[6] Because the

[1]La Touche & Kane, Swift & Co., Nuttall & McGuire, Hugh Henry & Co., Joseph Fade & Co., Burton & Falkiner.

[2]La Touche & Kane, Gleadowe & Co. (formerly Swift's Bank), Willcocks & Dawson (formerly Fade's Bank), Dillon & Ferrall, Lennox & French, Thomas Finlay & Co., Mitchel & Macarell, Richard & Thomas Dawson.

[3]William Gleadowe & Co., La Touche & Son; Thomas Finlay & Co., Sir George Colebrooke.

[4]Two banks in Cork (Tonson's, later called Warren's, Bank founded in 1768, and Roberts' founded about 1786), The Bank of Limerick in 1789, Hayden & Rivers in Waterford and two short-lived banks in Belfast (Belfast Bank, and Cunningham's Bank).

[5]*Report from the Select Committee on promissory notes in Scotland and Ireland,* p. 102, P.P. 1826 (iii) 402. On Belfast banking see also J.J. Monaghan, 'Social and economic history of Belfast', unpublished M.A. thesis, Queen's University pp. 170–82; Public Record Office of Northern Ireland, Downshire Papers, D. 607, nos. 704, 728, 856, 11 August, 2 September, 9 November 1796.

[6]The supply of specie in Ireland in 1774 was put at £1,500,000 by one writer (*Thoughts on a fund for the improvement of credit in Great Britain and the establishment of a National Bank in Ireland* (London, 1780) p. 24), a figure which represents a great increase on previous estimates. This figure also agrees substantially with

Irish banks were primarily discounting houses, the issue of notes was, in a sense, only incidental and had been adopted by the want of specie. Even allowing for some development of provincial banking in the second half of the century, and for the additional accommodation provided by the Bank of Ireland, itself in the first decade or more of its existence a bank of moderate size and confined in the main to the Dublin area, the discounting facilities made available by the banks were failing to keep up with the growth of internal and external trade. This gave rise in the second half of the century to a class of merchants with a specialized bill trade. Their functions were similar to those of the Irish banks, the only real difference being that they did not issue notes in discounting, largely because of an enlarged supply of gold coins. In an enquiry before the House of Commons in 1772 into the bankruptcy of William Howard a wine importer, for instance, a witness stated that Howard had 'set up the bill trade, that is, that he had become an acceptor and discounter of bills, and that country gentlemen lodged their money with him.'[1] One landlord, Pollard of Castlepollard in Co. Westmeath, had since 1767 been in the habit of paying his rents into Howard's hand, and drawing on him as often as he required. Howard frequently advanced sums to Pollard, and when he had occasion drew on Pollard in London.[2] These bill merchants also tended to support one another and in addition had recourse to the banks. Abraham Grier, for example, drew on the bank of Colebrooke to the amount of £50,000 a year, and owed £4,000 at the time of Howard's failure.[3]

From the beginning of the century onwards, provincial merchants

Young's statement that 'the specie of Ireland, gold and silver, is calculated by the Dublin bankers at £1,600,000' (Young, *Tour in Ireland*, pt. II, p. 146). There is evidence of a strong inflow of specie in the following decades and the supply in 1797 was put at £5,000,000 (*Report of the Committee on the circulating paper, specie and the current coin of Ireland*, 1804, reprinted 1826, p. 86). An important contributory factor was the removal of the prohibition on the export of English gold and silver to Ireland in 1780. Hitherto guineas could be shipped to Ireland only by stealth.

[1]Report on the bankruptcy of William Howard, 20 March 1772. *Journals of the Irish House of Commons,* vol. 8, app. cccclxv.

[2]Ibid., app. cccclxvii. Some idea of the extent of Howard's bill trade can be obtained from the evidence given by Patrick Ferril, book-keeper to the partnership of William and John Howard, before the parliamentary committee. According to the committee's summary of Ferril's evidence, Howard's receipts over the period 1 June to 15 November 1770, the latter the date of his bankruptcy, were £34,678 and his disbursements from notes and bills accepted in the same time, £60,513. (Ibid., app. cccclxxi).

[3]Ibid., app. cccclxxii.

14

had begun to have enlarged financial and commercial dealings with Dublin correspondents. This gave rise to an increased circulation of inland bills of exchange, and some of the Dublin merchants who acted as correspondents gradually developed a bill business to meet the various requirements of internal payments, as well as of external exchange. In 1770 the Cork merchant, Richard Pope, employed the bank of Thomas Finlay and Company as his Dublin correspondents, but had also some financial dealings with the Dublin firm of Williams and Sadleir, with whom 'I do all my merchantile (*sic*) business . . . and some bill business.'[1] The large Dublin merchant house of Joshua and Joseph Pim discounted bills on a very extensive scale. In the 'nineties they were discounting bills on English merchants for Courtenay and Ridgway, provision merchants in Waterford, and accepting drawings on them by butter merchants in the river valleys converging on Waterford, from whom Courtenay and Ridgway purchased corn and butter. Their business with Courtenay and Ridgway in 1792 amounted to almost £43,000 and when drawings on them tended to be in advance of bills discounted or negotiated, they drew on, or had sums remitted, from one or other of two London discount houses who also operated for Courtenay and Ridgway.[2] Important among the merchants who besides their functions in commodity trade provided indispensable services in the financing of trade and the remitting of money were the Dublin linen merchants.

The Dublin firm of Robert Shaw & Son had a country-wide business, dealt with large provincial firms and country bill merchants, and even acted as a correspondent for two banks in Cork, one in Limerick and one in Waterford. Shaw negotiated and rediscounted bills for the bankers, accepted their drawings on him, and regularly dispatched large consignments of guineas to the country. The volume of this business was large, amounting in the case of the individual bankers to annual totals varying between £80,000 and £200,000. At times, the country bankers allowed balances to accumulate in Shaw's hands, but he also advanced them large sums. In April 1792, for instance, Shaw agreed to extend the credit of Maunsell & Company, the Limerick bankers, to £20,000 'on particular occasions'. His

---

[1]Library of the Society of Friends, London. Gurney Papers, Section II, no. 330 E. Richard Pope to Richard Gurney, Cork, 6 Sept. 1770.

[2]Ledger of Courtenay and Ridgway, 1 June 1791–31 May 1792, in the possession of Mrs. Olive Ridgway, Rossmore, Mallow, Co. Cork. The London houses were Smith, Wright, Hammet & Co., and Peter Thellusson, Sons & Company.

dealings with his correspondent in London were rather limited, arising mainly from transactions on behalf of his country customers, or from English bills he had taken from them. These were normally negotiated on the Dublin market, or rediscounted at the Bank of Ireland, but at times Shaw appears to have held them to build up London balances. Shaw was a merchant in the inland flour trade, and advanced money to country merchants on receipt of their flour in Dublin. This was at the origin of his bill trade, and as early as 1785 he had developed a fairly considerable business which was totally unrelated to his commodity trade. By the 'nineties the Shaws' commodity trade had become a mere sideline to the growing volume of their discounting and accepting activities.[1] In 1797 Shaw junior wound up business on his own account and became a member in the partnership of Thomas Lighton & Company, which opened a bank in Dublin in the following year. The Shaws' business was exceptional only in its extent, for the nature and evolution of their operations were reflected in other Dublin and provincial mercantile houses at this time.

The pattern of Irish payments was to change radically in the nineteenth century. One of the most important features was, of course, the abolition of the separate Irish currency in 1826, which in the absence of an Irish mint had, in any case, been purely conceptual and not a physical reality. The existence of a course of exchange on London had imposed a strain on the Irish banks, which even the Bank of Ireland, despite its relatively large resources, felt severely.[2] The abolition of the Irish currency and hence of the exchange strengthened the Irish banking system and, in conjunction with other factors, altered the character of its business. Dublin, Cork and Belfast had all been centres of exchange with London in the eighteenth century, of which Dublin was overwhelmingly the most important, being linked by an organized bill trade with the provincial towns. The early nineteenth century, however, witnessed the decay of this structure in its internal as well as in its external branches. One of its first manifestations dates from 1797, when the suspension of gold payments in Ireland made the Belfast linen shippers, who had still to find gold to purchase their linens in the north of Ireland, where

[1]National Library, Dublin. Shaw MSS., 1785–97.
[2]See a long resolution made by the Court of Directors of the Bank in the light of a report from the Treasury Committee, the text of which is given in Hall, op. cit., pp. 107–8.

payment in gold remained the rule, decline to take bills on Dublin from their English customers.[1] Direct financial dealings from the various parts of Ireland continued to develop in the following years (reflecting the supersession of the specialist merchant and hence the less dominant position of Dublin in Irish overseas trade), and in 1822 the Court of Directors of the Bank of Ireland noticed that the inland bill trade was in decline, and direct payment to England more common than formerly.[2] This indicated an increased reliance on London, which was now beginning to replace Dublin in the control of the Irish financial system—a change which corresponded to the altered pattern of Irish overseas trade and to the increased dependence on England in political and economic matters generally.

[1]Public Record Office of Northern Ireland: William McCance to Jackson and Rushforth in Manchester, Belfast, 24 April 1797. (Copies of invoices of linen shipped by McCance, and of covering letters.)

[2]Text of the Court of Directors' resolution, Hall, op. cit., pp. 107-8. ' . . . that a considerable alteration appears to have taken place in the mode of transacting trade between England and Ireland, whereby payments are made more directly in the way of exchange and much fewer inland bills are made in Ireland, consequently so long as the Bank shall decline to discount bills on London, its discounts must bear a very small proportion to the trade of the country.'

CHAPTER XI

ANGLO-IRISH TRADE AND IRISH
ECONOMIC DEVELOPMENT

ANGLO-IRISH trade in the eighteenth century can be viewed as the main branch of Irish foreign trade or as the most indispensable factor in the country's economic development. The former aspect is in fact the superficial aspect of the considerable changes affecting Ireland in the economic context in the eighteenth century.

As far as Irish overseas trade is concerned, Anglo-Irish trade was mainly responsible for the expansion in its volume. The enhanced importance of European markets was a temporary phenomenon of the immediate aftermath of the Cattle Acts: as early as the 1690s it was clear that trade with England accounted again for a rising proportion of Irish exports. This upwards trend was halted seriously only during the economic stagnation of the 1720s. England was the most expansive market area in Europe: its textile industries offered a market for wool, worsted yarn and linen yarn, and exemption from import duties granted to Irish linen in 1696 gave the Irish linen industry an opportunity to overtake German linen in the one branch of the textile industries (apart from silk) in which England was weak. The continental market for Irish beef and butter was limited. Butter exports to Europe fell at the end of the century, and henceforth fluctuated within a static or declining trend. If beef exports recovered momentum in the 1720s, it was only because the expansion of the English and French plantations created new markets. Within Europe a somewhat better balance in agriculture[1] tended to reduce outlets for Irish livestock products. Indeed, by the 1780s with reduced demand for Irish butter in Europe and for beef in the West Indies, it is likely that but for the growth of English demand, severe depression would have occurred in the country's staple agricultural exports.[2]

As far as imports are concerned, the prominence of continental trade was largely the result of the importance of wine in the pattern of demand of an underdeveloped country. The consumer and capital

---

[1]B.H. Slicher Van Bath, *The agrarian history of Western Europe, A.D. 500–1850* (London, 1963) pp. 205–15.

[2]L.M. Cullen, 'The role of foreign trade in the eighteenth-century Irish economy', paper read to the Economic History Society Conference, Belfast, April 1967.

goods required by the Irish economy, growing and to an extent changing in the eighteenth century, could be obtained in greater quantity and at more competitive prices in England. Preferential tariffs and in some cases prohibitions on imports from other sources only helped to reinforce a trend that was in any event inevitable on economic grounds.

It seems clear that England's industrial expansion and Ireland's economic development in the eighteenth century are associated. Alternative markets for Irish products were few, and the English market, from the start the motor of expansion in the linen industry, came in the second half of the century to play the same role as far as Irish agricultural exports were concerned. At the time England's industrial expansion hardly appeared to threaten Ireland's industrial prospects. Indeed the growth in effective demand in Ireland made possible by enlarged export outlets appeared to strengthen industry, and, as the second half of the century progressed, larger units employing more capital and an extended division of labour replaced small and scattered units, many of which had succumbed to English competition in the middle of the century. It is these circumstances and not the policies or subsidies of Grattan's Parliament that accounted for the evidence of industrial growth in the closing decades of the eighteenth century.

Contemporary belief that Ireland could industrialize, overoptimistic though it was, was not wholly unrealistic, because it was far from clear at the time that England's advantages in industrialization were, as later proved to be the case, altogether disproportionate. Fuel costs in the Irish ports were, given the ease of importing coal by sea from England or Scotland, not excessive, and moreover it was still hoped that investment in mining and in the new 'fire engines' and further expenditure on canal building would help to industrialize the interior as well as reduce Ireland's dependence on imported coal itself. Fears among English businessmen that Irish industries might constitute serious competition were not exaggerated public attitudes (though they were that to some extent also) but a belief in a possibility which experience could not exclude. Within England itself the localization of industry was still very incomplete, and many of the early manifestations of the so-called Industrial Revolution took place outside what were to prove subsequently the main centres of industrial expansion. At the time English and Irish industrial expansion hardly seemed incompatible. Even cotton spinning, the main focus of the

Industrial Revolution at this stage, was greatly stimulated in Ireland by the new technological and organizational changes, and expanded rapidly. It was only in the course of the first three or four decades of the nineteenth century that the extent and nature of the threat to Irish industrial development made itself clearly evident. The removal of duties, subsequent to the Union in 1801, was in no way instrumental in this change, because the decisive factors lay in the gradual localization of industry on the coalfields and in the external economies that went with localization. Confidence was still general at the end of the eighteenth century, and there is a striking contrast between this buoyant outlook and the pessimistic attitudes that grew in the nineteenth century and that took refuge in the Union itself as an explanation of difficulties due solely to economic causes.

Within the eighteenth century, the growth of foreign trade promoted a considerable degree of economic development and brought on significant changes in economic organization. The radius of operation of merchants in the ports extended through a wider hinterland and their success in turn relied in part on the rise of inland merchants. Fairs and markets helped to make the changes effective. As markets developed, economic specialization became more pronounced. Such specialization was of course still embryonic. The typical merchant handled several commodities and discharged several mercantile functions. As opportunity offered, capital was switched from one activity to another. In a market which, though expanding, was still relatively small, especially in the provinces, and in which profit margins could fluctuate widely in the short run, it was of course only natural that merchants should take full advantage of the flexibility of operations made possible by the fact that their investment was primarily one of working capital. When depression in the linen trade in 1773 coincided with poor harvests, the bleaching firm of Andrews was able to switch most of their operations temporarily to their flour-milling business and to the import of grain from America; 'seeing there was no probability of making anything by them [linens] worthwhile and money in this country being exceeding scarce we thought we cou'd make more by employing our money in another trade'.[1] Instances could be multiplied, and would also illustrate how merchant capital helped to finance industrial development.

---

[1] Isaac Andrews & Sons Ltd., Belfast, Letter books. John and Michael Andrews to Thomas Bird, Sunderland. Comber, 22 October 1773.

Most striking of the incipient but incomplete trends towards specialization was the emergence of better defined banking and discounting activity. Fortuitous or subsidiary gains on the exchanges encouraged a number of merchants to expand their exchange activities, developing a remitting or discounting business well in excess of the financial requirements of their own commodity trade. Some of these merchants gradually developed a banking business connected with, though in some measure independent of, their commodity trade, and not a few in time concentrated their capital on the business of banking and exchange. The move from commodity trade to banking suggests that profits were higher in the latter activity. This is of course what one would expect. Banking was the more liquid trade, and the turnover much quicker than in the more sluggish business of exchanging commodities. Thus, Samuel Hoare, son of a Cork banker and partner in the business of Gurnell & Co. of London who were correspondents for several Irish banks, received a profit of £5,174 in the three years from 1 April 1744 to 1 April 1747, while his proportion of the partnership's stock was £8,000.[1] The return on his capital therefore averaged 21½ per cent for the three years. In the 5 years 1722-6 the Dublin bankers La Touche and Kane had an annual average profit of about £1,560 on a capital somewhat in excess of £8,000. These figures would suggest that returns on their capital were almost 20 per cent. Such profits appear to be well in excess of earnings in commodity trade: the move from trade to banking, although a perfectly logical extension of economic activity, was from the point of view of the individual merchant dictated first and foremost by considerations of profit.

As a very large proportion of Irish trade was on English account, commission earnings loomed large in the earnings of most Irish merchants. This reflects to a large extent the smaller capital resources of the Irish merchant community, and the fact that the market cost of capital—and the personal cost where self-financing was involved—was greater in Ireland than in England. The fact that commission earnings tended to predominate may have had psychological consequences with rather wide economic implications. Commission earnings, while reflecting changes in the prices of goods, were by comparison with the profits of trade on a merchant's own account, more immediately dependent on the volume of trade which fluctuated

[1]Public Museum, Cork. Ledger of Samuel Hoare of Cork and London, 1744-96.

relatively little, especially where agricultural commodities were concerned, than on prices which fluctuated sharply and could wipe out
profits altogether. The incomes of Irish merchants therefore tended
to be relatively stable by comparison with earnings acquired by trade
on merchants' own account, and especially by contrast to the
incomes of agricultural producers in the hinterland of Irish ports.
This relative stability of earnings may be one of the factors accounting
for the conservatism and want of enterprise of which Irish merchants
have been accused traditionally. Caution was the keyword, and where
the market was restricted there was justification for it: a merchant
in Waterford advised with regard to malt imports that 'we would
much prefer making a contract with our principal brewers than
encourage it to come for sale. In that case, as there are but a few of
them, they might blow on it'.[1]

Trends in merchants' returns in trade are difficult to assess, although there are many instances of profits for individual consignments or for short periods of time. Profits tended, as far as can be
judged, to be modest, and fluctuations between good and bad years
emphasized that high returns on occasion could hardly be taken as
representative of the business even of more successful merchants. In
any event high rates of return in many instances reflected higher costs,
the effects of the small scale of business of many merchants: 'the
bulk of our business is carried on by small and inconsiderable stocks,
and the merchants are forced to exact high prices per cent in order
to support themselves on such slender capitals'.[2] To the extent that
overheads had to be reckoned with, many merchants were prepared
to transact business for small returns. The oatmeal firm of Bogle
Oliphant & Co. in Glasgow and Ayr, for example, informed a
Drogheda merchant in 1769 that 'as we keep a man constantly for
retailing and being now out we would be glad to keep him employed
even for a small profit'.[3] Again, merchants were prepared to accept
low profits because much of their capital represented earnings
ploughed back into the business and in the absence of widespread
investment opportunities in the economy did not at first sight appear
to occasion a cost for the merchant. Small merchants working on

[1]Library of the Society of Friends, London. Gurney Papers, II/338E. Joseph
Jacob to Richard Gurney. Waterford, 20 October 1770.
    [2]*Reflections little to the purpose on a paper less to the purpose (by the author of
Seasonable remarks)* Dublin, 1729, p. 48.
    [3]Scottish Record Office, General Register House, Edinburgh. Letter book of
Alexander Oliphant. Ayr, 29 July 1769.

their own capital were much less likely to be deterred by low profits than larger merchants, some of whose resources entailed a real capital cost in a readily perceptible sense. As a worsted yarn merchant in Cork noted:

> When trade bears a profit adequate to the expence of raising money, at the rate you know it must cost some, things go on well; when profits are reduced under that, he who deals on an artificial capital must sink— he will not or can not stop his business till it stops him, but goes on, get or lose, and thereby the little trader, who employs his real capital only, is hard set to maintain his family, and often is reduced—formerly this trade was good, the great and the small got by it . . .[1]

Shipping employed in the coal trade was a particularly striking instance of low returns. Conditions had been particularly bad in the 1720s,[2] but even as late as 1744 Sir James Lowther remarked that the owners 'must be tired with advancing money for repairs and receiving no dividends'.[3] Although Lowther's firm opinion was that the coal trade could be profitable only to vessels specialized in the trade he had to admit in 1738 that the coal trade 'would be entirely ruined if great part of it was not carried on by ships that are frequently employ'd in other business by which they are greater gainers'.[4] The accounts of a Whitehaven vessel between 1762 and 1771 show that, despite larger earnings in intermittent voyages to European or American destinations, dividends paid to the owners were normally modest.[5] In such conditions, and especially where many of the vessels depended exclusively on the coal trade, intensive utilization was the only way of reducing the incidence of overhead charges, and coals continued to be shipped as long as there was any likelihood of some

[1]Library of the Society of Friends, London. Gurney Papers, II/484. Ebenezer Pike to Richard & John Gurney, Cork, 18 July 1772.

[2]Record Office, The Castle, Carlisle. Sir James Lowther's letters to his agent in Whitehaven. 26 January 1721 (no. 37); 29 October 1723 (no. 69). *Calculations relating to the coal trade being an account of what coals stand in per ton, delivered at the keys of Dublin by the Whitehaven ships. Computed according to the known rules of merchandising,* 1721 (copy in the Goldsmith Collection). Makey, op. cit., passim.

[3]Record Office, The Castle, Carlisle. Sir James Lowther's letters, 22 November 1744 (no. 102). Again in 1754 he referred to the owners 'raising more money voyage after voyage to carry on the ordinary repairs and business of the ships (ibid., 11 April 1754 (no. 44)).

[4]Ibid., 6 April 1738 (no. 6).

[5]Record Office, The Castle, Carlisle. Benson Papers. Trading accounts, 1762-71. The accounts of two Maryport vessels, the *Duke,* 1764-70 and *Nancy,* 1770-95, confirm this. National Library of Ireland, MSS. 1589-90.

surplus above working costs. The trade was still regarded as barely remunerative in 1794,[1] and the evidence of masters before the Dublin coal committee tends to corroborate this conclusion.[2] Because of the absence of investment outlets, a surplus of capital existed in relatively backward areas such as Cumberland. Poorly remunerated though capital invested in coal vessels appears to have been, the mere fact that any dividend was paid at all on shares in ships was sufficient to attract capital. Ownership was highly fragmented and diffused widely through the hinterland of the port among not only merchants and seamen but among widows, tradesmen and 'gentlemen' of small resources. In such circumstances continued investment in the shipping was a product both of isolation from areas offering more remunerative outlets for investment and of a poorly developed monetary evaluation of the costs of investment necessarily made by individuals who had no clear alternative outlet for their savings.

Scattered indications exist of what contemporaries regarded as acceptable profits. In 1673 Colonel Richard Laurence, when the exchange charged on bills on London was £10 per cent, proposed a method of saving half the cost of bills in remitting money to London by exporting Irish commodities instead of bills, remarking that 'that I believe is as much as most merchants gain by their adventure'.[3] Six years later, the Belfast merchant George Macartney, delayed remitting money to London, when exchange was £4½ per cent to £5 per cent and falling, observing that 'if it come to par its better than any trade whatever'.[4] A century later a northern bleacher John Andrews wrote to a London factor that 'at the price you have sold them when I deduct the interest of my money I have not more than 4 per cent clear profit. I leave you to judge if that is sufficient for my

[1]According to Hutchinson, writing in 1794, 'the profits to the shipping are very uncertain, no capital of such an extent makes so poor a return; it barely affords a living profit to the industrious and careful. The shares are divided into small parts, and are generally taken to oblige some individual rather than with the view of much advantage' (op. cit., vol. ii, p. 140). See also O. Wood, 'The development of the coal, iron and shipbuilding industries in Cumberland', unpublished Ph.D. thesis (Econ. Hist.) University of London, 1952, pp. 53, 93-4.

[2]Public Record Office of Ireland, Dublin. 1A-46-46. Committee books of the committee on the Dublin coal trade, 1793.

[3]H.M.C. *Ormonde MSS.*, new series, vol. 3, p. 333. Laurence was the author of the *The interest of Ireland in its trade and wealth* (Dublin, 1682).

[4]Linen Hall Library, Belfast. Letter book of George Macartney, Belfast 1679-81. p. 67, 16 July 1679.

trouble'.[1] These isolated quotations suggest that a level of profit regarded as acceptable in the difficult conditions of the 1670s had little appeal under better conditions a century later. What profits merchants might hope to attain is suggested by the Cork yarn merchant, George Newenham, having made a 'sketch' of his affairs in 1772, informing his Norwich correspondent that 'for these two years past I don't find I have made 15 per cent per annum on my capital'.[2] If this is a gross margin, it suggests at interest rates of 6 per cent a net return of 9 per cent[3] as the one which Newenham had hoped for but had failed to gain in what we know were the very competitive conditions of the trade in those years and against a background of general economic difficulty in both islands at the time. Fluctuations in profits suggest that the monopoly element typically was absent. Even discounting the claims made by merchants about low profits, business records suggest that in fact profit margins often proved disappointing. Moreover, low profits were encountered frequently not only during the recurrent trade recessions but even at the peak of economic activity.

High realised profits—as opposed to the anticipation of profits—do not appear to have been an important factor in promoting economic expansion. To the extent that high profits would have represented an element of monopoly they should in fact have proved conducive to a less than optimum expansion of output. In a sense the absence of monopoly conditions was a vital factor in securing a high rate of economic development. Low rates of return—as in shipping in the coal trade—were associated in practice with a striking expansion in capacity. The linen industry, the most remarkable instance of expansion in Anglo-Irish trade, is perhaps a case even more in point. Profits in the linen trade varied widely between good and bad years.[4] But even when conditions were favourable, competitive buying by drapers and bleachers tended to raise the prices of unbleached cloth, while at the same time the greater quantity of bleached cloth being put on the market damped the rise in prices, profit margins

[1]Andrews MSS. in possession of Messrs. Isaac Andrews and Sons Ltd., Belfast. John Andrews to Quintin Dick, London. Comber, 12 February 1790.

[2]Library of the Society of Friends, London. Gurney Papers, section 2, no. 377. George Newenham to R. & J. Gurney. Cork, 12 June 1772 (copy).

[3]Turnover was slow in the yarn trade, and hence a given outlay might be recouped only over a year or longer.

[4]Public Record Office of Northern Ireland, D. 468. Ledger and invoices of James Ferguson, 1771-84.

thus being squeezed from both ends. When drapers and bleachers reduced their purchases, this was not because reduced profits led to fewer purchases, but because a slower turnover of cloth already on the Dublin and London markets deprived them of the working capital that would have made it possible for them to keep the bleach greens full.

When sales were slow the bleacher was in something of a dilemma. On the one hand the absence of sales reduced his turnover and the consequent want of ready money limited his ability to replenish his greens with a fresh supply of unbleached cloth. On the other hand money could be obtained only by advances from the factors on the security of unsold goods in their warehouses, or by pushing sales through substantial abatements on the invoice prices. Both courses however reduced the profits, the former by heavy interest charges at a time when unsold goods were slow to clear, the latter by cutting the profit margin which the bleacher had allowed for in his invoicing. But in declining advances from the factors or in refusing to concede price abatements, the bleacher stood to gain little, for when the market picked up again, higher prices were a poor compensation for the long period during which the bleacher had impatiently awaited a return on his outlay. If the bleacher computed the interest on his outlay, the real returns were indeed poor. 'Linens seldom advance by keeping equall to the interest of money', complained a Comber firm in 1772.[1] Bleachers because of their efforts to achieve a turnover of their capital twice within the year, allowed themselves a relatively modest profit margin in order to push their sales on the very competitive markets. A Comber bleaching firm informed a London merchant house in 1790 that 'the very low prices at which I allow them to be sold requires quick returns',[2] and in 1792 another London house were told by the same firm that their price range 'leaves a very trifling profit indeed, shou'd our goods not be immediately disposed of, it is a business not worth attending to'.[3] Bleachers were therefore prepared to accept relatively small profit margins in return for quick sales. The measure of good trading conditions was quick returns

[1]Andrews MSS. in the possession of Messrs. Isaac Andrews & Sons Ltd., Belfast. John and Michael Andrews (to William Gregson, mcht., Dublin), Comber, 20 January 1772.

[2]Ibid., John Andrews to Hayter, Pearson & Sammam, London. 4 November 1790. See also a letter of 6 April 1791 to Hayter, and of 16 May 1791 to Quintin Dick.

[3]Ibid., John & J. Andrews to Quintin Dick, 20 June 1792.

rather than a large margin. When the trade was depressed both margins and returns were unsatisfactory. 'We join you in opinion', wrote a County Down bleaching firm to a London correspondent in 1792, 'that it is better to have quick returns if but small profits, but when there is no interest of money . . . we think it hard to sell'.[1]

It is against a background such as this that Anglo-Irish trade expanded. Monopoly profits were probably exceptional or temporary. Returns were typically modest, capital was accumulated painfully, and the ploughing back of some of the profits was an indispensable factor in business growth. Such circumstances can hardly have made merchants the happiest of men—the mortality of firms was in fact very high—but they were indispensable none the less in the economic expansion of the age.

The growth of Anglo-Irish trade is one of the most striking features of trade within the British Isles in the eighteenth century. Within the eighteenth century neither demographic growth nor the early stages of the Industrial Revolution adversely affected Ireland's development as a whole. In the case of the Industrial Revolution change was experienced not only indirectly through the expansion of the English market but directly by organizational changes which helped to make once declining industries such as glass and brewing competitive again and made it possible for the cotton industry to expand. In the early nineteenth century, conditions began to become distinctly less favourable. Population growth had already proceeded to an extent which was beginning to outrun the resources of a mainly rural economy. At the same time the fuller realization of the Industrial Revolution in England was about to undermine many Irish industries, including ones which had gained initially from the technological and organizational changes of the Industrial Revolution. Domestic industry, especially in textiles, widespread in the northern half of the country in particular and an ever more indispensable component of small incomes in rural areas as population grew, was of course also subject to the blast of competition. The vulnerability of domestic industry was all the greater because the threat to it came not only from outside the island but from linen spinning in factory units emerging around Belfast from the end of the 1820s. The effect of the Industrial Revolution was thus to undermine the prospects of industrialization at the very time when through continued population

[1]Ibid., John & J. Andrews to Quintin Dick, London. Comber, 4 August 1792.

growth new employment outlets off the land were more necessary than ever. The decay of domestic spinning generally and of weaving in the more peripheral areas was an important factor in the widening rural impoverishment of the decades preceding the Famine.

Anglo-Irish trade is a convenient medium through which to see the organizational and environmental changes affecting economic life. While the growth of trade and changes in organization gave a stimulus to development and even diversification at first, their long-term results proved quite different. The growth of trade led in the long run to striking transport improvements in the form of the railways and steam shipping in cross-channel trade and to the localization of industry. As the more self-contained economic communities within England or elsewhere in the British Isles were drawn into a wider market zone embracing the islands as a whole, industry in the less favoured locations became exposed to increased competition. With declining industry such areas ceased to be the semi-self-sufficient industrial units they had been and found themselves increasingly on the periphery of a much larger market. These changes were already anticipated in banking where even in the first quarter of the nineteenth century—before their full effects on industry were experienced—London was already replacing Dublin as the pivotal point around which payments between the two islands centred. The changes in financial relations were themselves simply a facet of the more flexible commercial relations in which direct contacts were replacing commodity exchanges arranged by intermediaries of the old type. The breakdown of the insular market and financial structure revolving around Dublin is a facet of the growing absorption of rural Ireland as of rural England into a single large market covering most of the production and exchanges within these islands. Such changes worked imperceptibly and often subtly. Contemporaries of the nineteenth century were not always aware of their significance, and above all political obsession in Ireland with the Union between the two islands which became effective on the first of January 1801 led few to realise or to accept their inevitability.

THE COMPARATIVE EVIDENCE AND VALUE OF EIGHTEENTH-CENTURY STATISTICS OF ANGLO-IRISH TRADE[1]

BROADLY speaking, the correspondence between the statistics on both sides of the Irish sea is quite satisfactory, though they are not at all stages strictly comparable. The ledgers of Irish imports and exports[2] give separate figures for England and Scotland up to and including 1731, but thereafter figures exist only for Great Britain till 1783 when the Irish statistics are again subdivided. From 1755 onwards, however, there is a run of statistics of Scottish overseas trade compiled in Edinburgh from data returned from the Scottish outports,[3] and these when taken in conjunction with the corresponding London figures for English trade,[4] afford a fairly satisfactory basis for comparison between Great Britain and Ireland in the years from 1755 onwards for quantities, though not for values. The quantities in the various statistics correspond reasonably well, and comparison is closest in commodities such as wool, which for reasons of commercial policy, and tobacco, tea, sugar and rum, which because of drawbacks on re-export from England and high import duties in Ireland, were subject to strict customs control and close liaison between the officers in the two countries. In these commodities, as in most others entering into Anglo-Irish trade, there is a tendency for exports on one side to exceed the corresponding imports on the other, but the excess is normally small enough to be accounted for by the inevitable delays between entry and physical shipment, losses at sea and forced changes of destination. For the other commodities of Anglo-Irish trade a similar correspondence exists, though on the whole in a less discernible degree. In some commodities the tendency for exports to exceed the corresponding imports on the other side appears to be reversed, and in a few items large discrepancies arise of a nature that varied over the century. The most striking variation is in hops but the discrepancy can be explained satisfactorily.[5] The mere failure of figures on both sides to correspond should not in itself be taken as a sign of smuggling between the countries. The abuses might be of purely local significance or might relate to smuggling to a third country or could simply be a statistical discrepancy caused by the method of recording the data. On the other hand, the fact that figures broadly agree on both sides does not necessarily signify that the statistics measure fairly accurately the total volume of trade

---

[1]For discussion of English foreign trade statistics see G. N. Clark, *Guide to English commercial statistics 1696–1782* (London, 1938) and Professor Ashton's introduction to Schumpeter, op. cit.

[2]P.R.O., *Customs* 15.   [3]P.R.O., *Customs* 14.

[4]P.R.O., *Customs* 2, 3, 17, Custom House Library, London, Ledgers of Imports and Exports.

[5]See chapter IV, pp. 77–8, n. 1.

between the two countries. In the case of coal, for example, the Irish customs normally accepted the masters' own entries or the figures entered on their English cocquets: the broad correspondence between the figures is, therefore, somewhat meaningless, and the Irish statistics totally fail to serve as a check on the undoubted abuses that existed in the English ports shipping coals to Ireland. A comparison of the statistical material on both sides also affords little evidence for an estimation of the volume of the smuggling trade in high-duty commodities. Such goods smuggled from Britain to Ireland were simply entered for a third country, and in Ireland goods destined for the British smuggling market, where entered at the Custom House at all, were as a rule entered for the Irish coastwise traffic. Statistical sources thus provide no real basis even for an attempt at measuring the clandestine traffic in high-duty commodities between the two islands.

Although in Irish exports to England a broad correspondence exists, important discrepancies arise in a few of the principal commodities. The fact that linen was free of duties on both sides appears to have led the linen exporters to make over-entries. But in the trade with England these over-entries are concealed or negatived by the fact that the linen merchants made under-entries with the knowledge of the customs officers to avoid the payment of local duties at Liverpool, Chester and Bristol, which were apparently determined by the amount expressed in the Irish merchants' cocquet. Over most of the century these two factors practically cancelled one another, as the statistics of exports of Irish linens normally exceed the corresponding figures for imports on the other side by above 5 to 10 per cent. These contrary tendencies appear to be well illustrated in the fact that in linen exports to Scotland, where the necessity for under-entries did not arise, the amounts apparently exported from Ireland greatly exceed the corresponding Scottish figures; and the figures on both sides only agree closely in the last four years of the century, when the Irish customs officers had become negligent in making full returns of linen exported and when, as a consequence, the volume of linen exports recorded for England had apparently for the first time fallen substantially below the corresponding English estimates for imports of linen.

Comparisons in the provision trade are seriously impaired by the fact that the rules governing entry of provisions appear to have been different on both sides or at any rate to have had a varying incidence on the recording of provisions for statistical purposes. The large discrepancies that frequently arise between the figures cannot consistently be explained away by any of the hypotheses that more commonly account for such variations, and the poor correspondence between the figures must arise from the official nature of much of the demand and from the importation of much beef, pork and some butter expressly for transhipment. In particular, the non-entry of purchases of provisions by the Admiralty Victualling Agent in Cork may explain how Irish export figures in the final decades of the century fall below the corresponding English figures, and on the other hand the apparent excess of Irish export over English import figures in the preceding period may possibly be accounted for by the export from Ireland

15

on nominal merchant account of provisions which were not entered on the English side in accordance with routine customs practice. On the other hand, figures for by-products of the provision trade such as raw hides and tallow, and for the small provision trade between Ireland and Scotland, tally reasonably well. But in the provision trade with England, the Irish estimates from the 1780s tend, on the whole, to fall much below the corresponding English figures. The general tendency in the period of Irish export figures for provisions to fall below the corresponding English figures would appear to confirm the growing importance relatively and absolutely of the Navy Victualling Agent in Cork, a reflection of the growing dependence of the Navy on direct official purchases in Ireland.

Exact quantitative comparison between the statistics on both sides of the Irish Sea is, of course, impossible. The English year ended on 25 December or after 1751, on 5 January, whereas in Ireland the year ending 25 December was employed only until 1706. Thereafter the Irish fiscal year ending on Lady Day, 25 March, was used until the end of the century. This difference of a quarter between the runs of statistics makes comparison very difficult. The difficulty is, of course, somewhat lessened by the trade being seasonally low in the first quarter of the year. In Irish wool exports in particular, this contributed to a very close correspondence between the statistics on both sides. But in most commodities the volume of off-season trade was large enough to reduce the degree of correspondence, and more so for imports into Ireland than for exports. A further difficulty is the long time elapsing between the date of entry of the same consignment in both countries, i.e. first in the country of export and subsequently in the country of import. As a result of factors of this nature, divergences of a fairly substantial nature can exist, even when the Customs year corresponds in both countries, as it did at the beginning of the century.

The statistics of the eighteenth century can be accepted as a fairly reliable guide to the volume of legal traffic in commodities which were subject to high duties or a strict control on both sides. In the case of other commodities, they are clearly less satisfactory, though they would still appear to serve as an acceptable general indication of the extent of trade. But comparison between the statistics affords practically no indication of the size of the smuggling trade between the two islands.

Though the statistics may therefore be taken as a guide to the volume of legal trade between the two islands in most individual commodities, they are extremely unreliable as a guide to the extent of this legal trade as a whole, because of the inadequacies of the official valuations. Moreover, as the valuations differed in the two countries, radically different conclusions concerning Anglo-Irish trade can be drawn from contemporary figures that otherwise broadly agree. Originally the Inspectors General in the two islands appear to have followed the same principle in forming valuations of commodities. Prices of exports were intended to represent the current wholesale prices of exports in the home ports, and valuations of imports were computed from the prices at which home merchants were supposed to have made their purchases overseas. However, there was some deviation from the principle, and in particular the English Inspectors

General completely abandoned from the opening of the eighteenth century the attempt to follow current prices. On the whole, the Irish prices appear to have followed the original plan fairly closely. The only obvious exception is coal, the valuation of which is based on the prices at which English coals were landed in Dublin and not the prices in the coal ports. This is a reasonable exception, as little or no coal was imported on Irish account, coals generally being sold to the Irish dealers at the Dublin quays out of the vessels of masters from the coal ports. In the English statistics a few departures from the principle are also readily detectable. The prices of herrings for instance, appear extraordinarily high by comparison with prices on the Irish side, and though coals appear to have been valued according to their price in the English ports in the first years, the valuations were soon altered to those of coals in the Irish ports. On the other hand the valuation employed in the Scottish statistics from the time of their inception in the 1750s is clearly that of coal in the Scottish ports.

In the early years the valuations employed in the English and Irish statistics correspond roughly, a reflection of the fact that valuations were based on current prices. But English valuations of imports tend to exceed the corresponding valuations employed in Ireland for Irish exports, even allowing for the difference in exchange rates, and the Irish valuations of imports from England appear to have been on the whole higher than those of English exports to Ireland. The result is that total Irish exports to England as computed in the Irish ledgers were, to the end of the first decade of the eighteenth century, generally less than total imports from Ireland as computed in the English statistics. On the other hand the Irish estimates of total imports from England exceed the corresponding English estimates. However, from the early 1720s, the estimates in the Irish Inspector General's ledgers of total imports from England fall increasingly below the corresponding estimates in London. The reason is that the valuations used in the Irish statistics reflect the fairly continuous fall of import prices, especially of colonial goods, in the first half of the country, whereas the English valuations which remained unaltered exaggerate the values of this trade. This fall in Irish valuations was so pronounced that from the early 1730s to the end of the 1770s the English estimates of exports to Ireland exceed the Irish figures for imports, despite the fact that over this period these latter figures included the growing volume of trade with Scotland as well as the English trade. The valuations of Irish imports rose again in the second half of the century and after 1783 the Irish estimates of imports from England exceed the corresponding English figures, though not by a substantial margin when allowance is made for the rates of exchange. The result of the English Inspector General's failure to adjust prices is most evident in the case of imports from Ireland. In the first decade of the eighteenth century, valuations of these exceed the Irish valuations and as a consequence the figures for total imports from Ireland exceed the Irish estimates of exports to England. But the Irish valuations of the commodities entering into the trade reflected the rise in actual prices, and when direct comparison between the Irish and English statistics again becomes possible from 1783 onwards, the Irish estimates of exports to England exceed by 50 per cent the corresponding English estimates of imports from Ireland.

Irish-Scottish trade was little larger in the early eighteenth century than it had been in the previous century. Exports and imports both hovered around the £10,000 to £30,000 mark, forming less than 10 per cent and at times less than 5 per cent of the corresponding figures for trade between Ireland and England. By the end of the century imports and exports both reached £200,000 to £350,000 per annum, even in those years when the statistics were most free of over-entries of Irish linen, and amounted to about 10 per cent of the corresponding figures for trade between England and Ireland. These figures appear to suggest that trade between Scotland and Ireland increased at a slightly faster rate than Anglo-Irish trade, and at the end of the century Irish trade with Scotland formed a somewhat larger portion of total Irish trade with Great Britain than it had at the beginning of the century. Statistics compiled in Scotland, which commenced only in 1755, employ a series of stable valuations, though they are independent of those used in the London statistics. These valuations, formed in 1755, are higher than those used by the Irish Inspector General. The valuations set on imports from Ireland were very high, and despite being left unaltered for the rest of the century they exceeded up to 1800 the corresponding Irish valuations, not only in the case of linen in which the Irish valuations were lagging behind actual prices from the middle of the century, but even in the case of livestock products in which several substantial, though inadequate, adjustments were made by the Irish Inspector General in the last 40 years of the century. Irish import valuations on the other hand correspond more closely to the Scottish valuations of exports The result is that Scottish estimates of total exports to Ireland only slightly exceed the corresponding estimate of imports in Ireland, even allowing for the rates of exchange, and by the end of the 'nineties as a result of further alterations of Irish valuations, Irish imports exceed the Scottish values of exports to Ireland, even allowing for the rates of exchange.

Figures for Scottish-Irish trade were seriously disturbed by factors affecting linen, the most important single commodity entering into Irish exports to Scotland. No local duties being levied in the Scottish ports on Irish linens, over-entries of linen for Scotland reached very large proportions, in some years Irish exports being twice or three times higher than the corresponding estimates in the Scottish statistics. On the other hand, the Scottish valuation of Irish linens at 2s. 1d. is a high one by comparison with the Irish one of 1s. 4d. per yard. As a result of the higher Scottish valuations for linens, Scottish figures for total imports exceed the corresponding Irish estimates except in those years when the over-entry of linens in Ireland was abnormally large.

BIBLIOGRAPHY

I. PRIMARY SOURCES

Administrative material

Administrative records may be divided into two principal categories:
(i) those emanating from the administration of the revenue or customs
establishments in these islands, and (ii) those referring to the general
administration of government.

The administrative aspects of Anglo-Irish trade can be documented
copiously from primary sources, despite the destruction of the Public
Record Office of Ireland in 1922, and the loss at one time or another of the
great bulk of the local customs records of the Irish ports and, on the other
side of the Irish sea, of the records of the ports of Liverpool and Bristol
and of the central customs administration in London. In particular, a
large number of the records of the Irish Revenue Commissioners found
their way to England in the early nineteenth century, including the ledgers
of imports and exports (Customs 15 in the Public Record Office in London)
and the voluminous minutes of the Irish Commissioners (Customs I in
the Public Record Office, London). On the English side, the ledgers of
exports and imports have survived (Customs, 2, 3, 17), and the letter books
of the customs establishments of some of the ports. To these should be
added the ledgers of exports and imports of Scotland (Public Record
Office, London, Customs 14), the port books of the Scottish ports (General
Register House, Edinburgh), and the letter books of the Scottish ports.

While these sources are voluminous in the amount of reference to trade,
they are, apart from the statistical sources, of limited value in illustrating
its evolution. The statistical material for Anglo-Irish trade in the eighteenth
century is particularly rich, and is more reliable than historians have
conceded. In addition to the statistics relating to the trade of England,
Scotland and Ireland as entities, a large number of port books survive
for many of the English and Scottish ports. This material has been little
used for this period. W.H. Makey's unpublished thesis 'The place of
Whitehaven in the Irish coal trade, 1600–1750' is the only instance of extensive use of this material to document an aspect of Anglo-Irish trade.
With a few isolated exceptions no port books have survived on the Irish
side, although the loss is made much less serious by the fact that the
ledgers of Irish exports and imports in addition to aggregates for the
country as a whole give figures for the traffic of each individual port in
Ireland in the various commodities imported and exported. As far as
Anglo-Irish trade is concerned, it is thus possible to establish the quantity
of exports and imports handled in each individual port in Ireland.

As far as general administrative records are concerned, the loss of most
of the Irish records is lessened by the fact that the Public Record Office in
London preserves the other half of the vast correspondence between
Dublin and London and also that many documents of an administrative
or political nature survive in private collections, published or unpublished,
and among manuscripts in the British Museum. These documents are

often concerned with issues touching on commercial questions. However, their interest is primarily political, and they generally throw little light either on the organisation or evolution of trade. Moreover, the information fed to politicians was often misleading or inaccurate, and intended to promote or deter a particular course of action. The interpretation of economic events affecting Ireland was already overcoloured by political preoccupations.

The great mass of administrative material is unpublished. Some contemporary printed sources such as the appendices to the Journals of the Irish House of Commons and English parliamentary papers contain a large amount of relevant information.

Public Record Office, London
Admiralty Papers
Board of Trade Papers
Colonial Office Papers
Customs 1 (Customs Minutes, Ireland)
Customs 2, 3 (Ledgers of Imports and Exports, England)
Customs 14 (Ledgers of Imports and Exports, Scotland)
Customs 15 (Ledgers of Imports and Exports, Ireland)
Customs 17 (States of Navigation and Commerce)
Port Books
Unbound Privy Council Papers
Shaftesbury Papers
Treasury Papers
Public Record Office of Ireland, Dublin
MSS Committee Books of the Committees of the Irish House of Commons
to enquire into the Dublin Coal Trade and Public Coal Yards, 1778,
1790, 1791, 1793, 1796. (1A–46–46)
Customs and Excise Papers (Administration), 1787–1837
Wyche Documents
Official Correspondence, 2nd series (1790–1831)
Private Letters on Irish Affairs (Letters to and from Lord Townshend
in 1779)
Series of 104 letters to Lord Townshend, 1767–72 (1A–41–134)
Public Record Office of Northern Ireland, Belfast
Transcripts of the State Papers, Ireland
An Account of timber, barrel staves, etc. shipt off in the ports of Belfast
and Coleraine 1683–95 (T. 552, p. 59)
Foster Papers (D. 562)
Macartney Letter Books (D. 572)
Customs Letter Book, Newcastle and Annalong, Board to Officers, 1786–
1821 (T. 1095/2)
Scottish Record Office, General Register House, Edinburgh
Port Import and Export Books, boxes 3, 9, 13, 28–30, 31
Customs Accounts, Scotland
Customs Account of bounty money paid out of the Customs to importers
of victual 1699 (2 portfolios)

H.M. Customs and Excise
CUSTOM HOUSE LIBRARY, LONDON
Ledgers of Imports and Exports, England
Irish Revenue Board: minute books 1696–8, 1700–1, 1701–3, 1712–14
Letter Book, Lancaster, 1728–32
Correspondence, London and Whitehaven, 1744–8 (letter book)
Letters from Whitehaven, 1775–85 (letter book)
Letter Book, Beaumaris, 1757–63
Correspondence London, Exeter and Bideford, etc., 1676–1702
Entries Inwards, Minehead, 1757–86
Letters Dublin and Newry, 1790 (letter book)
Customs Letters, Wicklow, 1795–1804 (letter book)
Selections from Record Offices, Dublin and Edinburgh, 1533–1781 (H. Atton, 1911)
Selections from outport Letter Books, 1662–1829 (H. Atton, 1912)
Selections from the records in the Scottish outports, 1921
Selections from Customs outport records, 1925
Selections from Customs outport records: south coast, 1922, northern England, 1924, west coast, 1926, southern Scotland, 1928, northern England, 1929–36
CUSTOM HOUSE, AYR
Letter Books, Ayr
CUSTOM HOUSE, BRISTOL
Letter Books, Barnstaple
CUSTOM HOUSE, GREENOCK
Letter Books, Greenock and Port Glasgow, and Rothesay
CUSTOM HOUSE, LIVERPOOL
Register of wool vessels, 1739–92
Subsidiary Shipping Register, 1796–1800
CUSTOM HOUSE, TROON
Letter Books, Irvine
CUSTOM HOUSE, WHITEHAVEN
Letter Books, Whitehaven
Shipping Registers, 1786–1800
Archives Department, Council House, Bristol
Mayor's Dues, 1792–1823
Town Duties, 1790–5
Bristol Reference Library
Bristol Presentments: exports 1773–80, 1790, 1795–6; imports 1775, 1778–80, 1795–6
Chester City Record Office
Memoranda book of protested bills of exchange, etc., 1639–65. (C/B/166)
Great Letter Book of Chester Corporation, vol. 4, 1674–1715
The Comptroller's Subsidy Book, Parkgate 1790–1802
Records of the Tanners' Company
C/Mc. 402–5, letters, 1696–7
Chester County Record Office
River Dee Navigation Book 1740–70

British Museum
Additional MSS
Harleian MSS
Lansdowne MSS
Sloane MSS

Printed material
Statutes at large, Ireland
Journals of the Irish House of Commons
Irish Parliamentary Register
Statutes at large, England (Great Britain)
Journals of the English (British) House of Commons
Reports from the British House of Commons, 1st series
Report of the Lords of the Committee of Council appointed for the con-sideration of all matters relating to trade and foreign plantations, 1785
Minutes of the Evidence taken before a Committee of the House of Commons, being a Committee of the whole House . . . [on] the adjustment of the commercial intercourse between Great Britain and Ireland, 1785
Minutes of the Evidence taken before a Committee of the House of Lords being a Committee of the whole House appointed to take into considera-tion the resolutions come to by the Commons relating to the adjustment of the commercial intercourse between Great Britain and Ireland, 1785
Accounts and Papers, House of Commons, 1785
Report of the Committee on the circulating paper, the specie and the current coin of Ireland, and the exchange between that part of the United Kingdom and Great Britain, 1804, reprinted 1826 P.P. 1826 (407) *V.* 461
Official and real or current value of the imports and exports of Great Britain to and from Ireland, 30 July 1804, P.P. 1803-4, VIII, 190
Account presented to the House of Commons respecting the official and the real or current value of the imports and exports of Ireland, 8 May 1804. P.P. 1803-4, VII, 93
Report from the Select Committee on the butter trade of Ireland, 1826. P.P 1826 (406) *V.* 135
Report, Appendix and Minutes of Evidence of Select Committee on the circulation of promissory notes under the value £5 in Scotland and Ireland, 1826. P.P. 1826 (402) III, 257
Third report of the committee of secrecy appointed to examine and state the total amount of outstanding demands on the Bank of England, 21 April 1797. *P. P.* 1826 *(III),* 26.
Registers of the Privy Council of Scotland, 3rd Series
Acts of the Privy Council of England, Colonial Series
Calendars of State Papers, Ireland.
Calendars of State Papers, Domestic
Calendars of State Papers, Colonial
Calendars of Home Office Papers
Calendars of Treasury Books
Calendars of Treasury Books and Papers

Journals of the Commissioners of Trade and Plantations
Irish Manuscripts Commission. Publications
Irish Manuscripts Commission. Analecta Hibernica (Journal of the Irish MSS Comm.) 1930 to date
Historical Manuscripts Commission. Reports and publications
Accounts of the Dublin Port and Docks Board for the Year 1932
The state letters of Hugh Earl of Clarendon, Lord Lieutenant of Ireland during the reign of King James the Second and his Lordship's diary for the years 1687, 1688, 1689 and 1690 (Oxford, 1763) vol. I
Letters written by His Excellency Hugh Boulter, D.D. Lord Primate of all Ireland, etc., to several Ministers of State in England and some others (Oxford, 1769–70) 2 vols .
LANDSDOWNE, MARQUIS OF (ed.), *The Petty Papers* (London, 1927) 2 vols.
—— *The Petty-Southwell Correspondence 1676–87* (London, 1928)

Business records

Administrative and political records at best, as in much of the customs material, reveal only a framework of economic activity. At worst, as in many of the reports and memorials scattered through political papers or in evidence before committees of enquiry, they often present information which can be very misleading. The records of actual business houses are essential to get a more intimate picture of the conduct of trade and of its environment. A problem in the use of business records is that unlike administrative and political material only a small quantity has survived. Moreover, with comparatively few exceptions the surviving material is very incomplete even for individual concerns. The material in consequence does not always lead to firm conclusions especially about long-term trends. However, business records are invaluable in the assessment of economic prospects, and in the study of economic fluctuations and of the economic background. Especially in the case of an agricultural country, the business records should include estate records. Apart from illustrating the organization and financing of trade, these records suggest a course of events and causation often in conflict with contemporary polemical assertions and with the picture accepted by subsequent Irish historians.

A useful guide to some of the manuscript sources is R.J. Hayes (ed.), *The manuscript sources for the history of Irish civilisation* (Boston, 1965). The Ainsworth Reports (typescript available in the National Library, Dublin) on MSS. in private keeping are also very useful. The publications of the Irish Manuscripts Commission, including *Analecta Hibernica,* list or catalogue a number of collections of estate or business papers: *the Kenmare MSS.* (ed. E. MacLysaght) are especially useful.

BELFAST: *Linen Hall Library*
Letter Books of George Macartney, merchant, Belfast, 1660–67, 1678/9–1681. (The library also has transcripts of these volumes, made by Sydney Andrews. For the most part, the transcripts have been consulted. Page references are to the transcripts.)
Public Record Office of Northern Ireland

Downshire Papers (D. 607)

Black Papers (T. 1073)

Copy invoices and ledger of James Ferguson, linen bleacher, Belfast, 1771–84 (D. 468)

Copy letters and invoices of linens shipped by William McCance, bleacher, Belfast, 1796–7

Greer Papers D., 1044

Copy invoices 1799–1801 in Letter Book of James McCleery

Mussenden Papers, uncatalogued collection and catalogued collection D. 354

Accounts of a Ballycastle merchant, 1751–54 (T. 1044)

Weir Papers, D. 1140

    In the possession of Messrs. Richardson Sons, & Owden Ltd., Murray St., Belfast

Cash Book of J. & J. Richardson of Lisburn, 1785–7

    In the possession of Messrs. Isaac Andrews & Son, Ltd.

Andrews MSS.

BORDEAUX: *Archives Départementales de la Gironde*

7 B 1779, 7 B 1800. Pelet Papers (letters received from Cork and London)

7 B 1575 Lalle Pierre Papers (letters received from Ireland)

BRISTOL: *University Library*

Pinney Papers

CARLISLE: *Record Office, The Castle*

Benson Papers (shipping accounts). See also under Whitehaven

CORK (City): *Public Museum*

Bills of lading, 1786

Ledger of Samuel Hoare of Cork and London, 1744–96

CORK (County): *In the possession of Mr. Adrian E.O. Waters, Kilmacsimon, Bandon, Co. Cork*

Letters from Eusebius Low to Dr. Eaton Edwards

    In the possession of Mrs. Olive Ridgway, Rossmore, Mallow, Co. Cork

Ledger of Courtenay and Ridgway 1791–92

DUBLIN: *Friends' Library, Eustace St.*

Copies of Quaker Wills

Sharp MSS.

    National Library of Ireland

Ainsworth Reports on MSS in private keeping

Abdy MSS (MS. 325)

Bellew Papers

Blake Papers

Fingall Papers

French Papers

La Touche & Kane: Abstract Ledger 1719–26 (MS. 2785)

Ormonde Papers

Shaw MSS

Handbook and farm accounts 1734–86 (MS. 498)

Letters received by the Dillon merchant and banking house 1730–55; bill book 1750–52, microfilm (N. 3142)

Accounts of the *Duke* and *Nancy* of Maryport, 1764–95 (MSS. 1589–1590)
  Public Record Office of Ireland
Sarsfield Vesey Papers
  Library, University College
O'Connell Papers
EDINBURGH: *National Library of Scotland*
Houston MSS
  Scottish Record Office, General Register House
Letter Book of Alexander Oliphant, 1766–71
LONDON: *British Museum*
Egmont Papers (Add. MSS. 46978–47014, 47042)
  Guildhall Library
Radcliffe Papers
Letter book of Thomas d'Aeth, senior and junior, merchants, London,
  1698–1704
  Library, Society of Friends, Euston Rd., N.W.1.
Gurney Papers
  London Corporation Record Office
Irish Society, Letter Book 4, 1708–1721
  Public Record Office
Chancery Masters' Exhibits:
  C 104/11, 12 Cleek *v.* Calpine
  C 105/15 Herne *v.* Barber
  C 105/24 Power *v.* Fitzgerald
  C 107/1, 2 Papers of James Rogers, merchant, Bristol
  C 107/104 French *v.* Davies
  C 107/161 Lloyd *v.* Nicholson
  C 110/46 St. George *v.* St. George
  C 110/181 Smith *v.* Blagden
  C 114/52 Unknown cause, estate of John Reay
LIVERPOOL: *Liverpool Record Office*
Norris Papers
MANCHESTER: *University of Manchester*
McConnel and Kennedy MSS:
  Letters from Irish correspondents, 1795–1803
  Belfast Sales, 1812–1827, 1850–57
RADSTOCK: *In the possession of Lord Hylton, Ammerdown Park, Radstock*
Irish invoices and bills of exchange, 1674–81 *in* Memoranda Book of
  James Twyford, merchant, Bristol
STOKE-ON-TRENT: *Wedgwood Museum, Barlaston*
Wedgwood Papers
TROWBRIDGE: *Wiltshire Record Office*
Hindley MSS.
WHITEHAVEN: *Mining Department, Somerset House*
Book for Seaton Colliery, 1770–82
  *Formerly at Lowther Estate Office, Penrith, now transferred to the
  Record Office, Joint Archives Committee for Cumberland and West-
  morland, The Castle, Carlisle*

Sir John Lowther's Letters from London to Whitehaven, 1693–7, 1697–8
Sir James Lowther's Letters from London to Whitehaven, 1706–54
John Speding, Letters to Mr. Lowther, 5 May 1725 to 29 October 1725
    (copies)
Letters from Whitehaven, 11 May 1726 to 24 March 1726–7; 19 May 1732
    to 11 March 1733 (nos. 24–101) (copies)
Abstract accounts for the Whitehaven and Parton collieries, 1701–50
Total account of the number of waggons shipped yearly from Howgill and
    Whingill collieries, 1782–1800
NEW YORK: *New York Historical Society Library*
Letter Book of Greg and Cunningham, 1756–7 (microfilm in National
    Library, Dublin)

Newspapers
Newspapers are helpful to the student of Anglo-Irish trade in many ways. They echo contemporary opinion, and thus supplement the information available in contemporary writings. More importantly, the newspapers, Irish as well as English, often provide information on shipping movements, prices and exchanges in addition to providing incidentally a mass of information on trade, industry, banking and economic conditions generally. Advertisements are helpful also, throwing light on trade, shipping, banking, the leasing of land etc. Dublin newspapers had a wide circulation, and in consequence news and advertisements throw light on provincial conditions as well as on conditions in the capital. Provincial newspapers often refer to events in Dublin. A drawback to newspapers as a source is that many papers were short-lived, or that few files are extant. A more serious drawback, however, is that within the extant files information on prices, stocks, exchanges, shipping is often given only intermittently. The haphazard appearance of news of an economic nature in contemporary newspapers limits their value, but employed in conjunction with other sources the information that can be gleaned from them is often invaluable. Most complete of the eighteenth-century newspapers are the *Belfast News Letter*, *Faulkner's Dublin Journal* and the *Freeman's Journal*.

The National Library, Dublin, and the British Museum have the largest collections of Irish newspapers. Important collections of local newspapers are in Cork and Belfast.

Belfast News Letter, 1739, 1750, 1754, 1771, 1776, 1778, 1780, 1782, 1784,
    1786, 1788, 1790, 1792, 1794, 1796
(Belfast) *Northern Star*, 1792
Chester Chronicle, 1775–6, 1777, 1789
Clonmel Gazette, 1788
Connaught Journal or Galway Advertiser, 1793, 1795
Cork Evening Post, 1757–8
Cork Hibernian Chronicle, 1770, 1789–92
Cumberland Chronicle, 1776–8
Cumberland Pacquet, 1776–7
Dublin Gazette, 1729–30
Dublin Intelligence, 1728–9, 1729–30

Esdall's [Dublin] News Letter, 1753, 1754
Faulkner's Dublin Journal, 1728–34, 1737–60, 1777–93
Finn's Leinster Journal, 1778, 1790
Munster Journal, 1750
New Cork Evening Post, 1792, 1799
Waterford Chronicle, 1771
Williamson's Liverpool Advertiser, 1760, 1775, 1780, 1790

Contemporary printed works

Few contemporary works deal directly with Anglo-Irish trade, although works such as those of Petty, Temple, Dobbs, Prior, Young, Caldwell, Hely Hutchinson, Sheffield and Newenham deal at length with commercial issues closely affecting at many points Anglo-Irish trade. Incidental reference to Anglo-Irish trade and payments and to their background abound, however, in contemporary writings.

Much eighteenth-century economic writing is very misleading because, even in the discussion of commercial issues, the political aspects were given primacy. The writings are especially misleading when they emanate from periods such as the 1720s and late 1770s when economic difficulties and political agitation coincided. An economic mythology established itself very quickly with the writings of the 1720s and the political concerns which manifested themselves in that decade providing the base of arguments which were repeated in subsequent writing. Swift's writings, Prior's *List of the absentees of Ireland* (probably the most influential economic tract of the eighteenth century in Ireland), Caldwell's and Hely Hutchinson's tracts in the 1770s, and Newenham's works, have through their widespread acceptance by historians resulted in considerable distortion in the presentation of the course of Irish economic history in the eighteenth century. Works dealing with the smuggling trade, wool smuggling in particular, are especially misleading, and with the exception of works appearing in 1698 are omitted from the bibliography.

For a discussion of the value of contemporary printed works, see: Cullen, L.M. 'The value of contemporary printed sources for Irish economic history in the eighteenth century', *Irish Historical Studies,* vol. XIV, no. 54 (September 1964).

The best guides to contemporary printed works are:

HANSON, L.W., *Contemporary printed sources for British and Irish economic history, 1701–1750* (Cambridge, 1963)
HIGGS, H., *Bibliography of economics, 1751–1775* (London, 1935)
WAGNER, H.R., *Irish economics, 1700–1783: a bibliography with notes* (London, 1907)

The contemporary works listed are from the British Museum; National Library, Dublin; Linen Hall Library, Belfast; Foster Collection, Queen's University, Belfast; Goldsmith Collection, Senate House, University of London; and the Library, London School of Economics.

Alexander the Coppersmith: remarks on the religion, trade, government, police, customs, manners and maladys of the city of Cork (Cork, 1737)

ANDERSON, A., *An historical and chronological deduction of the origin of commerce* (London, 1801) vol. iv.

An answer to a letter from a gentleman in the country to a member of the House of Commons (London, 1698).

Appendix to a short essay on coin (Dublin, 1737).

Bailey's northern directory, merchants' and tradesmen's useful companion for the year 1781.

BERKELEY, G., *The Querist*, 1735 (ed. J. Hone, Dublin, 1935).

BEWLEY, G., *A narrative of the Christian experiences of George Bewley, late of the city of Corke, written by himself* (Dublin, 1750).

BINDON, D., *Essay on the gold and silver coin currant in Ireland* (Dublin, 1729).

BROWNE, SIR JOHN, *Essay on trade in general and that of Ireland in particular by the author of seasonable remarks* (Dublin, 1728).

—— *Reply to the observer on seasonable remarks* (Dublin, 1728).

—— *Seasonable remarks on trade* (Dublin, 1728).

—— *The benefits which arise to a trading people from navigable rivers* (Dublin, 1729).

—— *A short review of the several pamphlets that have appeared this sessions on the subject of coin* (Dublin, 1729).

—— See also below *Reflections little to the purpose* ... and *Scheme of the money matters* ... (also by Sir John Browne)

Calculations relating to the coal trade being an account of what coals stand in per ton, delivered at the keys of Dublin by the Whitehaven ships. Computed according to the known rules of merchandising, 1721.

CALDWELL, SIR JAMES, *Enquiry into the restrictions on the trade of Ireland* (Dublin, 1779)

CARY, J., *Essay on the state of England in relation to its trade* (Bristol, 1695).

—— *Some considerations relating to the carrying on the linnen manufacture in the kingdom of Ireland by a joint-stock* (London, 1704).

Case of John Hay and the other separate creditors of Samuel Burton Esq., deceased (Dublin, 1740).

Case of the merchants trading in tobacco at Whitehaven in the county of Cumberland (1715?).

CASTAING, J., *The course of the exchange and other things* (London, 1697–1800).

CHILD, SIR J., *A new discourse of trade* (London, 1698).

COLLINS, JOHN, *A plea for the bringing in of Irish cattel and keeping out of fish caught by foreigners* (London, 1680).

COLLINSON, J., *History of the county of Somerset* (Bath, 1791) vol. 2.

A collection of tracts concerning the present state of Ireland (London, 1729).

Comparative view of the public burdens of Great Britain and Ireland (London, 1779).

Considerations on the duties levied in Ireland on wooll brought to England, humbly submitted to the Parliament (1720–23).

Considerations on the present calamities of this kingdom, and the causes of the decay of public credit (Dublin, 1760).

Considerations on the removal of the custom house (Dublin, 1781).

Considerations on the silk trade of Ireland with useful hints for the extension thereof adduced to the Dublin Society (Dublin, 1778).

Cork Directory, 1787.

DEFOE, D., *A plan of the English commerce* (London, 1728).

Discourse concerning Ireland and the different interests thereof in answer to the Exeter and Barnstaple petitions (London, 1698).

A discourse of the woollen manufacture of Ireland and the consequences of prohibiting its exportation (1698).

DOBBS, ARTHUR, *An essay on the trade and improvement of Ireland* (Dublin, 1729) in *A collection of tracts and treatises illustrative . . . of Ireland* (Dublin, 1861) vol. 2.

(Wilson's) Dublin Directory, 1751–1800.

DUBOURDIEU, J., *Statistical account of County Down* (Dublin, 1802).

DUNDONALD, EARL OF, *Thoughts on the manufacture . . . of salt* (Edinburgh, 1784).

EACHARD, L., *An exact description of Ireland* (London, 1691).

An enquiry how far it might be expedient, and at this time more particularly, seasonable, to permit the importation of Irish cattle (London, 1743).

An enquiry into the legality and consequences of an embargo: by a member of the Irish parliament (Dublin, 1780).

An enquiry into the reasons of the decay of credit, trade and manufactures in Ireland (Dublin, 1735).

Enquiries into the principal causes of the general poverty of the common people of Ireland (Dublin, 1725).

An essay concerning the establishment of a national bank in Ireland (Dublin, 1779).

Essays and observations on the following subjects, viz. on trade ... published by a society of gentlemen in Dublin (London, 1740).

FOSTER, JOHN, *An essay on the principle of commercial exchanges* (London, 1804).

A General Directory of the Kingdom of Ireland (Dublin, 1788) vol. ii.

Gentleman's and Citizen's Almanack, Dublin, 1733–1800.

The groans of Ireland (Dublin, 1741).

HARRIS, W., *Remarks on the affairs and trade of England and Ireland* (London, 1691).

HELY HUTCHINSON, J., *The commercial restraints of Ireland considered* (Dublin, 1779).

HUTCHINSON, W., *History of the county of Cumberland* (Carlisle, 1794) 2 vols.

HUTTON, E., *The merchant's magazine: or tradesman's treasure* (London, 1712).

Impartial considerations on the danger of multiplying banks here, by a member of the guild of merchants (Dublin, 1763).

The importance of the northern colleries in a letter to a noble lord (Dublin, 1764).

The interest of England as it stands with relation to the trade of Ireland considered . . . with short remarques on a book entituled some thoughts on the bill now depending before the Rt. Hon. the House of Lords (London, 1698).

JONES NEVILL, ARTHUR, *Some hints on trade, money and credit humbly addressed to the true friends of Ireland* (Dublin, 1762).

LAURENCE, R., *The interest of Ireland in its trade and wealth* (Dublin, 1682).

Letter to the author of a pamphlet entitled Some Thoughts on the Nature of Paper Credit (Dublin, 1760).

Letter to the Earl of Carlisle from William Eden Esq. on the representation of Ireland requesting a free trade (Dublin, 1779).

Letter from a gentleman in the country to a member of parliament in reference to the votes of the 14th inst. (1698).

Letter from a gentleman in Ireland to his brother in England relating to the concerns of Ireland in matter of trade (1677).

Letter to a member of parliament touching the late intended bank (Dublin, 1721).

Letter from a merchant of Dublin to the author of the remarks on the conduct of Messrs. W———cks and D———n (Dublin, 1755).

Letter from Hugh Boyd, Esq., of Ballycastle to a member of parliament on the scarcity of coals in Dublin (Dublin, 1749–50).

A letter in answer to a paper entitled Appeal to Swift . . . in Tracts concerning the present state of Ireland (London, 1729).

A letter sent to Mr. Garway (a member of the Rt. Hon. the House of Commons of England) by an English gentleman (27 Dec. 1673).

MAXWELL, H., *Reasons offered for erecting a bank in Ireland in a letter to Hercules Rowley, Esq.* (Dublin, 1721).

—— *Mr. Maxwell's second letter to Mr. Rowley, wherein the objections against the bank are answered* (Dublin, 1721).

MOLYNEUX, W., *Case of Ireland's being bound by Acts of Parliament in England stated* (Dublin, 1698).

NEVILL, JOHN, *Seasonable remarks on the linen trade of Ireland* (Dublin, 1783).

New Cork Directory, 1795.

NEWENHAM, T., *A statistical and historical enquiry into the progress and magnitude of the population of Ireland* (London, 1805).

—— *View of the national, political and commercial circumstances of Ireland* (London, 1809).

Observations on the brewing trade of Ireland, 1777.

Observations on coin in general (Dublin, 1729).

Observations on and a short history of Irish banks and bankers (Dublin, 1760).

Observations on raising the value of money (Dublin, 1718).

Paper credit considered, particularly relative to the late failures of bankers and receivers in Ireland (Dublin, 1760).

PETTY, SIR WILLIAM, *Writings*, in Hull, C.H., *Economic Writings of Sir William Petty* (Cambridge, 1899) 2 vols.

Plain reasons addressed to the people of Great Britain against the (intended) petition to parliament from the owners and occupiers of land in the county of Lincoln for leave to export wool (Leeds, 1782).

The present state of his majesty's revenue compared with that of some late years (Dublin, 1762).

PRIOR, T., *List of the absentees of Ireland* (Dublin, 1729) in *A collection of tracts and treatises illustrative . . . of Ireland* (Dublin, 1861) vol. 2.

A proposal for the restoration of public wealth and credit in a letter to a truely honourable member of the house of commons (Dublin, 1760).

Proposals humbly offered to Parliament for the restoration of cash and public credit to Ireland (Dublin, 1760).

Proposals humbly offered to his excellency Lord Townshend and to the present Parliament for the improvement of trade and restoration of cash and public credit to Ireland (Dublin, 1772).

Quæries proposed to the public on the reduction of the interest of money in Ireland (Dublin, 1766).

The question relative to the petition of the cities of Dublin and Corke and the town of Belfast for a new regulation of the Portuguese gold coin (Dublin, 1760).

Reasons against the scheme of reducing the interest of money in Ireland (1765).

Reasons for a new bridge (Dublin, 1761).

Reasons for and against lowering the gold and silver of this kingdom (Dublin, 1760).

Reasons offered for erecting a bank in Ireland in a letter to Hercules Rowley, Esq. (Dublin, 1721).

Reasons why we should not lower the coins now current in this kingdom (Dublin, 1736).

Reflections little to the purpose on a paper less to the purpose (by the author of Seasonable remarks) (Dublin, 1729).

Remarks on the conduct of Messrs. W———cks and D———n late bankers of the city of Dublin and Mr. R———d B———r their cashier by a country gentleman (Dublin, 1755).

Remarks on Mr Maxwell's and Mr Rowley's letters, setting forth the advantages of a bank and Lumbards in Ireland (Dublin, 1721).

Remarks on a pamphlet entitled Some Thoughts on the Interest of England, 1698.

Remarks on a pamphlet lately published entitled reasons against the establishing of a bank in the town of Belfast in a letter from a gentleman in Dublin to his friend in Belfast (1752).

Remarks on the present state of the linnen manufacture of this kingdom (Dublin, 1745).

Remarks on Willcocks and Dawson's estimates laid before the creditors the 5th of this instant at Guild-Hall and published in the newspapers the 8th of this instant (Dublin, 1755).

Representation of the state of the trade of Ireland laid before the house of lords of England (Dublin, 1750).

*16

ROE, R., *An answer to a pamphlet published by the Earl of Dundonald entitled Thoughts on the Manufacture and Trade of Salt and on the Coal Trade of Great Britain* (Dublin, 1786).

RUTTY, J., *Essay towards a natural history of the county of Dublin* (Dublin, 1772) 2 vols.

Scheme of the money matters of Ireland (Dublin, 1729).

SHEFFIELD, LORD, *Observations on the manufactures, trade and present state of Ireland* (London, 1785).

Short account of the reasons of the intended alteration of the value of the coins current in this kingdom (Dublin, 1729).

SIMON, J., *An essay towards an historical account of Irish coins* (Dublin, 1749).

SMITH, J., *Chronicon rusticum—commerciale, or memoirs . . . concerning the woolen manufacture and woolen trade in general* (1747).

Some account of the life of Joseph Pike with preliminary observations by John Barclay (London, 1837).

Some considerations on the improvement of the linen manufacture in Ireland (Dublin, 1735).

Some considerations relative to the coal trade in Dublin (Dublin, 1761).

Some reflections concerning the reduction of gold coin in Ireland (Dublin, 1737).

Some thoughts on the Bill depending before . . . the House of Lords for prohibiting the exportation of the woollen manufactures of Ireland (London, 1698).

Some thoughts on the importance of the linnen-manufacture of Ireland (Dublin, 1739).

Some thoughts on the tillage of Ireland (Dublin, 1738).

STEPHENSON, R., *A letter to the right honourable and honourable the trustees of the linen manufacture* (Dublin, 1759).

—— *Observations on the present state of the linen trade of Ireland* (Dublin, 1784).

—— *A letter to the right honourable and honourable the trustees of the linen manufacture* (Dublin, 1791).

The substance of the arguments for and against the bill prohibiting the exportation of woollen manufactures from Ireland to foreign parts (London, 1698).

SWIFT, (DEAN) J., *Writings* (ed. H. Davis).

TEMPLE, *Essay upon the advancement of trade in Ireland*, 1673, in *Miscellanea* (London, 1697).

Thoughts on the causes and consequences of the present high price of provisions (London, 1767).

Thoughts on a fund for the improvement of credit in Great Britain and the establishment of a national bank in Ireland (London, 1780).

TUNNICLIFF, W., *A topographical survey of the counties Stafford, Chester and Lancaster* (Nantwich, 1787).

Two and two make four, in a letter to the honest traders of Ireland (Dublin, 1757).

Unprejudiced enquiry into the nature and consequences of the reduction of our gold (Dublin, 1737).
View of the grievances of Ireland by a true patriot (Dublin, 1745).
A view of the present state of Ireland (London, 1780).
WAKEFIELD, E., *An account of Ireland, statistical and political* (London, 1812) 2 vols.
WALLACE, T., *An essay on the manufactures of Ireland* (Dublin, 1798).
YOUNG, A., *Tour in Ireland* (London, 1780).

II. SECONDARY WORKS

Anglo-Irish trade, despite its prominence in the economic life of the two islands, has received little attention in modern writings, although of course incidental reference is very frequent. W.H. Makey's unpublished thesis, 'The place of Whitehaven in the Irish coal trade, 1600–1750', is the only study at length of an aspect of Anglo-Irish trade. T.C. Smout's *Scottish trade on the eve of the union, 1660–1707* covers trade between Scotland and Ireland at that time. Professor R. Davis's articles on English trade are highly relevant to the study of Anglo-Irish trade.

Studies of agriculture and of individual industries and firms on both sides of the Irish Sea have with few exceptions only incidental reference to the trade within the Irish Sea. Andrews', Gill's and Green's works are however very useful for the linen trade. With regard to individual ports, McGrath's and Minchinton's work is very useful in illustrating the trade of Bristol with Ireland; Parkinson that of Liverpool; the writings of Ford, Makey, Hughes, and Williams cover at some length important aspects of the overseas trade of the Cumberland ports; and Stephens, Clark and Hoskins explore the trade of Exeter. On the Irish side, with the exception of Dr W. O'Sullivan's study of Cork, none of the ports has had detailed economic study.

As for the general background against which Anglo-Irish trade developed, most works are unsatisfactory, either because they are preoccupied with the political aspects of commercial issues, or because they accept contemporary preoccupations without assessment of the background. As a result the established picture of Irish economic history is highly unrealistic. The articles of Professor Joseph Johnston in *Hermathena* were a pioneering though incomplete attempt to break away from this version. Lynch and Vaizey's *Guinness's brewery in the Irish economy;* James' 'Irish smuggling in the eighteenth century', *Irish Historical Studies,* vol. XII, no. 48 (September 1961), and R.D. Crotty, *Irish agricultural production: its volume and structure,* while questioning aspects of the interpretation of the eighteenth-century economy, are still tentative.

For some assessment of the historiography of writings on Irish economic history, see:
CULLEN, L.M., 'The re-interpretation of Irish economic history', *Studies in Irish History, Topic, no. 13* (Spring 1967, Washington and Jefferson College, Washington, Pennsylvania).

16

—— 'Problems in the interpretation and revision of eighteenth-century Irish economic history', *Transactions of the Royal Historical Society* 5th series, vol. xvii (1967).

ANDREWS, S., *Nine generations: a history of the Andrews family, millers of Comber* (Belfast, 1958).

ASHTON, T.S., *An economic history of England: the eighteenth century* (London, 1955).

—— *Introduction* in E.R. Schumpeter, *English overseas trade statistics 1697-1808* (Oxford, 1960).

—— *Economic fluctuations in England, 1700-1800* (Oxford, 1959).

BARKER, T.C., 'Lancashire coal, Cheshire salt and the rise of Liverpool', *Transactions of the Historical Society of Lancashire and Cheshire,* vol. 103 (1951).

BENN, G., *History of Belfast* (Belfast, 1823).

BEVERIDGE, W., *Prices and wages in England,* vol. I, *Price Tables: Mercantile Era* (London, 1939).

BOLTON, G.C., 'Some British reactions to the Irish Act of Union', *Economic History Review,* second series, vol. xviii, no. 2, August 1965.

BOWDEN, P.J., *The wool trade in Tudor and Stuart England* (London, 1962).

—— 'Wool supply and the woollen industry', *Economic History Review,* second series, vol. IX, no. 1 (1956).

BURKE, J.F., *Outlines of industrial history of Ireland* (Dublin, 1940).

BUSTEED, J., 'Irish private banks', *Journal of the Cork Historical and Archaeological Society,* vol. 53 (1948).

CAMPBELL, R.H., *Scotland since 1707: the rise of an industrial society* (Oxford, 1965).

CARTE, T., *A history of the life of James, Duke of Ormonde* (London, 1735-6).

CHART, D.A., *Economic history of Ireland* (Dublin, 1920).

CLARK, E.A.G., *The ports of the Exe Estuary, 1660-1860* (Exeter, 1960).

—— 'The estuarine ports of the Exe and the Teign', Ph.D. thesis (geography), University of London, 1957.

CLARK, G.N., *Guide to English commercial statistics,* 1696-1782 (London, 1938).

COLE, G.D.H., *British trade and industry, past and future* (London, 1932).

CONNELL, K.H., *The population of Ireland, 1750-1845* (Oxford, 1950).

CROSS, A.L., *Eighteenth century documents relating to the royal forests, the sheriffs and smuggling* (New York, 1928).

COYNE, W. (ed.), *Ireland, industrial and agricultural* (Department of Agriculture, Dublin, 1902).

CROTTY, R.D., *Irish agricultural production: its volume and structure* (Cork, 1966).

CULLEN, L.M., 'An Ceangal Tráchtála idir Éire agus an Fhrainc, 1660-1800' (Trade relations between Ireland and France, 1660-1800), unpublished M.A. thesis, National University of Ireland (1956).

—— 'Tráchtáil idir iarthar na h-Éireann is an Fhrainc, 1660–1800' (Trade between the West of Ireland and France, 1660–1800), *Galvia*, vol. 4 (1957).

—— 'The overseas trade of Waterford as seen from a ledger of Courtenay and Ridgway', *Journal of the Royal Society of Antiquaries of Ireland*, vol. lxxxviii, part 2 (1958).

—— 'Privateers fitted out in Irish ports in the eighteenth century', *The Irish Sword*, vol. iii, no. 12 (1958).

—— 'The exchange business of the Irish Banks in the eighteenth century', *Economica*, November 1958.

—— 'Tráchtáil is Baincéaracht i nGaillimh san 18ú céad' (Trade and banking in Galway in the eighteenth century). *Galvia*, vol. 5 (1958).

—— 'The Galway smuggling trade in the 1730's', *Journal of the Galway Archaeological and historical society*, vol. xxx (1962).

—— 'The value of contemporary printed sources for Irish economic history in the eighteenth century', *Irish Historical Studies*, vol. XIV, no. 54 (September, 1964).

—— 'The re-interpretation of Irish economic history', *Studies in Irish History. Topic, no. 13* (Washington and Jefferson College, Washington, Spring 1967).

—— 'Problems in the interpretation and revision of eighteenth-century Irish economic history', *Transactions of the Royal Historical Society*, 5th series, vol. xvii (1967)

—— 'The role of foreign trade in the eighteenth-century Irish economy', paper read to the Economic History Society Conference, Belfast, April 1967.

CUNNINGHAM, W., 'The repression of the woollen manufacture in Ireland', *English Historical Review*, vol. 1 (1886).

DANIELS, G.W., 'The early records of a great Manchester cotton spinning firm', *Economic Journal*, vol. xxv (1915).

—— *The early English cotton industry* (Manchester, 1920).

DAVIS, R., 'English foreign trade, 1660–1700', *Economic History Review*, second series, vol. vii (1954).

—— 'English foreign trade, 1700–74', *Economic History Review*, second series, vol. xv, no. 2 (December, 1962).

—— 'The rise of protection in England, 1689–1786', *Economic History Review*, second series, vol. xix, no. 2 (August, 1966).

—— *The rise of the English shipping industry* (London, 1962).

DEANE, P. AND COLE, W.A., *British economic growth, 1688–1959: trends and structure* (Cambridge, 1962).

DELANY, V.T.H. AND D.R., *The canals of the south of Ireland* (Newton Abbot, 1966).

DICKSON, R.J., *Ulster emigration to colonial America 1718–1775* (London, 1966).

DILLON, M., *The history and development of banking in Ireland* (London and Dublin, 1889).

DUNN, M., *An historical, geological and descriptive view of the coal trade of the North of England* (Newcastle-upon-Tyne, 1844).

DUNLOP, R., 'A note on the export trade of Ireland in 1641, 1665 and 1669', *English Historical Review,* vol. XXII (1907).

FETTER, F.W., *The Irish pound* (London, 1955).

FONTAINE, J., *Memoirs of a huguenot family* (New York, 1853).

FORD, P., 'Tobacco and coal: a note on the economic history of White-haven', *Economica,* vol. IX (1929).

FRANKLIN, D., 'Extracts from the letter book of Joseph Ffrancklyn, mayor of Cork in 1708', *Journal of the Cork Historical and Archeological Society,* second series, vol. I (1895).

FUSSELL, G.E., and GOODMAN, CONSTANCE, 'Eighteenth-century traffic in livestock', *Economic History* (Supplement to the *Economic Journal*) vol. 3, no. 11.

—— —— 'The eighteenth-century traffic in milk products', *Economic History* (Supplement to the *Economic Journal*) vol. 3, no. 12.

FOX BOURNE, H.R., *English merchants* (London, 1866) 2 vols.

GAUTIER, C., 'Un investissement genevois: la tontine d'Irlande de 1777', *Bulletin de la Societé d'histoire et d'archeologie de Genève,* tome X, 1951.

GILBART, J.W., *History of banking in Ireland* (London, 1836).

GILL, C., *Rise of the Irish linen industry* (Oxford, 1925).

GOODBODY, O., 'Anthony Sharp, a quaker merchant of the liberties', *Dublin Historical Record,* vol. XIV (June, 1955).

—— 'Anthony Sharp, wool merchant, 1643–1707, and the quaker community in Dublin', *Journal of the Friends Historical Society,* vol. 48, no. 1 (Spring, 1956).

GREEN, E.R.R., *The Lagan valley* (London, 1949).

—— *Industrial archaeology of county Down* (Belfast, 1963).

—— 'The cotton handloom weavers in the north-east of Ireland', *Ulster Journal of Archaeology,* 3rd series, vol. VII (1944).

GRUBB, I., 'Social conditions in Ireland in the seventeenth and eighteenth centuries as illustrated by early Quaker records' (unpublished M.A. thesis, University of London, 1916).

—— *Quakers in Ireland* (London, 1927).

—— 'An unpublished memoir', *Friends Quarterly Examiner,* vol. LIX (London, 1925).

—— *Quakerism and English industry before 1800* (London, 1930).

HALDANE, A.R.B., *The drove roads of Scotland* (London and Edinburgh, 1952).

HALL, F.G., *The Bank of Ireland, 1783–1946* (Dublin, 1949).

HAMILTON, H., *An economic history of Scotland in the eighteenth century* (Oxford, 1963).

HANSON, L.W., *Contemporary printed sources for British and Irish economic history* (Cambridge, 1963).

HARPER, L.A., *The English navigation laws* (New York, 1939).

HAYNES-THOMAS, G.M., 'The port of Chester', *Transactions of the Lancashire and Cheshire Antiquarian Society,* vol. LIX (1947).

HEATON, H., *The Yorkshire woollen and worsted industries* (Oxford, 1920).

HOON, E.E., *The organisation of the English customs system, 1696–1786* (New York, 1938).

HORNER, J., *The linen trade of Europe during the spinning-wheel age* (Belfast, 1920).

HOSKINS, W.G., *Industry, trade and people in Exeter, 1688–1800* (Manchester, 1935).

HUGHES, E., *North country life in the eighteenth century*, vol. I, *the northeast, 1700–50* (London, 1952); vol. 2, *Cumberland and Westmorland, 1700–1830* (London, 1965).

JAMES, F.G., 'Irish smuggling in the eighteenth century', *Irish Historical Studies*, vol. XII, no. 48 (September, 1961).

—— 'The Irish lobby in the early eighteenth century', *English Historical Review*, vol. LXXXI (July, 1966).

JARVIS, R.C., 'Illicit Trade with the Isle of Man, 1671–1765', *Transactions of the Lancashire and Cheshire Antiquarian Society*, vol. 58 (1945–6).

—— *Customs letter-books of the port of Liverpool, 1711–1823* (Manchester, 1954).

—— 'Cumberland shipping in the eighteenth century', *Transactions of the Cumberland and Westmorland Antiquarian and Archaeological Society*, vol. 54.

JOHN, A.H., 'The London Assurance Company and the marine assurance market of the eighteenth century', *Economica*, May, 1958.

—— 'The course of agricultural change, 1660–1760' in *Studies in the Industrial Revolution* (London, 1960), ed. L.S. Pressnell, pp. 125–55.

JOHNSTON, J., 'Irish currency in the eighteenth century', *Hermathena*, vol. 52 (1938).

—— 'Commercial restriction and monetary deflation in eighteenth-century Ireland', *Hermathena*, vol. 53 (1939).

KEARNEY, H.F., 'The political background to English mercantilism, 1695–1700', *Economic History Review*, 2nd series, vol. XI, no. 3.

—— *Strafford in Ireland, 1633–41* (Manchester, 1959).

KEITH, T., *Commercial relations of England and Scotland, 1603–1707* (Cambridge, 1910).

KIERNAN, T.J., *History of the financial administration of Ireland to 1817* (London, 1930).

LANE, H.J., 'Life and writings of John Cary', unpublished M.A. thesis, 1932, Bristol University.

LANSDOWNE, MARQUIS OF, *Glanerought and the Petty-Fitzmaurices* (London, 1937).

LARGE, D., 'The wealth of the greater Irish landowners, 1750–1815', *Irish Historical Studies*, vol. XV, no. 57 (March, 1966).

LATIMER, J., *The history of the Society of Merchant Venturers of the City of Bristol* (Bristol, 1903).

LECKY, W.E.H., *A history of Ireland in the eighteenth century* (London, 1892).

LE FANU, T.P., 'The story of Peter Lunell, a huguenot refugee, and his son William', *Proceedings of the Huguenot Society of London*, vol. xiv.

LIPSON, E., *The history of the woollen and worsted industries* (London, 1921).

LYNCH, P. AND VAIZEY, J., *Guinness's brewery in the Irish economy* (Cambridge, 1960).

McCUTCHEON, W.A., *The canals of the north of Ireland* (Dawlish, 1965).

McGRATH, P., *Merchants and merchandise in seventeenth-century Bristol* (Bristol, 1955).

MacLYSAGHT, E., *Irish life in the seventeenth century* (Cork, 1949).

MAKEY, W.H., 'The place of Whitehaven in the Irish coal trade, 1600–1750' (unpublished M.A. thesis, University of London, 1952).

MARMION, A., *The ancient and modern history of the maritime ports of Ireland* (London, 1855).

MARWICK, W.H., *Scotland in modern times* (London, 1964).

MATHIAS, P., *Brewing industry in England 1700–1830* (Cambridge, 1959).

MAXWELL, C., *Country and town in Ireland under the Georges* (London, 1940).

MINCHINTON, W.E., *The trade of Bristol in the eighteenth century* (Bristol, 1957).

MITCHELL, B.R. AND DEANE, P., *Abstract of British historical statistics* (Cambridge, 1962).

MONAGHAN, J.J., 'Social and economic history of Belfast'—unpublished M.A. thesis, Queen's University of Belfast.

—— 'The rise and fall of the Belfast cotton industry', *Irish Historical Studies,* vol. 3, no. 9 (March, 1942).

MURRAY, A.E., *History of the commercial and financial relations between England and Ireland from the Restoration* (London, 1903).

NAMIER, L.B., 'Anthony Bacon, M.P., an eighteenth-century merchant', *Journal of Economic and Business History,* vol. 2, no. 1 (November, 1929).

NEF, J.U., *The rise of the British coal industry* (London, 1932), 2 vols.

NÍ CHINNÉIDE, S., 'A Frenchman's impression of Limerick town and people in 1791', *Journal of the North Munster Antiquarian Society,* 1948.

O'BRIEN, G., *Economic history of Ireland in the eighteenth century* (Dublin, 1918).

—— *Economic history of Ireland in the seventeenth century* (Dublin, 1919).

—— *The economic history of Ireland from the Union to the Famine* (London, 1921).

—— 'The Irish free trade agitation of 1779', *English Historical Review,* vol. 38 (1923), vol. 39 (1924).

—— 'The last years of the Irish currency', *Economic History* (Supplement to the *Economic Journal*) no. 2 (May 1927).

O'CONNELL, M.R., *Irish politics and social conflict in the age of the American Revolution* (Philadelphia, 1965).

O'CONNOR, T.M., 'The embargo on the export of Irish provisions, 1776–9', *Irish Historical Studies,* vol. 2, no. 5 (March 1940).

O'DONOVAN, J., *Economic history of livestock in Ireland* (Cork, 1940).

O'KELLY, E., 'The old Limerick private bankers', *Journal of the Old Limerick Society,* vol. 1, no. 1 (December 1946).

—— *The old private banks and bankers of Munster* (Cork, 1959).

OLDHAM, C.H., *The woollen industry of Ireland* (Dublin, 1909).

OWEN, D.J., *Short history of the port of Belfast* (Belfast, 1917).

—— *History of Belfast* (Belfast and London, 1921).

O'SULLIVAN, W., *The economic history of Cork* (Cork, 1937).

PARKINSON, C.N., *The rise of the port of Liverpool* (Liverpool, 1952).

PINKERTON, W., 'Contribution towards a history of Irish commerce', *Ulster Journal of Archaeology*, vol. 3 (1855).

PRENDEVILLE, P.L., 'Select bibliography of Irish economic history: the 17th and 18th centuries', *Economic History Review*, first series, vol. 3, no. 3 (April 1932).

PRICE, J.M., 'The rise of Glasgow in the Chesapeake tobacco trade', *William and Mary Quarterly*, 3rd series, April 1954.

RAISTRICK, A., *Quakers in science and industry* (London, 1950).

RAMSAY, G.D., *The Wiltshire woollen industry in the 16th and 17th centuries* (Oxford, 1943).

—— *English overseas trade during the centuries of emergence* (London, 1957).

ROBERTSON, M.L., 'Scottish commerce and the American war of independence', *Economic History Review*, second series, vol. IX, no. 1 (1956).

SALMON, J., 'Early Irish bankers and banking', *New Ireland Review*, vol. XII (1899–1900).

SCHUMPETER, E.B., *English overseas trade statistics, 1697–1808* (Oxford, 1960).

SCOTT, W.R., *The constitution and finance of English, Scottish and Irish joint-stock companies to 1720* (Cambridge, 1910–12), 3 vols.

SIGERSON, G., *Last independent parliament of Ireland* (Dublin, 1918).

SIMMS, J.G., *The Williamite confiscation in Ireland 1690–1703* (London, 1956).

SLICHER VAN BATH, B.H., *The agrarian history of western Europe, A.D. 500–1850* (London, 1963).

SMOUT, T.C., *Scottish trade on the eve of the Union* (Edinburgh and London, 1963).

SMYTH, G.L., *Ireland, historical and statistical* (London, 1844).

STEPHENS, W.B., *Seventeenth-century Exeter* (Exeter, 1958).

SUTHERLAND, L.S., 'Sir George Colebrooke's world corner in alum, 1771–3', *Economic History* (supplement to the *Economic Journal*), vol. 3, no. 11, February, 1936.

TENISON, C.M., Articles on Irish banks and bankers in *Journal of the Cork Historical and Archaeological Society*, 1892–5, and *Journal of the Institute of Bankers in Ireland*, 1900–10.

TROW-SMITH, P., *A history of British livestock husbandry to 1700* (London, 1957).

—— *A history of British livestock husbandry, 1700–1900* (London, 1959).

URWICK, W., *Biographical sketches of the late James Digges La Touche Esq., banker, Dublin* (Dublin, 1868).

VIGNOLS, L., 'L'importation en France au dix-huitième siécle du boeuf salé d'Irlande', *Revue historique*, 1928.

Victoria county history, Cumberland.

Victoria county history, Somerset.

WADSWORTH, A.P., AND J. DE L. MANN, *The cotton trade and industrial Lancashire, 1600–1780* (Manchester, 1931).

WAGNER, H.R., *Irish economics, 1700–83: a bibliography with notes* (London, 1907).

WALL, M., 'The rise of a catholic middle class in eighteenth-century Ireland', *Irish Historical Studies*, vol. XI (September, 1958).

WARBURTON, J., WALSH, R., AND WHITELAW, J., *History of the city of Dublin* (London, 1818), 2 vols.

WEBB, J.J., *Industrial Dublin since 1698 and the silk industry in Dublin* (Dublin, 1913).

WESTROPP, M.S.D., 'Glassmaking in Ireland', *Proceedings of the Royal Irish Academy*, vol. 29, section C (1911–12).

—— 'Notes on the pottery industry', *Proceedings of the Royal Irish Academy*, vol. 32, section C (1914–16).

—— 'Notes on Irish moneyweights and foreign coin current in Ireland', *Proceedings of Royal Irish Academy*, vol. 33 (1916–17), Section C.

WILLAN, T.S., *The English coasting trade, 1600–1750* (Manchester, 1938).

WILLIAMS, J.E., 'The growth and decline of the port of Whitehaven, Cumberland, 1650–1900', unpublished M.A. thesis, Leeds University, 1951.

—— 'Whitehaven in the eighteenth century', *Economic History Review*, second series, vol. 8 (1955–6).

WILSON, C.H., *Anglo-Dutch commerce and finance in the eighteenth century* (Cambridge, 1941).

WOOD, O., 'The development of the coal, iron and shipbuilding industries in Cumberland', unpublished Ph.D. thesis, University of London, 1952.

INDEX